# HOME MEASURES

**The Essential Reference Guide
to Sizes and Measurements
for Home, Office and Kitchen**

**Shirley Bond**

**Grub Street • London**

Published by Grub Street
The Basement, 10 Chivalry Road
London SW11 1HT

Copyright © 1996 Shirley Bond
Jacket design and illustrations: Nicci Walker
Design copyright © 1996 Grub Street
Book design: Nick Denchfield

**British Library Cataloguing in Publication Data**

Bond, Shirley
Home Measures: the essential reference guide to sizes and
measurements for home, office and kitchen.
1. Weights and measures  2. Weight and measures - Tables
3. Metric System - Conversion tables  4. Mensuration
I. Title
530.8'1
ISBN 1 898697 43 4

Printed and bound in Great Britain by Biddles Ltd, Guildford and King's Lynn

The chart on page 198 is reproduced by kind permission of the
Health Education Authority, which is the copyright holder.

Whilst every effort has been made by the author and publisher to ensure
that the information contained in this book is accurate neither can
accept responsibility for any errors contained herein.

## About the Author

Shirley Bond is a Nutritionist, State Registered Dietitian and Home Economist. She is a member of the British Dietetic Association and The Nutrition Society and a Fellow of the Institute of Home Economics whom she represents on the Consumers' Committee of the Meat and Livestock Commission. After working for several years as a dietician in hospitals she became a lecturer in nutrition and home economics for the Flour Advisory Bureau in London.

She was a member of the Government Nutrition Task Force Working Group on Information and Education for the public, schools and media and now represents the consumer on the MAFF Food Authenticity Working Group for Meat and Meat Products.

The award of a Winston Churchill Memorial Fellowship in the late 80's enabled her to visit Scandinavia and Holland to study the ways in which healthy eating guidelines were promoted in those countries.

Now working as a Food and Nutrition Consultant she has written several books and numerous articles for magazines and newspapers on all aspects of food and nutrition. She is also a member of the Guild of Food Writers.

# At a Glance Contents

**⑩**

# HOME AND HOBBIES    147

**⑪**

# THE STUDY    166

# INTRODUCTION

All around the home, but especially in the kitchen, there are numerous situations where correct measures, sizes and temperatures are important and timings vital.

What litre or pint size pie dish is needed to make a pie for six people and how much pastry in ounces or grams is needed to cover it? How can a recipe with the ingredients written in American cups be 'translated' into metric measures? How many glasses of wine are obtained from one bottle? How can recipes be adjusted for timing in the microwave? What is the recommended safe temperature for a refrigerator? With Imperial, metric and American measures in use in Britain everyone needs help with measuring and conversion problems.

As well as measures for the cook, other useful measures around the home have been included in this book.

Just how is body temperature expressed in °C now it has changed from ° F ? How do you buy a valance to fit a bed when there is no standard bed height, or cope with fitted sheets made to metric sizes and so unsuitable for an imperial sized bed? Is 23°C a hot, warm or cold day ? Just how many rolls of wallpaper (still made to imperial measures) are needed to paper a room ? What is the time in Hong Kong when it is 9.00 a.m. in Britain?

Much of the confusion at the present time, especially in the kitchen, is due to the partial and very slow introduction of the metric system into Britain. As there is no co-ordinated policy for Britain to 'go metric' we have a dual system of measures in place which leaves most consumers completely confused. Older people find the need to convert Imperial measures into metric measures and young people who have been taught metric measures find they need to translate these into Imperial units when buying or using items that are not yet metricated.

Until the day comes when everything is only made and sold in metric quantities and all recipes specify just metric ingredients, this book will be invaluable.

# BACKGROUND TO METRICATION

## Early weights and measures

The bushel and peck, the drachm and scruple, the pennyweight, rood, furlong and chain, were all units of measurement in Britain at one time. But years ago they were declared no longer lawful for use in trade or business. The only one of these which has stood the test of time is the furlong which is still regularly used in horse racing; 'Only one furlong to go'.

The cubic yard, stone and hundredweight were in use more recently, until legislation also removed them as legal units of measurement for trade transactions in Britain.

## Imperial system of measures

The Imperial system of weights and measures evolved over centuries even before proper means of exact measuring were available. The inch was the breadth of a man's thumb and the yard was the distance from the nose to the end of the outstretched arm of Henry I. A man's foot was generally about a third of this distance so three feet were taken as making up one yard.

Weights originated in a similar way, derived from the weight of grains taken from an ear of wheat. In the reign of Henry III a pound was 6750 grains, but this changed to 7000 grains and 56 pounds in the reign of Elizabeth I. Volumes, areas and capacities were arrived at in a similar way. Some would call it an accumulation of folklore which needs replacing.

## Metric system of measures

The French realised that using parts of the body as a measure would never be consistent, so introduced the metric system based on more standard measures. Napoleon introduced the metric system to Europe and wherever he established his Empire the metre was adopted.

## Metrication in Britain

**1790** The British were invited by the French to establish an international system of weights and measures but no action was taken.

**1871** A bill to make metric measures legal in Britain was defeated in Parliament by just five votes. If this bill had been passed everyone in Britain would have converted to using metric measures over one hundred years ago. Despite the setback many people persisted in trying to get Britain metricated. Manufacturers who were exporting more and more of their goods to Europe were especially keen as they realised the benefits of all the goods they made being of suitable size wherever they were sold.

**1965** A plan to metricate was launched with Government approval.

**1969** A Metrication Board was set up to begin the process of educating all businesses and members of the public in metric measures.

**1972** A White Paper on Metrication stated the Government's intention to complete a metrication programme by the end of 1975.

**1976 The Weights and Measures Act** gave the Government power to phase out Imperial units for trade except for the gallon, pint, mile, foot and inch.

**1979** A general election resulted in a change of Government and the new Government stated that they would only support metrication on a voluntary basis.

The Metrication Board which was producing all the necessary educational material for school and public use was disbanded in 1980. Metrication went into limbo and the ambition of many that Britain would be fully metricated around the same time as we joined what is now the European Union has not been realised.

## Present situation

Today the European Union wants Britain to use metric measures so that all countries in the Single European market use the same weighing and measuring system. But Britain still has both the Imperial and metric systems in operation and will have until at least the turn of the century because of present legislation in place. If something remains voluntary, not mandatory, then few are going to make a great effort to change, especially when change will involve a great deal of expense.

Large industries such as the car industry, which export products, or use parts from the Continent, have to use metric measures and for them there is no problem. However, as no guidance has been given to the general public on when or how to use metric measures, or how to work out necessary conversions in everyday situations such as baking a cake or buying clothes, most of Britain's consumers just muddle along. This is not a problem that will just go away. Eventually some sort of educational back up will be required to get everyone familiar with metric measures. It is necessary for everyone to learn to 'think metric' and get familiar with it.

It was recognised that school children should be taught to work in metric to get familiar with the system, but the Government White Paper also stated that school children should have a working knowledge of Imperial measures for many years to come. This means that conversion charts are often used the opposite way by young people who learn about kilograms and so on at school, but then find that shops are still selling items loose in pounds and ounces.

The problem is not helped by many manufacturers, tradesmen and shop keepers who continue to think Imperial. We still buy some of our food in Imperial weights. People such as estate agents give sizes of rooms in feet and inches in their sale literature as they know people will understand these and will be able to relate the size to the room sizes they have previously lived in. Yet builders usually use metric measurements when building houses.

## Future legislation

In July 1992, 'A Consultative Document on Metrication' was issued by the Department of Trade and Industry. This gave proposals for Amending Weights and Measures, Units of Measurement and Price Marking Legislation. Discussions following this consultation resulted in a Parliamentary Announcement on Metrication by the Secretary of State for Trade and Industry. He announced to Parliament that legislation phasing out the use of imperial units was to be introduced. This is happening very, very slowly and a dual system will still be in operation for many years to come.

Just two examples are that the pint of milk will remain all the time it is in a returnable container on the doorstep but will be sold in litre cartons in shops. Distances and speeds on road signs and maps will remain in miles, yards and feet and not change to kilometres even though petrol is sold in litres.

Certain changes to the selling of pre-packed foods in shops have now been authorised and many other changes will take place every year until further legislation which comes into place at the end of 1999. The United States of America is in the process of changing to metrication so Americans will also find the information in this book useful. Information regarding the conversion to the metric system of cup sizes, US pints and gallons are given.

To help the consumer see a job right through to successful completion many other measuring problems around the home are highlighted in these pages. For instance as well as giving metric sizes for varying widths of material, information is given regarding the number of widths of material needed when making curtains. Safety has not been forgotten and the new colours used in electrical wiring are given, safe temperatures for food in refrigerators and the new markings used on microwaves which correspond to similar marks on convenience foods and meals.

Under one cover are solutions to all manner of measuring problems that people are likely to encounter around the home but especially in the kitchen. It will be invaluable to every cook and homemaker for many years to come and help to clear the Great Metric Muddle.

# 1

# BRITISH AND INTERNATIONAL STANDARDS OF EXACT WEIGHTS AND MEASURES

## BRITISH STANDARD NUMBERS

The British Standards Institute (BSI) was incorporated by Royal Charter. It is the independent national body for the preparation of British Standards and is the UK member of the International Organisation for Standardisation (ISO). Compliance with a British Standard does not of itself confer immunity from legal obligations.

The British Standards Institute give numbers to each item for which a specific standard has been achieved. The specifications and criteria which have to be met in order for a number to be given, are thoroughly discussed with everyone involved in each industry before being published. Anyone who feels that his goods or services comply with these standards can apply for the appropriate BS number to be given him. Standards are continually under review and are updated as necessary. Copies of all British Standard documents are kept in large reference libraries around the country.

**The BSI Kitemark** This is one of the two marks of the British Standards Institute. This is proof that the product has been made under an approved system of control, that testing has been carried out, and that the BSl has  periodically inspected the maker's work to ensure it complies with the relevant British Standard. Look for it when buying oil heaters, fireguards for open coal fires, pressure cookers, harnesses for prams, push chairs, and high chairs, carry cots and stands.

**The BSI Safety Mark** This is the symbol of safety from the British Standards Institute. It appears on products which conform to BSI safety standards. Look for it on domestic light fittings, (table lamps, pendant lamps etc) and domestic gas appliances (cookers, fires, water heaters etc).

## BS 5750

This BS number has always been regarded as the ideal for which everyone should aim. Those whose product or services achieve this standard are justly proud. It was adopted as a hallmark several years ago by the International Standards Organisation (ISO) of which the British Standards Institute was a founding member.

The European Standards body is called CEN. CEN stands for Comité Européan de Normalisation (European Committee for Standardisation). Its headquarters are at Rue Bréderode 2, B - 1000 Brussels, Belgium. CEN also adopted the idea of awarding standard numbers so until now there have been three different numbers all standing for virtually the same thing. To avoid confusion between the three there is now to be one similar number for each standard in the series.

For instance BS5750 part 1:1987 will now be known as BS EN ISO 9001:1994. This indicates that the standard was checked and updated as necessary in 1994 and has the new triple status as a national, European and International standard. Changes will occur as standards are renewed and revised.

## Statutory instruments

Statutory Instruments are created under the authority of a statute. Sometimes they are referred to as Rules, Regulations and Orders and they can be amended and revoked as necessary.

Over 2,000 Statutory Instruments are issued each year covering all manner of subjects and they are numbered sequentially from the first of January each year.

Each SI carries a commencement date and source of authority. They are available for reference in all main libraries in the United Kingdom.

## Standard Abbreviations

### BRITISH STANDARD 350: PART 1 AND BS 1991: PART 1

| | | | |
|---|---|---|---|
| acre | acre | metre | m |
| centilitre | cl | mile | mi |
| centimetre | cm | milligram | mg |
| cubic centimetre | cm³ | millilitre | ml |
| cubic foot | cu ft or ft³ | millimetre | mm |
| cubic inch | cu in or in³ | minute | min |
| cubic kilometre | km³ | ounce | oz |
| cubic metre | m³ | pint | pt |
| cubic mile | mi³ | pound | lb |
| cubic millimetre | mm³ | quart | qt |
| cubic yard | yd³ | square centimetre | cm² |
| foot | ft | square foot | ft² |
| gallon | gal | square inch | in² |
| gram | g | square kilometre | km² |
| hectare | ha | square metre | m² |
| hundredweight | cwt | square mile | sq mile |
| hour | h | square millimetre | mm² |
| inch | in | square yard | yd² |
| kilogram | kg | ton | ton |
| kilometre | km | tonne | tonne |
| litre | l | yard | yd |

# WEIGHTS AND MEASURES

The system of weights and measures in Britain has traditionally been the Imperial system. This evolved over many years from units with different origins which were appointed by statute in 1838 to be used throughout the United Kingdom.

The Imperial System is gradually being superceded by the International System commonly known as the metric system based on the unit of ten. This is known as the Système Internationale d'Unités, abbreviated to SI.

## Système Internationale l'Unités

One of the main advantages of SI is that there is a unique symbol for each unit. Because these are international symbols they are never translated into other languages. For instance 'm' means 'metre' anywhere in the world. (See above for 'Standard Abbreviations').

There are exact conversion figures to enable any measurement from the imperial system to be changed into the equivalent metric measure and vice versa. Many of these figures include several decimal points which make everyday calculations impractical and also difficult without a calculator.

So for ease of use the exact figure is not always taken and figures are rounded up or down a little to the nearest whole number or 0.5 (½). In many instances this rounding up or down will not matter and it is easier to use whole numbers or numbers with just one decimal point.

However in some instances it is vital to be exact.

All figures given in this chapter are exact, so they form an essential reference point in the whole area of metrication. In the following chapters most figures have been rounded up or down a little to provide convenient usable quantities of measurement. The book is written as a practical guide, not a mathematical text book.

## The metric system

The main benefit of the metric system lies in its simplicity and universality. It is simple because all relationships between a unit and its multiples and sub-multiples in the system are in powers of 10. This is rather more sensible and certainly much easier to work out than the imperial measurement system which involves practices such as measuring the length of an object in inches, dividing the total inches by twelve to get the number of feet and then dividing the number of feet by three to get the number of yards.

> **There are four main metric measures**
>
> The **metre** is the unit for length, breadth or height
>
> The **litre** is the unit of volume
>
> The **kilogram** is the unit of weight
>
> **°C** is the measure of temperature

## MEASUREMENTS OF MASS OR WEIGHT

This is the unit of measure most used in recipes and around the kitchen in general. The conversion figures given are exact, to form a mathematical reference, but it will be seen in the text that for all practical purposes rounded up figures are used. Official legislation has been passed for the ounce to be taken as equivalent to 25 g for all practical purposes in the kitchen. These are given in the appropriate places in the book.

# Mass or weight

**1 ounce** equals   28.3495 grams
0.0625 pounds
0.028350 kilograms

**1 gram** equals   0.035274 ounces

**1 pound** equals   16 ounces
453.592 grams
0.453592 kilograms

**1 kilogram** equals   2.20462 pounds
35.2740 ounces
0.019684 hundredweight

**1 hundredweight** equals   50.8023 kilograms
112 pounds
1792 ounces
50802.3 grams
0.056 US tons (short ton)
0.05080 tonnes
0.05 UK tons

**1 US ton** equals   0.907185 tonnes
0.892857 UK tons
17.8571 hundredweight
907.185 kilograms
2000 pounds
32000 ounces
907185 grams

**1 tonne** equals   0.984207 UK tons
1.10231 US tons
19.6841 hundredweight
1000 kilograms
2204.62 pounds
35273.9 ounces

**1 UK ton** equals   1.01605 tonnes
1.12 US tons
20 hundredweight
1016.05 kilograms
2240 pounds
35840 ounces

The pound and ounce will not be authorised for use for goods sold loose from bulk after 31st December 1999.

The troy ounce will continue to be allowed for transactions in precious metals.

Since 1st October 1995 all pre-packed catchweight products, by law, have to be weighed and labelled in metric measures. The British Retail Consortium have decided to use the conversion factor of 1 pound equals 0.5 kilograms.

The table below gives the number of grams to the nearest round figure in each Imperial ounce and also the recommended gram conversion to the nearest 25 g as commonly used in recipes.

| Imperial / Metric Weight Conversions | | |
|---|---|---|
| OUNCE (OZ) | GRAM (HIGHEST ROUND FIGURE) | GRAMS (RECOMMENDED TO NEAREST 25G) |
| 1 oz | 28 g | 25 g |
| 2 | 57 | 50 |
| 3 | 85 | 75 |
| 4(¼ lb) | 113 | 100 - 125 |
| 5 | 142 | 150 |
| 6 | 170 | 175 |
| 7 | 198 | 200 |
| 8(½ lb) | 227 | 225 |
| 9 | 255 | 250 |
| 10 | 284 | 300 |
| 11 | 311 | 325 |
| 12(¾ lb) | 340 | 350 |
| 13 | 368 | 375 |
| 14 | 396 | 400 |
| 15 | 425 | 425 |
| 16(1 lb) | 453 | 450 |

## MEASUREMENTS OF VOLUME

Liquids are measured by volume and whether measuring a little milk to add to a recipe or petrol to put in the car, the following list of equivalent volumes will enable you to convert easily from imperial to metric quantities or vice versa. Exact measures have been given although many decimal points are involved and in practice the figures are rounded off to the nearest 0.5.

It is important to have the exact equivalent measures for reference.

# Equivalent measures

| | | |
|---|---|---|
| **1 litre** equals | 1000 millilitres | |
| | 0.2642 US gallons | |
| | 0.2200 UK gallons | |
| **1 US gallon** equals | 3.785 litres | |
| | 3785 millilitres | |
| | 0.8327 UK gallons | |
| **1 UK gallon** equals | 1.201 US gallons | |
| | 4.546 litres | |
| | 4546 millilitres | |
| **1 US barrel** equals | 42 US gallons | |
| | 34.97 UK gallons | |
| **1 fluid ounce** equals | 28.41 millilitres | |
| **1 UK pint** equals | 568.2 millilitres | |
| **1 litre** equals | 1.760 UK pints | |

**NB:** Since 31st December 1994 the following units of volume measurement are not authorised. The pint except to dispense draught beer and cider and milk in returnable containers. The fluid ounce and pint are not to be used for beer, cider, waters, lemonades and fruit juices in returnable containers unless specifically specified.

## How to use these Figures

The litre is the unit of volume or capacity. The short way to write litre is l.

### Decilitres
It can be divided into decilitres written dl. Deci means 10 so there are 10 decilitres in 1 litre.
1 decilitre = ½ American cup

### Centilitres
1 litre can also be divided into centilitres written cl. Centi means one hundred so there are 100 centilitres in 1 litre.

### Millilitres
1 litre can also be divided into millilitres written ml.
Milli means one thousand so there are one thousand millilitres in 1 litre and therefore there are five hundred millilitres in ½ litre.

| | |
|---|---|
| 10 millilitres (ml) | = 1 centilitre (cl) |
| 10 centilitres (cl) | = 1 decilitre (dl) |
| 10 decilitres (dl) | = 1 litre (l) |
| 10 litres (l) | = 1 decalitre(dal) |
| 10 decalitres (dal) | = 1 hectolitre (hl) |
| 10 hectolitres (hl) | = 1 kilolitre( kl) |

When measuring small amounts of liquid such as in recipes, the millilitre, centilitre, decilitre and litre are most commonly used.

However in British recipes it is usual to find only millilitres and litres used, while the centilitre and decilitre are more common in European and American recipes.

## Fluid ounces and pints

The Imperial measure for liquids is the pint which is divided into fluid ounces. This quick reference chart shows the number of fluid ounces in pint measures and the number of millilitres each represents.

**1 pint** = 20 fluid ounces = 568 ml

**¾ pint** = 15 fluid ounces = 426 ml

**½ pint** = 10 fluid ounces = 284 ml

**¼ pint** = 5 fluid ounces = 142 ml

0.88 pints = ½ litre

**1.76 pints** - just over 1¾ pints = 1 litre

**8 pints** = 1 gallon which is just over 4½ litres

Although there are 568 ml in 1 Imperial pint it is very common in recipes to find the 1 pint equivalent given as 600 ml where the exact amount of liquid used is not too important such as in the making of a rice pudding.

**The chart below shows the exact conversion figures** to change fluid ounces to millilitres, and the nearest rounded practical figures from 1 fl oz to 10 pints. These are especially useful in the kitchen.

## Imperial / Metric Volume Conversions

| IMPERIAL MEASURE | EXACT ML FIGURE | ROUNDED OFF ML MEASURE |
|---|---|---|
| 1 fl oz | 28.413 ml | 25 ml |
| 2 | 56.826 | 50 |
| 3 | 85.239 | 75 - 85 |
| 4 | 113.652 | 100 - 125 |
| 5 fl oz ( ¼ pint) | 142.065 | 150 |
| 6 | 170.478 | 175 |
| 7 fl oz ( ⅓ pint) | 198.891 | 200 |
| 8 | 227.305 | 225 |
| 9 | 255.718 | 250 |
| 10 fl oz ( ½ pint) | 284.131 | 300 |
| 15 fl oz ( ¾ pint) | 426.196 | 425 |
| 20 fl oz ( 1 pint) | 568.261 | 575 |
| 25 fl oz (1¼ pints) | 710.326 | 700 |
| 30 fl oz (1½ pints) | 852.392 | 850 |
| 35 fl oz (1¾ pints) | 994.457 | 1 litre |
| 2 pints | 1136.523 | 1.1 litres |
| 2¼ pints | 1278.588 | 1.3 litres |
| 2½ pints | 1420.654 | 1.4 litres |
| 2¾ pints | 1562.719 | 1.6 litres |
| 3 pints | 1704.784 | 1.7 litres |
| 3¼ pints | 1846.849 | 1.8 litres |
| 3½ pints | 1988.915 | 2.0 litres |
| 3¾ pints | 2130.98 | 2.1 litres |
| 4 pints | 2273.046 | 2.3 litres |
| 4¼ pints | | 2.4 litres |
| 4½ pints | 2557.177 | 2.6 litres |
| 4¾ pints | | 2.7 litres |
| 5 pints | 2841.307 | 2.8 litres |
| 5¼ pints | | 3.0 litres |
| 5½ pints | | 3.1 litres |
| 5¾ pints | | 3.3 litres |
| 6 pints | 3409.568 | 3.4 litres |
| 6¼ pints | | 3.5 litres |
| 6½ pints | | 3.7 litres |
| 6¾ pints | | 3.8 litres |
| 7 pints | 3977.83 | 4.0 litres |
| 8 pints (1 gallon) | 4546.092 | 4.5 litres |
| 9 pints | 5114.353 | 5.1 litres |
| 10 pints | 5682.614 | 5.7 litres |

| | |
|---|---|
| **1 litre** equals | 1.76 pints - <br> a little more than 1¾ pints |
| **½ litre** equals | 0.88 pints |
| **4½ litres** equals | just under 1 gallon |
| **1 litre** equals | 4½ American cups |

To change litres to gallons and gallons to litres see page 188 - 189.

The chart below shows the reverse to the above chart converting millilitres to fluid ounces.

| ML | FLUID OUNCES | ML | FLUID OUNCES |
|---|---|---|---|
| 1 | 0.035 | 8 | 0.282 |
| 2 | 0.070 | 9 | 0.317 |
| 3 | 0.106 | 10 | 0.352 |
| 4 | 0.141 | 20 | 0.704 |
| 5 | 0.176 | 28.413 | 1 fluid ounce |
| 6 | 0.211 | 30 | 1.056 |
| 7 | 0.246 | | |

## MEASUREMENTS OF LENGTH, BREADTH & HEIGHT

Whether measuring the width across a cake tin, the depth of an oven, or the height of a room when wallpapering, it is measurements of length that are involved.

**Length** is the distance between two points whether measuring the length of a running track or a baking tin. When measuring a rectangular item such as a tin, the length is always the longer of the two sides.

**Breadth** is the term used for the width of something; the measurement across a running track or the shorter of the two sides of a rectangular tin.

**Height** or depth is a vertical measure; for instance the distance from the top of a building to the ground or from the top rim of a cake tin to the base.

The table below provides a quick reference to enable various measures of length to be converted from one to another quickly and easily, regardless of whether the length is tiny or very large or whether imperial or metric measures are preferred. Exact measures have been given in this section. This book is for practical use and therefore a lot of 'rounding off' has been done following the recommendations in legislation. However it is necessary that the reader has available the exact equivalent figures for reference.

# Equivalent measures

**1 centimetre** equals
10 millimetres
0.393701 inches
0.032808 feet
0.010936 yards
0.01 metres

**1 inch** equals
2.54 centimetres
25.4 millimetres
0.083333 feet
0.027778 yards
0.0254 metres

**1 foot** equals
12 inches
30.48 centimetres
304.8 millimetres
0.333333 yards
0.3048 metres

**1 yard** equals
3 feet
36 inches
91.44 centimetres
914.4 millimetres
0.9144 metres

**1 metre** equals
1.09361 yards
3.28084 feet
39.3701 inches
100 centimetres
1000 millimetres

**1 kilometre** equals
1000 metres
1093.61 yards
3280.84 feet
39370.1 inches
100,000 centimetres

**1 mile** equals
1.60934 kilometres
1609.34 metres
1760 yards
5280 feet
63360 inches
160934 centimetres

The mile, yard, foot and inch ceased to be authorised for use after December 1994 for economic, public health, public safety and administrative purposes except for continued use for road traffic signs and related distance and speed measurements. (see page 186.)

## How to use these Figures

The short way to write metre is m

1 yard is 3 feet or 36 inches
1 metre is just over 1 yard or 39.37 inches

Rounding this long figure to the nearest whole number means
1 metre equals 39 inches.

### To convert metres to feet

Multiply the number of metres by 3.2808 for an exact answer or 3.3 for an approximate answer.

### To convert metres to yards

Multiply the number of metres by 1.0936 for an exact answer or 1.1 for an approximate answer.

### To convert feet to metres

Multiply the number of feet by 0.3048 for an exact answer or 0.31 for an approximate answer.

### To convert yards to metres

Multiply the number of yards by 0.9144 for an exact answer or 0.9 for an approximate answer.

The chart below provides a quick reference to change feet and yards to metres

| FEET | METRES | YARDS | METRES |
|------|--------|-------|--------|
| 1 | 0.305 | 1 (3 feet) | 0.914 |
| 2 | 0.610 | 2 | 1.829 |
| 3 (1 yard) | 0.914 | 3 | 2.743 |
| 4 | 1.219 | 4 | 3.658 |
| 5 | 1.524 | 5 | 4.572 |
| 6 (2 yards) | 1.829 | 6 | 5.486 |
| 7 | 2.134 | 7 | 6.401 |
| 8 | 2.438 | 8 | 7.315 |
| 9 (3 yards) | 2.743 | 9 (27 feet) | 8.230 |
| 10 | 3.048 | 10 | 9.144 |

The chart below provides a quick reference to change metres to feet and yards

| METRES | FEET | YARDS |
|--------|--------|--------|
| 1 | 3.281 | 1.094 |
| 2 | 6.562 | 2.187 |
| 3 | 9.843 | 3.281 |
| 4 | 13.123 | 4.374 |
| 5 | 16.404 | 5.468 |
| 6 | 19.685 | 6.562 |
| 7 | 22.966 | 7.655 |
| 8 | 26.247 | 8.749 |
| 9 | 29.528 | 9.843 |
| 10 | 32.808 | 10.936 |

The metre can be divided into 100 parts each called a centimetre.

## Centimetres

The short way to write centimetre is cm
Centi means one hundreth so 1 metre can be divided into
100 centimetres written as 100 cm
1 centimetre is exactly equal to 0.3937 inches or 0.4 inches when rounded to the nearest inch.

## To convert centimetres to inches

Multiply the number of centimetres by 0.3937 for an exact answer or multiply by 0.4 for an approximate answer.

## To convert inches to centimetres

Multiply the number of inches by 2.54 for an exact answer or multiply by 2.5 for an approximate answer.

## To convert feet to centimetres

Multiply the number of feet by 30.48 for an exact answer or multiply by 30.5 for an approximate answer.

## To convert yards to centimetres

Multiply the number of yards by 91.44 for an exact answer or multiply by 91.5 for an approximate answer.

Once any answer or figure is more than 100 cm it is usual to express the answer in metres and centimetres rather than a very large number of centimetres.

**For example**

If you need 4 yards of material in Imperial measurement you would
need to buy: 4 yards x 91.44 = 365.76 centimetres.

Divide by 100 as there are 100 centimetres in each metre. This comes to 3
metres 65.76 centimetres or rounded to the nearest whole number = 3
metres 66 cm. As shopkeepers usually sell material in blocks of 10 cm you
would need to ask for 3 metres 70 cm of fabric.

A rough guide for everyday quick calculations is:
2½ centimetres are just under 1 inch
30 centimetres are just under 1 foot
90 centimetres are just under 3 feet or 1 yard.

The chart below provides a quick reference to change inches to millimetres
and centimetres.

| INCHES | MILLIMETRES | CENTIMETRES |
|--------|-------------|-------------|
| 1 | 25.4 | 2.54 |
| 2 | 50.8 | 5.08 |
| 3 | 76.2 | 7.62 |
| 4 | 101.6 | 10.16 |
| 5 | 127.0 | 12.70 |
| 6 | 152.4 | 15.24 |
| 7 | 177.8 | 17.78 |
| 8 | 203.2 | 20.32 |
| 9 | 228.6 | 22.86 |
| 10 | 254.0 | 25.40 |
| 20 | 508.0 | 50.80 |
| 30 | 762.0 | 76.20 |
| 40 | 1016.0 | 101.60 |
| 50 | 1270.0 | 127.00 |
| 60 | 1524.0 | 152.40 |
| 70 | 1778.0 | 177.80 |
| 80 | 2032.0 | 203.20 |
| 90 | 2286.0 | 228.60 |
| 100 | 2540.0 | 254.00 |

## Millimetres

The short way to write millimetre is mm
1 centimetre can be divided into 10 millimetres
1 metre can be divided into 1,000 millimetres
1 millimetre is equal to 0.0394 inches
1 inch is equal to 25.4 millimetres.

## To convert millimetres to inches

Multiply the number of millimetres by 0.0394 for an exact answer or
multiply by 0.04 for an approximate answer.

## To convert inches to millimetres

Multiply the number of inches by 25.4 for an exact answer.

When the answer is larger than 10 it is usual to express the answer in
centimetres and millimetres rather than a very large number of millimetres.

## For example

If a piece of wood is 3½ inches long it is 3½ x 25.4 = 889 mm long.
Divide 889 mm by 10 to discover that this is equal to 88.9 cm or rounded to
the whole number = 89 cm.

## Measuring various shapes

These formulae enable measurements of circular and spherical objects
to be calculated.

($\pi = 22 \div 7$ or 3.14)

## To find the:

circumference of a circle use the formuae $2\pi r$

area of a circle     $\pi r^2$

volume of a sphere   $\pi r^3$

surface of a sphere    $4\pi r^2$

volume of a cylinder   $\pi r^2 h$

# MEASUREMENTS OF TEMPERATURE

The Fahrenheit scale has historically been the most commonly used measure of temperature in Britain and other English speaking countries. The centigrade scale has been favoured by scientists throughout Europe and is now being gradually introduced into weather forecasting.

Most people still think in degrees Fahrenheit if they want to know whether the day is going to be warm or chilly and much equipment is still marked in this way. So it is useful to know the centigrade equivalents and to know how to convert quickly from one to another.

The Centigrade scale is called this because it is divided into 100 divisions.

Its correct name is the Celsius scale named after the Swedish astronomer and physicist Anders Celsius (1701 - 1744). Some thermometers are marked in Celsius (centigrade) **and** Fahrenheit scales.

| Comparative Temperatures | | | |
|---|---|---|---|
| **CENTIGRADE** | **FAHRENHEIT** | **CENTIGRADE** | **FAHRENHEIT** |
| 0° | 32° | 45° | 113° |
| 5° | 41° | 50° | 122° |
| 10° | 50° | 55° | 131° |
| 15° | 59° | 60° | 140° |
| 20° | 68° | 70° | 158° |
| 25° | 77° | 80° | 176° |
| 30° | 86° | 90° | 194° |
| 35° | 95° | 100° | 212° |
| 40° | 104° | | |

To avoid having to look up equivalent temperatures on a chart, or when a chart is not available, there is a quick way to convert from one temperature scale to the other temperature scale.

**To change Celsius to Fahrenheit**

Multiply the Celsius figure by 9, divide that answer by 5 and add 32. The answer is °Fahrenheit.

Put as an equation   $°F = 9/5 \, (°C + 32)$

## To change Fahrenheit to Celsius

Subtract 32 from the Fahrenheit figure, multiply by 5 and divide this figure by 9. The answer is °C.

Put as an equation   $°C = 5/9 (°F - 32)$

## Two temperatures are easy to remember and provide a good guide.

16°C = 61°F; and 28°C = 82°F

For the conversion of oven temperatures see page 84.

## Commonly used temperatures

The boiling point of water is 100° C or 212° F

The freezing point of water is 0° C or 32° F

Temperatures below freezing (0° C) have a minus sign in front.

## 'Normal' weather temperatures

| | |
|---|---|
| a very cold winters night is i.e. below freezing point | -5°C or 27°F |
| a cool night is about | 5°C or 41°F |
| a cool summer day and a mild winters day are around | 15°C or 59°F |
| a warm day is around | 20°C or 68°F |
| a hot day | 27°C or 80°F |
| a heatwave is as hot as | 30°C or 86°F or above |

## Room temperatures

These vary according to personal taste but recommended healthy temperatures are:

bedrooms about 18° C (64° F)

living rooms about 22° C (72° F)

A hot bath would be 43°C (109°F)

Washing up water would be about 48°C (118°F).

# MEASUREMENTS OF AREA

An area is always called 'square', a square foot, a square centimetre and so on. It is used around the house when measuring for flooring or wall coverings or similar. The little 'two' above the measure symbol means 'squared'. The table below gives all the equivalents of metric and imperial measures for area in exact equivalents. When measuring any large surface it is wise to use the exact, even if rather long figure, and then round off the answer. This way the answer is more precise(see note at end).

## Equivalent measures

| | |
|---|---|
| **1 cm²** equals | 100 millimetres² |
| | 0.1550 inches² |
| **1 inch²** equals | 6.4516 centimetres² |
| | 645.16 millimetres² |
| **1 foot²** equals | 144 inches² |
| | 929 centimetres² |
| | 92903 millimetres² |
| | 0.1111 yards² |
| | 0.09290 metres² |
| **1 yard²** equals | 9 feet² |
| | 1296 inches² |
| | 8361 centimetres² |
| | 836127 millimetres² |
| | 0.8361 metres² |
| **1 metre²** equals | 1.196 yards² |
| | 10.764 feet² |
| | 1550 inches² |
| | 10,000 centimetres² |
| **1 kilometre²** equals | 100 hectares |
| | 247.1 acres |
| **1 mile²** equals | 2.590 kilometre² |
| | 259.0 hectares |
| | 640 acres |
| **1 acre** equals | 4047 metres² |
| | 4840 yards² |
| | 43560 feet² |
| | 0.4047 hectares |
| **1 hectare** equals | 2.471 acres |
| | 10,000 metres² |
| | 11,960 yards² |
| | 107,639 feet² |

(see page 31 for acre equivalents for hectares and hectare equivalents for acres)

## Measurement of land area

Since 31st December 1994 the measurement of an acre has not been authorised for general use. It is authorised for continued use without time limit for land registration purposes only. Now only the hectare will be used, so refer to the following tables to convert one measure to the other.

1 acre = 4047 m$^2$

1 acre = 4840 square yards.

Equivalent measures are taken to the nearest 0.001.

| ACRES | HECTARES | HECTARES | ACRES |
|-------|----------|----------|--------|
| 1 | 0.405 | 1 | 2.471 |
| 2 | 0.809 | 2 | 4.942 |
| 3 | 1.214 | 3 | 7.413 |
| 4 | 1.619 | 4 | 9.884 |
| 5 | 2.023 | 5 | 12.355 |
| 6 | 2.428 | 6 | 14.826 |
| 7 | 2.833 | 7 | 17.297 |
| 8 | 3.237 | 8 | 19.769 |
| 9 | 3.642 | 9 | 22.240 |
| 10 | 4.047 | 10 | 24.711 |
| 20 | 8.094 | 20 | 49.421 |
| 30 | 12.140 | 30 | 74.132 |
| 40 | 16.187 | 40 | 98.842 |
| 50 | 20.234 | 50 | 123.553 |

# WEIGHTS AND MEASURES FOR COOKS

In some situations it is possible to use the exact conversion figure when converting from Imperial measures to metric measures. However, when weighing food for cooking, it is silly if not impossible to weigh for instance 57 g of flour in place of 2 oz flour as stated in a recipe, even though it is virtually the exact arithmetical equivalent. So in 1972 it was officially decided that throughout Britain the 1 oz weight would be replaced by 25 g when cooking ingredients were being weighed. As the metric system is based around units of 5 and 10 this makes good sense and makes measuring far more practical.

This means that throughout all recipes, multiples of 5 are always used when metric measurements are being used. (If exact conversion figures are required for some reason see page 17).

At times this can make recipes seem very inaccurate, as the metric figure may be far removed from the exact Imperial equivalent it is replacing. For this reason, those people developing new recipes or translating 'old' recipes, have to test both methods of measure. This can often result in a recipe which when written looks arithmetically incorrect but in fact works. This is why it is always recommended that those preparing the recipes should follow **either** the imperial measures or the metric measures **or** cups but not use a mixture of measures.

This is especially important when making baked items where correct proportions are usually essential. When making savoury items such as casseroles or pasta dishes it is not usually so important.

When everyone is familiar with metric measures and owns metric equipment the imperial measures will gradually be omitted from recipes.

## BRITISH AND AMERICAN EQUIVALENT MEASURES

There are many American cookery books on sale in Britain and Europe. There are also many British cookery books on sale in America. In order to enjoy all these recipes it is necessary to understand the cookery terms used and to be able to translate the American measures into Imperial or metric measures and vice versa.

(For translation of American cookery terms to British cookery terms see page 34).

(For quantities of food in one American cup see page 51)

## Chart for converting imperial to metric measures in recipes

As more foods are being sold in metric weights and many favourite recipes are written in Imperial measures there will often be the need to convert from one kind of measure to another when cooking. Exact conversion figures are not suitable for cooking as one cannot weigh to the nearest gram or quarter ounce, indeed there is no need.

So to change quantities from one type of measure to another a conversion chart is necessary.

## How to use this chart

To convert from Imperial to metric or metric to Imperial, look up the amount in the column to be changed and read off the amount alongside. Where no amount is given, obtain the total by adding two numbers together. For instance if the recipe states that 5½ ounces are needed, in grams this would be 150 + 15 = 165 grams.

Equivalents are given to the nearest 5 grams and are not necessarily mathematically correct.

| Converting ounces and pounds to grams and kilograms and vice versa | | | |
|---|---|---|---|
| **IMPERIAL** | **METRIC** | **IMPERIAL** | **METRIC** |
| ⅛ ounce | 5 grams | 12 | 350 grams |
| ¼ | 10 | 13 | 375 |
| ½ | 15 | 14 | 400 |
| ¾ | 20 | 15 | 425 |
| 1 | 25 | 16 oz (1 lb) | 450 |
| 2 | 50 | 1¼ lb | 550 |
| 3 | 75 | 1½ lb | 675 |
| 4 | 100 - 125 | 2 lbs | 900 |
| 5 | 150 | 2¼ lbs | 1 kilogram |
| 6 | 175 | 2½ lbs | 1¼ |
| 7 | 200 | 3 lbs | 1½ |
| 8 | 225 | 3½ lbs | 1¾ |
| 9 | 250 | 4 lbs | 1¾ |
| 10 | 275 | 4½ lbs | 2 |
| 11 | 300 | 5 lbs | 2¼ |

## Converting fluid ounces and pints to litres and millilitres and vice versa

| IMPERIAL | METRIC | IMPERIAL | METRIC |
|---|---|---|---|
| 1 fluid ounce | 25 ml | 1 pint milk exact measure | 568 ml |
| 2 | 50 | 20 fluid ounces (1 pint) | 600 |
| 3 | 75 | 1½ pints | 850 |
| 4 | 125 | 1¾ pints | 1 litre |
| 5 | 150 | 2 pints | 1.1 litres |
| 6 | 175 | 2½ pints | 1.4 litres |
| 7 | 200 | 3 pints | 1.7 litres |
| 8 | 225 | 3½ pints | 2 litres |
| 9 | 250 | 4 pints | 2.3 litres |
| 10 fluid ounces (half pint) | 275 | 4½ pints | 2.6 litres |
| 12 | 350 | 5 pints | 2.8 litres |
| 14 | 400 | 6 pints | 3.4 litres |
| 16 | 450 | 7 pints | 4 litres |
| 18 | 500 | 8 pints (1 gallon) | 4.5 litres |

## Translation of British / American Cookery Terms

| BRITISH | AMERICAN | BRITISH | AMERICAN |
|---|---|---|---|
| ale | light ale or beer | bicarbonate of soda | baking soda |
| almonds - ground | almonds - finely ground | bilberries | blueberries |
| | | biscuits | cookies |
| almonds - flaked | slivered almonds | bread rusks | zwieback crackers |
| anchovy essence | anchovy paste | broad beans | windsor or fava beans |
| apples - cooking | green apples | butter beans | lima beans |
| apple pips | apple seeds | butter - unsalted | sweet butter |
| aubergine | egg plant | | |
| avocado stone | avocado seed | cake tins | cake pans |
| | | cauliflower sprigs | cauliflowerets |
| bacon joint | baked ham | cherries - cooking | tart or sour |
| baking powder | baking powder | cherry stones | cherry pits |
| beans - french or green | snap beans | chick peas | garbanzo beans |
| | | chicken joint | chicken quarter |
| beans - haricot | white beans | chicory | Belgian endive |
| beetroot | beet | chocolate - plain | semi-sweet chocolate pieces |
| beef olives | roulades | | |
| beef stock cubes | beef bouillon cube | | |

## Translation of British / American Cookery Terms

| BRITISH | AMERICAN | BRITISH | AMERICAN |
|---|---|---|---|
| chocolate - cooking | unsweetened chocolate | glace cherries | candied cherries |
| cider | apple cider | golden syrup | none use corn syrup - light or dark |
| coconut - desiccated | flaked or grated | | |
| coriander - fresh | cilantro | grill | skillet |
| cornflour | corn starch | grilling | broiling |
| cos lettuce | romaine | | |
| courgettes | zucchini | ham - parma | prosciutto |
| crayfish | crawfish | haricot beans | navy beans |
| cream crackers | oyster crackers | hazel nuts | cob nuts or filberts |
| cream - double | heavy cream or whipping | icing sugar | confectioners sugar |
| cream - single | light cream | | |
| crystallised fruits | candied fruits | | |
| cucumber pickles | dill pickles | jam | jelly or preserves |
| custard powder | no equivalent use cornstarch + yellow colouring | jelly | jello |
| | | joint of meat | roast |
| curd cheese | farmer's cheese | ketchup | catsup |
| curly endive | chicory | | |
| | | macerate | steep |
| dairy produce | dairy products | made-up dishes | prepared dishes |
| dates - stoned | dates - pitted | maize - flour | cornmeal |
| demerara sugar | light brown sugar | groats | hominy grits |
| desiccated coconut | shredded coconut | mangetout | snow peas |
| digestive biscuits | Graham crackers | marrow | large zucchini or summer squash |
| drop scone | pancake | | |
| egg - hard boiled | hard cooked | minced beef | ground beef |
| | | muesli | granola |
| endive | chicory | mustard-French | prepared |
| entrecote steak | Porterhouse steak | mustard- dry English | dry |
| fats e.g. lard | shortening | | |
| flaked almonds | sliced almonds | oatmeal | rolled oats |
| flour - plain | all purpose flour | oil - groundnut | peanut |
| flour - self raising | self rising flour | offal | variety meats |
| french beans | snap beans | onion - Spanish | Spanish or Bermuda |
| full fat cheese | cream cheese | | |
| gelatine | gelatin | onion - spring | scallion or green |
| ginger nuts | ginger snaps | onion - button | pearl onion |

## Translation of British / American Cookery Terms

| IMPERIAL | METRIC | IMPERIAL | METRIC |
|---|---|---|---|
| orange and lemon pips | orange and lemon seeds | starter | appetizer |
| pancake | crêpe | starters | hors d'oeuvres |
| peach stone | peach pit | sticks celery | stalks |
| persimmons | sharon fruit | streaky bacon rashers | bacon slices |
| pig's trotters | pig's shanks | stock | broth |
| plain chocolate | semi-sweet chocolate | stoned olives | pitted olives |
| plain flour | all-purpose flour | sugar – caster or granulated | granulated |
| pork fillet | pork tenderloin | soft brown | light brown |
| porridge oats | rolled oats | demerara | light brown |
| potatoes - creamed | potatoes - mashed | cube sugar | sugar cubes |
| prawns | shrimps | icing | confectioners |
| prune stone | prune pit | suet | chopped beef suet |
|  |  | sultanas | seedless white or golden raisins |
| rice – round grain or Carolina rice | short-grain rice | swede | turnip or rutabaga |
| runner beans | green beans | sweetcorn | corn |
|  |  | swiss roll | jelly roll |
| salty biscuits | soda crackers | tomato ketchup | catsup |
| semi-skimmed milk | part skim milk | tomato puree concentrate | tomato paste |
| semolina | semolina flour not widely available - use farina | treacle | molasses |
|  |  | tunny fish | tuna fish |
| single cream | light cream | vanilla essence | vanilla extract |
| soured cream | sour cream | vanilla pod | vanilla bean |
| soya beans | soy beans | vermicelli | fettucine |
| soya sauce | soy sauce |  |  |
| sponge fingers | ladyfingers | walnuts | english walnuts |
| spring greens | spring cabbage | wholemeal | wholewheat |
| spring onions | scallions |  |  |
| stalk - apples, cherries etc | stem | yogurt - natural | plain yogurt |

## General Terminology

| BRITISH | AMERICAN | BRITISH | AMERICAN |
|---|---|---|---|
| biscuit mixture | cookie dough | kitchen paper | paper towel |
| bottling | canning | icing | frosting |
| butter muslin | cheese cloth | omelette | omelet |
| cake mixture | cake batter | piping bag | decorators bag |
| chop finely | to mince | pinch of | dash of |
| first course | appetisers | to mince | to grind |
| flan | 1 crust pie or pastry shell | mincer | grinder |
| | | mould | mold |
| fork prongs | fork tines | pudding basin | ovenproof bowl |
| fresh | raw | puddings | desserts |
| greaseproof paper | nearest to it - waxed paper | scones | biscuits |
| | | tin | can |
| to grill | to broil | trifle sponge | use 1 jelly roll |
| jelly cubes | jelly crystals | to whisk or whip | to beat |

An American pancake is like a large English drop scone.
For English pancakes use the word 'crêpes' not pancakes.

## British/American Terminology for Cooking Equipment

| BRITISH | AMERICAN | BRITISH | AMERICAN |
|---|---|---|---|
| Baking tray | Cookie sheet | Swiss Roll tin | Jelly roll pan |
| Frying pan | Skillet | Tartlet tin | Muffin pan |
| Grill pan | Broiler tray | Always use the word pan in place of tin in America | |
| Ring mould | Tube pan | | |
| Sandwich tin | Layer cake pan | i.e. loaf tin - loaf pan | |

## American measures

| 1 | American cup is equivalent to 8 American fluid ounces |
|---|---|
| 1 | American pint equals 16 British fluid ounces or just over ¾ of a British pint |
| 3 | American teaspoons equals 1 American tablespoon |
| 16 | American tablespoons equals 1 American cup |
| 2 | American tablespoons equals 1 American fluid ounce. |

## Alcoholic measure

| 1½ | American fluid ounces equals 1 jigger. |
|---|---|

## British/American Equivalent Measures

| BRITISH | AMERICAN |
|---|---|
| 1 teaspoon | 1¼ teaspoons |
| 1 tablespoon | 1½ tablespoons |
| ¼ pint or 142 ml | ⅝ cup |
| ½ pint or 284 ml | 1¼ cups |
| ¾ pint or 426 ml | 1⅞ cups |
| 1 pint or 568 ml | 2½ cups |

## A to Z of British and American Food Equivalents

| IMPERIAL | METRIC | AMERICAN |
|---|---|---|
| **Almonds** - whole blanched | | |
| 4 oz | 100 g | ¾ cup |
| **Almonds** - ground | | |
| 2½ oz | 70 g | ½ cup |
| **Bacon** - diced raw | | |
| 2 oz | 50 g | ⅓ cup |
| **Breadcrumbs** - fresh | | |
| 2 oz | 50 g | 1 cup |
| **Breadcrumbs** - dried | | |
| 2 oz | 50 g | ¾ cup |
| **BUTTER, MARGARINE AND WHITE FATS** | | |
| ½ oz | 15 g | 1 tablespoon |
| ¾ oz | 20 g | 1½ tablespoons |
| 1 oz | 25 g | 2 tablespoons |
| 1½ oz | 40 g | 3 tablespoons |
| 2 oz | 50 g | 4 tablespoons |
| 2½ oz | 70 g | 5 tablespoons |
| 3 oz | 85 g | 6 tablespoons |
| 4 oz | 100 g | ½ cup |
| 5 oz | 125 g | ⅝ cup |
| 6 oz | 150 g | ¾ cup |
| 8 oz | 225 g | 1 cup |
| **CEREALS** | | |
| 4 oz pearl barley/tapioca | 100 g | ½ cup |
| 6 oz corn meal | 150 g | 1 cup |
| 6 oz cracked wheat | 150 g | 1 cup |

## A to Z of British and American Food Equivalents

| IMPERIAL | METRIC | AMERICAN |
|---|---|---|
| 6 oz semolina/ground rice | 150 g | 1 cup |
| 3 oz oatmeal | 75 g | 1 cup |
| **CHEESE** | | |
| **grated hard** | | |
| ½ oz | 15 g | 2 tablespoons |
| 1 oz | 25 g | ¼ cup |
| 2 oz | 50 g | ½ cup |
| 4 oz | 100 g | 1 cup |
| **Parmesan** | | |
| 1 oz | 25 g | 3 tablespoons |
| 2 oz | 50 g | ⅓ cup |
| 4 oz | 100 g | ⅔ cup |
| **Cottage** | | |
| 2 oz | 50 g | ⅓ cup |
| 4 oz | 100 g | ⅔ cup |
| 6 oz | 150 g | 1 cup |
| **CORNFLOUR/CORNSTARCH** | | |
| ½ oz | 15 g | 1½ tablespoons |
| 1 oz | 25 g | 3 tablespoons |
| 2 oz | 50 g | 6 tablespoons |
| 4 oz | 100 g | ¾ cup |
| **CREAM** | | |
| 2 fl oz | 56 ml | 4 tablespoons or ¼ cup |
| 3 fl oz | 85 ml | 6 tablespoons |
| 4 fl oz | 114 ml | ½ cup |
| 5 fl oz (¼ pt) | 142 ml | ⅝ cup |
| ½ pt | 284 ml | 1¼ cups |
| 1 pt | 568 ml | 2½ cups |
| **Sour** | | |
| 5 oz carton | 142 ml | 1 cup |
| **CURRY POWDER** | | |
| ½ oz | 15 g | 1 tablespoon |
| 1 oz | 25 g | 2 tablespoons |
| **DRIED FRUIT** | | |
| **Currants, raisins** | | |
| 1 oz | 25 g | 2 tablespoons |
| 2 oz | 50 g | ⅓ cup packed |
| 4 oz | 100 g | ⅔ cup packed |
| 6 oz | 150 g | 1 cup packed |

| A to Z of British and American Food Equivalents | | |
|---|---|---|
| **IMPERIAL** | **METRIC** | **AMERICAN** |
| **Prunes** | | |
| 2 oz | 50 g | ⅜ cup |
| 6 oz | 150 g | 1 generous cup |
| **Dried Apricots** | | |
| 2 oz | 50 g | ⅜ cup |
| 4 oz | 100 g | ¾ cup |
| 6 oz | 150 g | 1 generous cup |
| 8 oz | 225 g | 1½ cups |
| **Candied peel** | | |
| 2 oz | 50 g | ½ cup |
| 4 oz | 100 g | 1 cup |
| **Glace cherries** | | |
| 4 oz | 100 g | bare ½ cup |
| 8 oz | 225 g | good ½ cup |
| **Apple rings** | | |
| 2 oz | 50 g | 1½ cups |
| 4 oz | 100 g | 2⅔ cups |
| **EGG WHITES** | | |
| 1 egg white | | 2 tablespoons |
| 4 egg whites | | ½ cup |
| **FLOUR** | | |
| Plain/all purpose (sifted before being measured) | | |
| ½ oz | 15 g | 2 tablespoons |
| 1 oz | 25 g | 4 tablespoons |
| 2 oz | 50 g | good ½ cup |
| 3 oz | 75 g | good ¾ cup |
| 3½ oz | 90 g | 1 cup |
| 4 oz | 100g | 1 cup + 2 tbs |
| 8 oz | 225 g | 2¼ cups |
| 1 lb | 450 g | 4½ cups |
| **GELATINE** | | |
| ½ oz | 15 g | 2 tablespoons |
| 1 oz | 25 g | 4 tablespoons or ¼ cup |
| **HONEY, JAM, SYRUP** | | |
| 4 oz | 100 g | ⅜ cup |
| 6 oz | 150 g | ½ cup |
| 8 oz | 225 g | ¾ cup |
| 12 oz | 340 g | 1 cup |
| 1 lb | 450 g | 1⅜ cups |

## A to Z of British and American Food Equivalents

| IMPERIAL | METRIC | AMERICAN |
|---|---|---|
| **ICE CREAM** | | |
| 6 oz | 150 g | 1 cup |
| **LOBSTER** | | |
| 4 oz | 100 g | ½ cup |
| 8 oz | 225 g | 1 cup |
| **PASTA** | | |
| 8 oz | 225 g | 1⅔ cups |
| **MEAT** | | |
| **Diced cooked meat** | | |
| 3 oz | 75 g | ½ cup |
| 6 oz | 150 g | 1 cup |
| 8 oz | 225 g | 1⅓ cups |
| **Minced (Ground) meat** | | |
| 4 oz | 100 g | ½ cup |
| 8 oz | 225 g | 1 cup |
| 12 oz | 340 g | 1½ cups |
| 1 lb | 450 g | 2 cups |
| **NUTS** | | |
| **Walnuts** | | |
| 2 oz - shelled | 50 g | ½ generous cup |
| 4 oz - shelled | 100 g | 1 generous cup |
| **ground nuts** | | |
| 2 oz | 50 g | ½ cup |
| 4 oz | 100 g | 1 cup |
| **small nuts** *see* **almonds** | | |
| **OLIVES** | | |
| 2½ oz | 70 g | ½ cup |
| 4 oz | 100 g | 1 cup |
| **PULSES** | | |
| **haricot beans** | | |
| 6 oz | 150 g | 1 cup |
| **kidney beans** | | |
| 11 oz | 310 g | 1 cup |
| **lentils** | | |
| 6 oz | 150 g | 1 cup |

| A to Z of British and American Food Equivalents | | |
|---|---|---|
| **IMPERIAL** | **METRIC** | **AMERICAN** |
| **RICE** | | |
| **Long grain** | | |
| 2 oz | 50 g | ¼ cup |
| 4 oz | 100 g | ½ cup |
| 8 oz | 225 g | 1 good cup |
| **Note**: 1 cup of raw rice yields approx. 3 cups cooked rice | | |
| **Short grain** | | |
| 2 oz | 50 g | ¼ cup |
| 4 oz | 100 g | ½ cup |
| 8 oz | 225 g | 1 cup |
| **SUGAR** | | |
| **Caster/granulated** | | |
| 1 oz | 25 g | 1 tablespoon |
| 2 oz | 50 g | ¼ cup |
| 3 oz | 75 g | ⅓ cup |
| 4 oz | 100 g | ½ cup |
| 5 oz | 140 g | ⅔ cup |
| 6 oz | 170 g | ¾ cup |
| 7 oz | 198 g | bare 1 cup |
| 8 oz | 225 g | 1 cup |
| **Icing/confectioners sugar (sifted)** | | |
| 1 oz | 25 g | ¼ cup |
| 2 oz | 50 g | bare ½ cup |
| 3 oz | 75 g | ⅔ cup |
| 4 oz | 100 g | ¾ cup |
| 5 oz | 140 g | bare cup |
| 6 oz | 170 g | 1 cup |
| 7 oz | 198 g | 1⅓ cups |
| 8 oz | 225 g | 1⅔ cups |
| 12 oz | 340 g | 2½ cups |
| 1 lb | 450 g | 3⅓ cups |
| **Soft brown/dark brown (firmly packed)** | | |
| 1 oz | 25 g | 2 tablespoons |
| 2 oz | 50 g | ¼ cup |
| 3 oz | 75 g | ⅓ cup |
| 4 oz | 100 g | ½ cup |
| 6 oz | 170 g | ¾ cup |
| 8 oz | 225 g | 1 cup |
| 12 oz | 340 g | 1½ cups |
| 1 lb | 450 g | 2 cups |

## A to Z of British and American Food Equivalents

| IMPERIAL | METRIC | AMERICAN |
|---|---|---|
| **SHRIMPS** | | |
| 4 oz - shelled | 100 g | ¾ cup |
| 8 oz - shelled | 225 g | 1½ cups |
| **TOMATO PUREE CONCENTRATE** | | |
| ¾ oz | 20 g | 1½ tablespoons |
| 2¼ oz | 60 g | 3 tablespoons |
| 3 oz | 75 g | 6 tablespoons |
| 3¾ oz | 85 g | 7½ tablespoons |
| 4½ oz | 115 g | 9 tablespoons |
| 9 oz | 255 g | 18 tablespoons |

## British and American Equivalent Weights and Measures

### FRESH FRUIT AND VEGETABLES

| IMPERIAL | METRIC | AMERICAN |
|---|---|---|
| **Apples** | | |
| 1lb eating - peeled & sliced | 450 g | 2⅔ cups |
| 1lb cooking - peeled & sliced | 450 g | 3 medium sized |
| 1lb eating | 450 g | 4 medium sized |
| **Asparagus** | | |
| 1lb - fresh | 450 g | 12 -14 spears |
| **Cabbage** | | |
| 8 oz - sliced | 225 g | 3 cups - pressed down |
| **Carrots** | | |
| 1lb - sliced | 450 g | 3 - 4 cups |
| **Celery** | | |
| 2 sliced celery stalks | | ¾ - 1 cup |
| **Courgettes** | | |
| 1lb | 450 g | 4 large |
| **Cucumber** | | |
| 1 British | | 2 American |
| **Mushrooms** | | |
| 8 oz fresh sliced | 225 g | 2½ cups |
| 8 oz fresh diced | 225 g | 2 cups |
| **Onions** | | |
| 8 oz - sliced | 225 g | 2 cups |
| 1lb - sliced | 450g | 4 cups |
| 8 oz - chopped | 225 g | 1 cup |

| British and American Equivalent Weights and Measures | | |
| --- | --- | --- |
| FRESH FRUIT AND VEGETABLES | | |
| IMPERIAL | METRIC | AMERICAN |
| **Peas** | | |
| 10 oz pack frozen | 283 g | 2½ cups |
| **Peppers** | | |
| 1 large - diced | | ¾ - 1 cup |
| **Potatoes** | | |
| 1lb - sliced | 450 g | approx. 3 cups |
| 1lb - diced | 450 g | approx. 4 cups |
| **Soft fruits** are sold in America as pints or quarts | | |
| 4 cups = 1 quart | | |
| **Raspberries** | | |
| 5 oz | 140 g | 1 cup |
| **Redcurrants** | | |
| 4 oz | 100 g | 1 cup |
| **Blackcurrants** | | |
| 4 oz | 100 g | 1 cup |
| **Strawberries** | | |
| 6 oz | 170 g | 1 cup |
| **Spinach** | | |
| 1lb cooked | 450 g | 1 cup |
| **Tomato** | | |
| 1lb | 450 g | 3-4 medium sized American tomatoes |
| 1lb fresh -peeled, seeded and chopped | 450 g | 1½ cups tomato pulp |
| **Turnips** | | |
| 1lb - peeled and quartered | 450 g | 2½ cups |
| **Watercress** | | |
| 1 bunch | 1½ cups | |

## 'E' NUMBERS AND THEIR MEANING

'E' stands for Europe, and 'E' numbers are given to various substances such as flavourings and preservatives which are added to our food. Each substance is thoroughly checked before it is allowed to be added and by reading the number the consumer can tell just what is present in the food she is buying.

All food manufacturers across Europe use the same E number system. So foods that are moved from country to country, food bought abroad or imported can be bought with confidence and everyone knows what those foods contain.

# What are E numbers?

The 'E' number system is like a shorthand way of writing down long chemical names of additives. By noting the numbers and looking them up on the list you know just what has been added to a food and why it is there.

Similarly, if a substance has to be avoided for some reason such as an allergy to tartrazine colouring (E102) one can look up its E number and avoid all foods with that number on the label.

### What use are E numbers?

The 'E' number system is especially useful for describing the contents of products such as yogurts. These usually have colourings or flavourings added but have very limited space to list them on the label.

Despite the presence of this system some names of additives are still written in full, but the use of numbers is now very widespread and is increasing. Either way the consumer is able to find out just what he or she is eating.

Not every number is used in the list. Gaps have been left in each section for new substances to be added as necessary.

### Colourings

One natural 'E' number is E101 which is vitamin B12. It plays an important part in a healthy diet and occurs naturally in food. It is a yellow-orange colour often used to colour processed cheese.

All substances which are colourings have E numbers between E100 and E180 inclusive.

### Preservatives

Preservatives protect against microbes which may spoil food and cause food poisoning. They also increase the storage life of foods such as pie fillings, yogurts, pizzas and cakes.

All substances which are preservatives have E numbers between E200 and E283 inclusive.

### Anti-oxidants

Many of the chemicals with E numbers are found naturally, for instance vitamin C, a most important vitamin which should be eaten every day is number E300. The chemical name for vitamin C is ascorbic acid. It is found naturally in many fruits and vegetables but is also an anti-oxidant.

This means that if it is used as an additive it can help prevent many of our ready packed foods from being spoilt by being exposed to oxygen in the air. All substances which are anti-oxidants have numbers between E300 and E321 inclusive.

### Emulsifiers and stabilisers

There are many foods such as ice cream, salad dressings, cake coatings and instant desserts which need emulsifiers and stabilisers to give them a creamy and smooth texture. All substances which are emulsifiers and stabilisers have E numbers between E400 and E495 inclusive.

### Sweeteners

Some sweeteners are natural products and are necessarily added to food to add bulk as in cake making. Intensive sweeteners like saccharin are added in very small amounts to items such as soft drinks. However some people need to know of their presence as they wish to avoid them. All substances which are sweeteners have E numbers E420 and E421.

These are the main categories of additives but there are others which while not fitting under these headings still play an important part in making our food safe, tasty and a pleasing texture. For instance savoury food often contains flavour enhancers to make the flavour stronger. Monosodium glutamate E621 is naturally found in foods but is added to others to make the natural flavours stronger. The list is being added to all the time as more substances pass through the testing regulations.

The Ministry of Agriculture, Fisheries and Food (MAFF) produce a booklet, Your Guide to Additives(Ref no.PB 0552(1) which lists all E numbers in numerical order. It is available from MAFF on request.

## Quantity guide for snacks or party buffets

### Bread

1 large sliced loaf (2 pound size) provides about 20 slices of bread depending on the thickness they are cut.

Use medium sliced cut for standard sandwiches, thin sliced for rolled sandwiches and thick slices are usually the most popular for toast and open sandwiches.

French sticks can be cut into approximately 20 x 2 cm (1 inch) slices.

### Butter

100 g (4 oz) creamed butter or margarine will butter 20 slices of bread.
225 g (8 oz) creamed butter or margarine will butter 24 rolls.

## Basic Fillings for 12 Rolls or Sandwiches

| | |
|---|---|
| 350 g  (12 oz) | smoked fish pâté or minced meat  such as ham or poultry |
| 350 g  (12 oz) | ham or tongue thinly sliced |
| 350 g  (12 oz) | cream cheese |
| 150 g  (6 oz) | grated hard cheese |
| 400 g  (15 oz) | canned tuna fish |
| 150 g  (6 oz) | pâté de fois gras |
| 10 | hard boiled eggs mashed with 50 g (2 oz) butter |
| 350 g  (12 oz) | chicken roll or corned beef sliced thinly |
| 250 g  (10 oz) | salami thinly sliced |
| 225 g  (8 oz) | cole slaw spread thinly |
| 350 g  (12 oz) | dressed crab with 150 ml (¼ pint) thick mayonnaise |
| 450 g  (1 lb) | medium sized tomatoes yield approximately 35 - 40 slices |

## Guidelines for quantities for a Buffet

| | For 25 | For 50 | For 100 | For 150 |
|---|---|---|---|---|
| Bread - sliced | 3 loaves | 4 loaves | 6 loaves | 10 loaves |
| French sticks - long | 6 | 12 | 24 | 36 |
| Butter or margarine | 2 lb | 4 lb | 8 lb | 12 lb |

The amounts listed below are average portion sizes if a variety of food is served. If choice is limited, for instance the only meat offered is chicken, then the portions should be larger.

**Soup**
allow 200 ml (⅓ pt) per person

**Cold meats**
allow 75 g (3 oz) per person

**Cold poultry**
1.35 kg (3 lb) bird gives 6-8 carved portions

**Stewing meats**
450 g (1 lb) meat for every 4 portions

**Pâté**
allow 50 g (2 oz) per person

**Cheese board**
allow 25 g (1 oz) per person

### Fruit salad
Home made is best using at least 5 varieties of fruit - whatever is in season. If canned is used then a 820 g (1¾ lb) can will serve about 20 people.

### Stewed fruit
450 g (1 lb) for every 4 portions

### Custard
600 ml (1 pt) will serve 8-10 portions

### Sponge cake
1 x 18cm (7 in) sponge cuts into 6-8 portions

### Round cake
A 22 cm (9 in) round cake cuts into 20 slices

### Square cake
A 22 cm (9 in) square cake cuts into 54 slices

### Amounts to serve per guest
As an average guide serve 6-8 savoury items and 2 sweet items per guest if the gathering such as a wedding reception is in the afternoon.

If the reception is at lunch time then more items and more substantial fare may be needed.

### Wedding cakes
1 lb (450 g) cooked mixture provides 8 - 10 portions as each portion is small and not as large as a normal portion of cake.

(see pages 67-69 for fruit cake recipes and recommended sizes of tiers of wedding cakes).

### Storage, freezing and thawing times for sandwiches
It can save a lot of time and bother to plan ahead and have sandwiches ready prepared in the freezer. All varieties of bread can be frozen but crisp breads are liable to lose their crispness when thawed. Fillings which are not suitable for freezing are hard boiled eggs which become rubbery, and foods with a high water content such as mayonnaise or salads like lettuce and cucumber. Add these at the last moment.

### To freeze sandwiches
They may be made and finished ready to serve but it is often better to freeze them in large squares or rolls and cut them up after defrosting. Leave the crusts on and then as the sandwiches defrost, just before serving them, cut them into the shapes desired, remove crusts if wished and garnish appropriately.

## To wrap

Wrap in foil or clingfilm.

Label with the type of filling or spread, the quantity and the date.

Sandwiches for a party such as asparagus rolls are best packed closely and frozen together on a tray to prevent them unrolling. Seal with foil.

Freeze pinwheels, club and ribbon sandwiches uncut and wrapped tightly in foil.

Sandwiches may be packed individually if they are likely to be used for a lunch box, or stacks of sandwiches with the same filling may be packed together with cling film or polythene between.

To prevent items breaking in the freezer it is wise to pack them into an ice-cream container or similar box to keep their shape.

## Storage time

All sandwiches should freeze well for about 2 months.

## To thaw sandwiches

Thaw them in their packaging. They are best thawed slowly at room temperature or overnight in a refrigerator. Individual sandwiches will thaw quicker than a large packet so times vary greatly.

## Approximate thawing times are

| | |
|---|---|
| 2 | hours for individually wrapped sandwiches |
| 6-7 | hours for stacks of 4-6 sandwiches |
| 4-5 | hours for rolled sandwiches |
| 3-4 | hours for pinwheels, club and ribbon sandwiches which cut more easily when partially thawed. |

## Toasted sandwiches

Place frozen, unwrapped sandwiches under a hot grill and they thaw whilst toasting.

If you prefer, fillings can be prepared and frozen separately from the bread and the sandwiches made up near to the time of eating. Pack the spreads into sealed polythene containers, label carefully and keep for 1-2 months depending on the filling.

Leave frozen fillings to defrost at room temperature for 2-3 hours or overnight in a refrigerator depending on the filling.

## Beverage Guide

### Non-alcoholic beverages

| | |
|---|---|
| **Tea** | 40 g (1½ oz) loose tea per gallon of water, depending on the variety of tea and the strength of brew required. |
| **Milk** | 1.1 litre (2 pt) per 4.5 l (1 gallon) of tea approximately 30 ml (1 fl oz) of milk is required per cup |
| **Ground Coffee** | 225 g - 275 g (8-10 oz) per 4.5 litres (1 gallon) of water, |
| **Instant Coffee** | 50 - 75g (2 - 2½ oz) per 4.5 litres (1 gallon) of water |
| **Cokes** | 1 per person |

### Servings per bottle

**Note** - the number of servings obtained from a bottle depends a great deal on the size of the glasses and the generosity of the pourer. Therefore the quantities below are an average guide.

| | |
|---|---|
| **Sherry** | 14 per 70cl bottle |
| **Spirits** | 24 per 70cl bottle |
| **Port** | 12 - 15 per 75cl bottle |
| **Vermouth** | 12 - 16 per 75cl bottle |
| **Liquers** | 32 per bottle |
| **Wine** | 6 per 75cl bottle |
| **Champagne** | 6 per bottle |
| **Sparkling Wine** | 6 per 75cl bottle |
| **Cokes** | 1 can per person |

1 pt (568 ml) fruit juice serves 4-6 glasses
1 bottle fruit squash when diluted serves between 20 - 26 glasses.

## Quantities of Food Equivalent to 1 American Cup Measure

To follow recipes in which the measures used are not familiar, it is necessary to be able to translate the quantities to the desired form. Each of the quantities listed is the equivalent to 1 American cup

e.g. 1 cup of peeled and sliced cooking apples = 100 g or 4 oz
    1 cup of dried and chopped apricots = 175 g or 6 oz

All figures have been rounded off to the nearest 5 g

| FOOD | METRIC | IMPERIAL |
| --- | --- | --- |
| Apples, cooking - peeled and sliced | 100 g | 4 oz |
| Apricots - dried and chopped | 175 g | 6 oz |
| Banana - mashed | 225 g | 8 oz |
| Bananas - sliced | 175 g | 6 oz |
| Beans - dried | 175 g | 6 oz |
| Biscuit crumbs, e.g. digestives | 100 g | 4 oz |
| Breadcrumbs - dried | 140 g | 4½ oz |
| Breadcrumbs - fresh | 50 g | 2 oz |
| Bran | 50 g | 2 oz |
| Butter | 225 g | 8 oz |
| Cabbage - raw, shredded | 100 g | 4 oz |
| Carrot - raw, sliced | 150 g | 5 oz |
| Cheese - cottage | 225 g | 8 oz |
| - Cheddar, grated | 100 g | 4 oz |
| - cream, curd | 225 g | 8 oz |
| - Parmesan, grated | 100 g | 4 oz |
| Cherries - whole, glâcé | 200 g | 7 oz |
| Cocoa powder | 100 g | 4 oz |
| Coconut - desiccated | 90 g | 3½ oz |
| Cornflour | 140 g | 4½ oz |
| Cornflakes | 25 g | 1 oz |
| Cranberries | 100 g | 4 oz |
| Cream - single and double | 225 ml | 8 fl oz |
| Currants - dried | 150 g | 5 oz |
| Dates - whole, dried, stoned | 175 g | 6 oz |
| Eggs (see under 'eggs' page 56) | | |
| Figs - dried | 175 g | 6 oz |
| Flour - plain and self raising | 150 g | 5 oz |
| Flour - wholewheat | 165 g | 5½oz |
| Honey | 350 g | 12 oz |
| Jam | 350 g | 12 oz |
| Lard or dripping | 225 g | 8 oz |

| Quantities of Food Equivalent to 1 American Cup Measure | | |
| --- | --- | --- |
| **FOOD** | **METRIC** | **IMPERIAL** |
| Lentils | 200 g | 7 oz |
| Macaroni - raw | 100 g | 4 oz |
| Marmalade | 300 g | 11 oz |
| Mayonnaise | 225 g | 8 oz |
| Milk - fresh | 225 ml | 8 fl oz |
|    - evaporated | 250 ml | 9 fl oz |
|    - condensed | 300 ml | 11 fl oz |
|    - powdered - low fat | 90 g | 3½ oz |
| Mincemeat | 300 g | 11 oz |
| Mixed peel | 175 g | 6 oz |
| Mushrooms - fresh sliced | 50 g | 2 oz |
| Mushrooms - canned and drained | 225 g | 8 oz |
| Muesli | 150 g | 5 oz |
| Noodles - uncooked | 75 g | 3 oz |
| Nuts - almonds, whole blanched | 150 g | 5 oz |
|    - flaked | 100 g | 4 oz |
|    - ground | 90 g | 3½ oz |
| Nuts - Brazil, whole shelled | 150 g | 5 oz |
|    - cashews, whole shelled | 150 g | 5 oz |
|    - hazelnuts, whole shelled | 150 g | 5 oz |
|    - peanuts, roasted and salted | 150 g | 5 oz |
|    - walnuts, halved | 100 g | 4 oz |
| Oats - rolled | 75 g | 3 oz |
| Oils | 225 ml | 8 fl oz |
| Olives - green, stuffed | 150 g | 5 oz |
|    - black | 175 g | 6 oz |
| Onions - chopped | 150 g | 5 oz |
| Peaches - fresh, sliced | 150 g | 5 oz |
|    - canned, sliced and drained | 225 g | 8 oz |
| Peas - frozen | 100 g | 4 oz |
|    - split, dried | 200 g | 7 oz |
| Peppers - sliced | 100 g | 4 oz |
| Potatoes - cooked and mashed | 225 g | 8 oz |
| Prunes - dried | 200 g | 7 oz |
| Prunes - cooked and stoned | 225 g | 8 oz |
| Raisins - seedless | 165 g | 5½ oz |
| Rhubarb - raw sliced | 200 g | 7 oz |
| Rice - long grain, uncooked | 200 g | 7 oz |
| Rice - short grain, uncooked | 215 g | 7½ oz |
| Sago | 190 g | 6½ oz |
| Salmon - canned, drained and flaked | 175 g | 6 oz |
| Semolina | 190 g | 6½ oz |

| Quantities of Food Equivalent to 1 American Cup Measure | | |
|---|---|---|
| **FOOD** | **METRIC** | **IMPERIAL** |
| Spaghetti - broken, uncooked | 100 g | 4 oz |
| Strawberries - fresh whole | 150 g | 5 oz |
| Suet - shredded | 100 g | 4 oz |
| Sugar - granulated | 200 g | 7 oz |
|     - caster | 200 g | 7 oz |
|     - icing | 100 g | 4 oz |
|     - brown | 200 g | 7 oz |
|     - demerara | 200 g | 7 oz |
| Sultanas | 175 g | 6 oz |
| Syrup and treacle | 350 g | 12 oz |
| Tapioca | 175 g | 6 oz |
| Tomatoes - canned in juice | 225 g | 8 oz |
|     - fresh, peeled and quartered | 150 g | 5 oz |
| Tuna fish - canned, drained and flaked | 200 g | 7 oz |

| Recommended Temperatures of Fat for Deep Frying Various Foods | | |
|---|---|---|
| **FOOD** | **OIL TEMPERATURE** | **BREAD TEST** **1in(2.5cm) cube** |
| Uncooked mixture (doughnuts, fritters etc) | 360°F (180°C) | 1 minute |
| Egg and crumbed fish cakes, croquettes and whitebait | 375°F (190°C) | 45 seconds |
| Fish fillets and fish in batter | 370°F (188°C) | 40 seconds |
| Potatoes - Blanching until soft | 375°F (190°C) | 1 minute |
| Frying until crisp and brown | 390°F (200°C) | 30 seconds |
| Scotch Eggs | 360°F (180°C) | 1 minute |

The bread test is a simple way of finding out whether the fat is hot enough when you don't have a proper fat thermometer.

For instance if a 1 in (2.5 cm) cube of bread turns brown when left in the fat for 45 seconds then the fat will be at a temperature of around 375°F (190°C).

### Importance of correct fat temperature

The temperature of the fat is important. If it is too hot then the outside of the food will brown and cook on the outside but the inside will be uncooked. If the fat is not hot enough then the food will become soggy as it will absorb the fat, will take a long time to cook and will not turn crispy and brown.

### Healthy frying

For good health use oil for frying rather than hard fat such as lard or dripping. Oil is a polyunsaturated fat which is better for health than saturated fats.
Cook the food so it is crispy, not soft from absorbed fat and drain the food well before serving.

### Chips

Chips are best blanched first at a lower temperature to cook them. Drain off the oil. Then just before serving immerse them in fat at a higher temperature to brown them quickly and give them a crispy texture.
Large, plain cut chips are more healthy than small, thin chips as there is less surface area in touch with the fat during cooking, therefore reducing the amount of fat absorbed and eaten.

## The weight of dry ingredients

The weights of dry ingredients in a recipe are often given in ounces or grams. Yet it can be quicker and more convenient to measure them out in tablespoons.

All tablespoon measures are level tablespoons as these are more accurate than heaped tablespoons.

1 tablespoon is equivalent to 15 ml.

The following number of spoon measures provide approximately 1 oz (25 g) of the ingredient.

| Measure | Ingredient |
| --- | --- |
| 1 level tablespoon | Rice |
| 2 level tablespoons | Flour, custard powder or cornflour |
| 2 level tablespoons | Semolina |
| 2 level tablespoons | Caster, granulated or brown sugar |
| 6 level tablespoons | Breadcrumbs - fresh |
| 3 level tablespoons | Breadcrumbs - dried |
| 5 level tablespoons | Cheese - grated, hard variety |
| 3 level tablespoons | Icing sugar - sifted |
| 5 level tablespoons | Desiccated coconut |
| 2 level tablespoons | Cocoa powder |
| 1 level tablespoon | Syrup, honey, treacle and jam |
| 4 level tablespoons | Ground almonds, hazelnuts, walnuts and mixed nut |
| 2 level tablespoons | Dried fruits, raisins, sultanas and currants |
| 4 level tablespoons | Porridge oats |
| 1 level tablespooon | Salt |

# 3

# MEASURES AND WEIGHTS OF FOOD

## EGGS

The use of the correct size egg in a recipe may seem unimportant but in fact can make quite a difference to the finished result. There is not an 'average' egg, but if the recipe does not state a specific size then it can be presumed that a Size 3 or 4 would be suitable. This is also a suitable size for serving as a hard boiled or poached egg for breakfast, or hard boiled in a salad.

### Egg Sizes and Weights

| | |
|---|---|
| Size 1 | 70 g or over |
| Size 2 | 65 g and under 70 g |
| Size 3 | 60 g and under 65 g |
| Size 4 | 55 g and under 60 g |
| Size 5 | 50 g and under 55 g |
| Size 6 | 45 g and under 50 g |
| Size 7 | under 45 g |

EU weight regulations use the term 'Grades' instead of 'Size' but the information is just the same as above, i.e. Grade 1 is the same weight as Size 1 and so on.

## Egg quality grading

### Grade A or Class A (First Quality)
Naturally clean fresh eggs, internally perfect with intact shells and an air cell not exceeding 6 mm (¼ in) depth.

### Grade B or Class B (Second Quality)
Eggs which have been down-graded because they had to be cleaned or preserved, or because they were in some way internally imperfect, cracked or had air cells exeeding 6 mm - but not more than 9 mm - in depth.

### Grade C or Class C (Third Quality)
Eggs which are fit for breaking out for manufacturing purposes but cannot be sold in their shells to the public.

### Source of the eggs

Eggs packed in a UK packing station will have on the box a number beginning with the figure 9, followed by a regional number and the packing station identification number.

Egg boxes may also show the date of packing by indicating the EEC week number. Week numbers are calculated from the first Sunday in January, 2 is the second full week and so on. Each box containing eggs should carry a 'Best Before' date and sometimes each egg may have a 'Best Before' date stamped on it.

**American Measures**

1 egg yolk = 1 tablespoon
1 egg white = 1½ tablespoon
12 - 14 egg yolks = 1 cup average-
depending on size
8 - 10 egg whites = 1 cup average -
depending on size
4 - 6 eggs = 1 cup average -
depending on size

### Liquid egg

Bought liquid egg may be all white, all yolk or both yolk and white. Use according to the recommendations on the packet. Pay special attention to the storage conditions and date stamp.

### Boiling eggs

Boiling an egg is thought to be the simplest thing to do but in fact needs careful timing to produce a good result.

### Time of cooking for soft boiled or hard boiled eggs

To prevent an egg from cracking during cooking, especially if it has been taken straight from a refrigerator, a pin or a specially made 'egg piercer' can be used to put a tiny hole in the blunt end of each shell.

### In simmering water

Size 2 and 3 eggs will take 4 minutes to become soft boiled or 12 minutes to become hard boiled

Size 4 and 5 eggs will take 3 minutes to become soft boiled or 10 minutes to become hard boiled

To prevent a dark ring forming between the white and yolk of a hard boiled egg, remove the egg from the hot water, crack the shell to let the steam escape, then plunge it into cold water.

# PASTRY

Nothing can beat home made pastry, but working out how much to make in various situations can be confusing. Making the wrong quantity can lead for instance to the pastry being insufficient to cover a pie dish adequately or having so much pastry over that you make a batch of jam tarts you don't really want.

### To calculate the amount of pastry needed

**Home made:** If a recipe requires a stated amount of pastry this refers to the quantity of flour used to make the pastry, e.g. if you need 225 g (8 oz) shortcrust pastry then you need to start with 225 g (8 oz) flour.

**Bought pastry:** To calculate the amount of pre-prepared bought pastry needed for the same results, add together the weights of flour, fat and water used to make the pastry from a basic recipe.

**Shortcrust pastry:** 225 g (8 oz) flour + 100 g (4 oz) fat + water = approximately 350 g (14 oz) prepared pastry.
To make the same item from pre-prepared puff pastry you will need to buy:

**Puff pastry :** 225 g (8 oz) flour + 225 g (8 oz) fat + water = approximately 500 g (1¼ lb) prepared puff pastry. As a general rule you need just over half as much again in weight if bought pastry is used.

### Quantity of Pastry required to cover and/or line various size dishes

All measures and yields are approximate

### Short crust pastry

| Dish | Size | Pastry quantity |
| --- | --- | --- |
| Oval pie dish | ½ litre (1 pt) dish | 125 g (5 oz) covers |
| | 750 ml (1½ pt) dish | 150 g (6 oz) covers |
| | 1 litre (2 pt) dish | 225 g (8 oz) covers |
| | 1½ litre (3 pt) dish | 250 g (10 oz) covers |
| Pie plate | 18 cm (7 in) plate | 125 g (5 oz) lines **or** covers |
| | 22 cm (9 in) plate | 150g (6 oz) lines **or** covers |
| | 18 cm (7 in) plate | 225g (8 oz) lines **and** covers |
| | 22 cm (9 in) plate | 250g (10 oz) lines **and** covers |
| Tarts | 225 g (8 oz) pastry | makes 18 x 6 cm (2½ in) tarts **or** 12 x 8 cm (3 in) tarts |

## Flan pastry

| | | | | | |
|---|---|---|---|---|---|
| 100 g (4 oz) Flan pastry | lines a | 15 cm | (6 in) | flan ring | |
| 125 g (5 oz) Flan pastry | lines an | 18 cm | (7 in) | flan ring | |
| 150 g (6 oz) Flan pastry | lines a | 20 cm | (8 in) | flan ring **or** | |
| | lines a | 15 cm | (6 in) | flan ring **and** | |
| | makes | 6 x 6 cm | (2½ in) | tartlet cases | |
| 200 g (7 oz) Flan pastry | lines a | 20.5 cm | (8 in) | flan ring | |
| 250 g (9 oz) Flan pastry | lines a | 23 cm | (9 in) | flan ring | |

The above amounts also apply if shortcrust pastry is used

## Puff pastry

| Item | Pastry | | Yield |
|---|---|---|---|
| Oval pie dish | 100 g (4 oz) | covers | 1 x 1 litre (2 pt) dish |
| Sausage rolls | 225 g (8 oz) | makes | 12 x 8 cm (3 in) |
| Vol au vents | 225 g (8 oz) | makes | 12 x 8 cm (3 in) |
| (round or oval) | | **or** | 10 x 9 cm (3½ in) |
| | 450 g (1 lb) | makes | 30 x 8 cm (3 in) **or** |
| | | | 20 x 9 cm (3½ in) |
| Bouchées | 225 g (8 oz) | makes | 30 x 5 cm (2 in) |
| (round shaped) | 450 g (1 lb) | makes | 60 x 5 cm (2 in) |
| Cream horns | 225 g (8 oz) | makes | about 10 if pastry rolled to 25 x 45 cm (10 x 18 in) oblong and rolled ¼ cm or (⅛ in) thick |

When using bought puff pastry, roll it out a bit thinner than you would home made pastry; about 0.2 - 0.4 cm ($^1/_{16}$- ⅛ in) as it rises very well.

**Sausage rolls** made from the above recipe require 225 g (8 oz) of sausage meat for filling.

**Mince pies** each about 2½ in (6.5 cm) diameter made from 12 oz (350 g) shortcrust or flaky pastry need ¾ - 1 lb (350 g - 450 g) mincemeat for filling.

## Suet pastry

| Item | Pastry | Yield |
|---|---|---|
| Dumplings | 225 g (8 oz) makes | 16 medium dumplings |
| Suet pudding | 225 g (8 oz) | Lines and covers a 750 ml (1½ pt) pudding basin |
| | 350 g (12 oz) | Lines and covers a 1.4 litre (2½ pt) basin |
| Roly-poly pudding | 225 g (8 oz) makes | 1 x (30.5 cm) 12 in roll from pastry rolled out to a 25 cm x 30 cm (10 x 12 in) rectangle |

## Choux pastry

| Item | Pastry | Yield |
|---|---|---|
| Eclairs | 65 g (2½ oz) makes flour recipe | 10 x 10 cm (4 in) long 25 x 4 cm (1½ in) long |
| Choux Buns | 65 g (2½ oz) makes flour recipe | 10 x 5 cm (2 in) diameter |
| Profiteroles | 65 g (2½ oz) makes flour recipe | 20 x 3 cm (1¼ in) diameter |

Each of the above recipes for eclairs, choux buns or profiteroles require ¼ pt (5 fl oz) (142 ml) of double cream, whipped with 4 tbs (60 ml) single cream or top of the milk for the filling.

## Mince Pies

Below is a guide for quantities of shortcrust pastry and mincemeat necessary to produce three batches of mince pies.

| Number of pies | Shortcrust pastry weight | | Mincemeat |
|---|---|---|---|
| 2½ in (6 cm) diameter | Homemade from | Prepared | |
| 10 | 225 g (8 oz) | 400 g (14 oz) | 225 g (8 oz) |
| 20 | 450 g (1 lb) | 700 g (1½ lb) | 450 g (1 lb) |
| 50 | 1 kg (2 lb) | 1.5 kg (3½ lb) | 1 kg (2¼ lb) |

# POULTRY

## Number of portions served from various kinds and sizes of poultry

### Turkey

10 - 14 lb (4.5 - 6.3 kg) oven ready turkey will serve 14 people as part of a main meal. It will serve double this number if served as cold meat and accompanied by other sliced meats.

16 - 20 lb (7.3 - 9.0 kg) oven ready turkey will serve about 25 people when served at a main meal.

When choosing or ordering a turkey remember that the parts that are discarded during the dressing of the bird to make it ready for the oven will weigh around 3 - 4 lb (1.4 - 1.8 kg). These form part of the total weight and are paid for even though they are discarded.

As the turkey carcass is so large it is not profitable to buy a small bird as the amount of meat obtained from it as a percentage of the total cost is very small.

### Goose

10 - 12 lb (4.5 - 5.4 kg) oven ready goose will serve about 8 people.

### Duck

1 lb (450 g) dressed duck is needed for each portion. A 4 - 6 lb (1.8 - 2.7 kg) duck as bought will serve 3-4 people.

A young duckling weighing 3½ - 4 lb (1.6 - 1.8 kg) will serve two people.

### Poussins

These are young chicken about 6 - 8 weeks old weighing 1 - 2 lb (450 - 900 g) and one will serve 1 or 2 people.

### Broilers

These are twelve-week-old chicken weighing between 2½ and 3 lb (1.1 - 1.4 kg). Each will serve 3 to 4 people.

### Large roasting chickens

Weighing about 4 - 5 lb (1.8 - 2.3 kg) each bird should serve six or seven people.

### Capons

Capons are 10-12 weeks old and will serve 8 - 10 people. They usually weigh around 6 - 8 lb (2.7 - 3.6 kg)

### Guinea fowl

Guinea fowl are small birds weighing 1¼ - 3¼ lb (550 g - 1.7 kg). An average sized bird will serve 4 people.

# GAME

### Grouse
An average sized grouse will serve 1 or 2 portions.

### Partridge
A young roasted partridge will provide 1 or 2 portions.

### Quail
One bird per person is served.

### Pheasant
An average sized pheasant will provide 2 portions but larger pheasants can be bought to serve 4 people.

| Roasting Times for Turkey | | | |
|---|---|---|---|
| **WEIGHT** | | **COOKING TIMES IN HOURS** | |
| | | 325°F (160°C) Gas Mark 3 | 450°F(230°C) Gas Mark 8 |
| **kg** | **lb** | **(slow method)** | **(quick method)** |
| 2.7 - 3.6 | 6 - 8 | 1½ - 3 | 2¼ - 2½ |
| 3.6 - 4.5 | 8 - 10 | 3½ - 3¾ | 2½ - 2¾ |
| 4.5 - 5.4 | 10 - 12 | 3¾ - 4¼ | 2¾ - 3 |
| 5.4 - 6.3 | 12 - 14 | 4 - 4¼ | 3 - 3¼ |
| 6.3 - 7.3 | 14 - 16 | 4¼ - 4½ | 3¼ - 3½ |
| 7.3 - 8.2 | 16 - 18 | 4½ - 4¾ | 3½ - 3¾ |
| 8.2 - 9.0 | 18 - 20 | 4¾ - 5½ | 3¾ - 4 |
| 9.0 - 10.8 | 20 - 24 | 4¾ - 5½ | 4 - 4¼ |

It is very important that turkeys and in fact all poultry and game are thoroughly defrosted before stuffing and cooking.

One week before you want to eat the turkey check its weight and plan how long it will take to defrost. There will then be no last minute panic, or worse, a bird being put in the oven which is still frozen inside.

It is best to let it defrost slowly in a cool place. A kitchen is often too hot especially if it is just before Christmas; the oven is on a lot and also central heating on in the house. A utility room or garage is often suitable as long as the bird is well covered.

| Time it takes to defrost frozen turkeys at room temperature or in a refrigerator | | | | |
|---|---|---|---|---|
| Oven Ready Weight: | | No of | Thawing Time in: | |
| lb | kg | servings | Cool Room | Refrigerator |
| 3 - 5 | 1.5 - 2.25 | 4 - 6 | 20 hours | 18 hours |
| 6 - 7 | 2.75 - 3.0 | 7 - 9 | 30 | 30 |
| 8 - 9 | 3.6 - 4.0 | 10 - 14 | 36 | 48 |
| 10 - 11 | 4.5 - 5.0 | 15 - 16 | 45 | 48 |
| 12 - 13 | 5.4 - 5.8 | 17 - 18 | 48 | 60 |
| 14 - 17 | 6.3 - 7.7 | 19 - 25 | 48 | 72 |
| 18 - 22 | 8.1 - 9.96 | 26 - 37 | 48 | 84 |
| 23 + | 10.4 + | 38 + | 48 | 96 |

**Defrosting in a Microwave**

Poultry can be defrosted in a microwave on a defrost cycle but it is advisable to check the manufacturer's instructions with your cooker first.

Allow approximately 8 minutes per lb (450 g). Before relying on this method check that the turkey will fit into your microwave. Start to defrost it in its polythene bag. Allow about 30-45 minutes standing time to complete the defrosting process.

Do not refreeze any part of the bird unless it is cooked first.

# PULSES

There are many varieties of peas and beans and although there are many similarities they each require different soaking and cooking times (see chart below).

Most, if not all, pulses can be bought in cans and are ready to eat. They should be rinsed under cold water and then used in salads or incorporated into recipes. Canned varieties are very convenient but are a more expensive way of eating pulses especially if they are eaten frequently.

## Measures of dried pulses

### Dried weight per portion

Dried beans such as butter beans, haricot beans and kidney beans, also peas, lentils and split peas:

Allow 1 - 2 oz (25-50 g) dry weight per person depending on what else is being served.

If dried beans are being served as a vegetable accompaniment to a meat dish, then 1 oz (25 g) dry weight per portion is sufficient.

A vegetarian using beans as a main dish should use 2 oz (50 g) dry weight per portion.

### Soaking
Dried pulses, except lentils and split peas, need to be soaked for varying lengths of time.

### Overnight
They can be soaked overnight if you have planned your meals far enough ahead.

### Cold water soak
Place the pulses in a large pan with a lot of water, and leave to soak for 6-8 hours.

### Hot water soak
Place pulses in a large pan with a lot of water, bring to the boil, boil for 2 minutes, remove from the heat and leave to soak in the same water for 45 - 60 minutes until cold. Then they can be drained and cooked (see cooking chart).

The addition of 2 tbs (30 ml) oil to the water will prevent the beans from foaming and will give them a glossy appearance.

### Cooking
Place the soaked, rinsed pulses in a large saucepan with lots of cold fresh water. Bring the water to the boil and boil rapidly for 10 minutes which will destroy any toxins which may be present in some beans especially red kidney beans. Then follow the chart below for cooking times. These can vary a bit according to the freshness of the beans.

| Cooking Times | | | |
|---|---|---|---|
| Aduki beans | 1 - 1½ hours | Lentils - brown | 25 - 30 minutes |
| Black beans | 1 - 1½ hours | split red | 20 - 30 minutes |
| Black-eyed peas | 25 - 30 minutes | Mung beans | 25 - 30 minutes |
| Butter beans | 45 - 60 minutes | Whole peas | 45 - 60 minutes |
| Cannellini beans | 1 - 1½ hours | Red kidney beans | 1 - 1¼ hours |
| Chick peas | 1 - 2 hours | Soya beans | 1 - 3 hours |
| Flageolet beans | 30 - 60 minutes | Split peas | 25 - 30 minutes |
| Haricot beans | 1 - 1½ hours | | |

## Cooking beans in a pressure cooker

A pressure cooker is excellent for cooking pulses since it saves a lot of time.
Allow 2 pints (1.1 litres) fresh cold water to every 1 lb (450 g) beans.
Bring the water to boiling point and add the beans. Bring to the boil
again, uncovered, and remove any scum. Put on the lid and cook for the
required time.

| Type of Bean | Cooking Time at High (15lb) Pressure |
|---|---|
| Aduki beans | 10 minutes |
| Black - eyed peas | 20 minutes |
| Butter beans | 25 minutes |
| Cannellini beans | 15 minutes |
| Chick peas | 20 minutes |
| Flageolet beans | 20 minutes |
| Haricot beans | 20 minutes |
| Lentils - brown | 15 minutes |
| - split red | 15 minutes |
| Red kidney beans | 20 minutes |
| Split peas | 15 minutes |

## Cooking pulses in the microwave

Weigh out amount of pulses required.
Rinse the pulses thoroughly in several changes of cold water and drain well.

## Cold soak

Place in a large bowl full of cold water and leave to soak for 4 hours.

## Hot soak

To each 4 oz (100 g) beans or peas in the bowl add ¾ pt (425 ml) hot water.
Cover and heat on full power for about 4 minutes until boiling. Remove
lid, cook for a further 3 minutes on Full Power then cover and leave to soak
for at least an hour.

After this time rinse the beans very well again in several changes of cold
water. They are now ready to cook.

**NOTE - It is essential that beans from the kidney bean family are fast
boiled first for at least 10 minutes to remove toxins. After this time they
can be cooked for the remaining time in the microwave.**

### Cooking

After the ten minute boiling time if this is required, or after soaking and rinsing, place the peas or beans into a very large bowl.

To every 8 oz (225 g) peas add 1½ pt (850 ml) hot water and 1 teaspoon oil. Cover the bowl with film or a loose fitting lid and cook on High (Full Power) for 30 minutes. Leave to stand for 10 minutes, remove lid, drain, rinse and drain again.

## Sugar and sweets

Sweets are made from a sugar mixture which has been boiled to a high temperature. The temperature required during preparation depends on the type of finished sweet desired.

### Making sugar products, sweets and caramel

The basic process is to dissolve sugar in water in a pan and then slowly bring the mixture to the desired temperature according to the finished product one is making. As the temperature rises so the liquid evaporates off, causing a syrup to form and thicken. This becomes darker as the temperature rises. It is very dark brown caramel when it reaches 350°F (175°C).

### Thermometers

It is advisable to use a special sugar boiling thermometer to ensure success. It should be graduated from 16°C (60°F) to 182°C (360°F). They are usually made in brass and have a hook at the top from which the thermometer can be suspended in the sugar mixture.

Homely tests can be used if you do not have a thermometer.

### The cold water test

Care must be taken not to burn your fingers when using homely tests. To carry out the cold water test, dip the fingers in cold water and then very quickly into the syrup.

### OR

Drop a teaspoon of toffee into a saucer of cold water and if it immediately sets into a soft pliable ball the toffee is ready.

Check results on the chart opposite.

| Sugar Temperatures | | | |
|---|---|---|---|
| **STAGE** | **TEMPERATURE** | **SWEET** | **COLD WATER TEST** |
| Soft ball | 235°F - 245°F (113°C - 118°C) | Fudge and fondants | Firm enough to form into a pliable ball and flatten when pressed between thumb and forefinger |
| Firm ball | 245°F - 265°F (118°C - 130°C) | Caramel marshmallows soft nougat | Firm but yields when pressed |
| Soft crack | 270°F - 290°F (132°C - 143°C) | Chewy toffee | Holds its shape but is still pliable, not brittle |
| Very brittle hard crack | 290°F - 310°F (149°C - 154°C) | Hard toffees Rock | When a drop of syrup is put into cold water it separates into threads which are hard and brittle |
| Caramel | 310°F (154°C) | | |
| Spun sugar | | | The threads falling from the spoon will snap |

Different kinds of sugar are used for different sweets, fondants and fudges and individual recipes should be followed for these.

### Caramel
To make basic caramel for a pudding such as a Caramel Custard, dissolve 4 oz (100 g) sugar in ¼ pt (150 ml) water over a low heat. Bring to the boil without stirring until it gradually turns a rich golden brown colour. Transfer carefully to the required tin or use to coat the surface of a dessert.

## Wedding cakes

A rich, dark, fruit cake is traditional for a wedding cake but a lighter fruit cake is perfectly acceptable if prefered. What is important is the sizes of the tiers, so that when assembled the whole cake is in proportion and doesn't look top heavy.

### Three-tier cake
The most favoured sizes for a three tier - cake are -

12 in (30.5 cm) for the bottom tier
9 in (23 cm) for the middle tier and
6 in (15 cm) for the top tier.

### Two-tier cake

A two-tier cake can be -

12 in (30.5 cm) for the bottom tier
8 in (20.5 cm) for the top tier
OR
10 in (25.5 cm) for the bottom tier
6 in (15 cm) for the top tier.

In order not to look too heavy the depth of the cakes must be in proportion, with the bottom tier deeper than the higher ones.

### Depths of cakes

The bottom tier should be 3 in (7.5 cm) deep.
Cakes which are 7-9 in (18-23 cm) in diameter should be 2½ in (6.5 cm) deep. Cakes which are 6 in (15 cm) diameter should be 2 in (5 cm) deep.

### Portions of cake

Each cake should be placed on a board 1 in (2.5 cm) larger than the cake.
From each 1 lb (450 g) of cooked mixture you can cut 8-10 portions of cake.

### To cut the cake

Whether round or square:
Cut the cake in half.
Cut this huge wedge into thick slices about 2 in (5 cm) wide.
Cut each of these slices into ½ in (1 cm) slices.
A traditional recipe is very rich and it is not usual to serve large slices at a wedding as you would if you were having friends to tea.

### To make a rich fruit cake

Follow the ingredients list on page 69 for the desired cake size and shape. Use the creaming method to make the cake.

See diagrams below for how to line a cake tin - essential for rich fruit cakes. Bake at 300°F (150°C) for about 3¾ hours.

## Ingredients for a Fruit Cake per Size of Tin

| Round tin | 15 cm | 18 cm | 20 cm | 23 cm | 25 cm | 28 cm | 30 cm | |
|---|---|---|---|---|---|---|---|---|
| **Square tin** | 12.5 cm | 15 cm | 18 cm | 20 cm | 23 cm | 25 cm | 28 cm | 30 cm |
| *glacé cherries | 65 g | 75 g | 100 g | 150 g | 200 g | 250 g | 350 g | 375 g |
| plain flour | 175 g | 200 g | 250 g | 300 g | 450 g | 600 g | 725 g | 825 g |
| currants | 150 g | 175 g | 225 g | 275 g | 400 g | 525 g | 675 g | 750 g |
| sultanas | 200 g | 250 g | 350 g | 425 g | 600 g | 800 g | 1 kg | 1.1 kg |
| raisins | 75 g | 75 g | 100 g | 150 g | 200 g | 275 g | 350 g | 400 g |
| *mixed peel | 50 g | 50 g | 50 g | 75 g | 100 g | 150 g | 175 g | 200 g |
| *chopped nuts | 25 g | 25 g | 50 g | 75 g | 75 g | 100 g | 175 g | 175 g |
| butter | 150 g | 175 g | 225 g | 275 g | 400 g | 525 g | 675 g | 750 g |
| caster sugar | 150 g | 175 g | 225 g | 275 g | 400 g | 525 g | 675 g | 750 g |
| weight of eggs | 150 g | 175 g | 225 g | 275 g | 400 g | 525 g | 675 g | 750 g |

| Round tin | 6 in | 7 in | 8 in | 9 in | 10 in | 11 in | 12 in | |
|---|---|---|---|---|---|---|---|---|
| **Square tin** | 5 in | 6 in | 7 in | 8 in | 9 in | 10 in | 11 in | 12 in |
| *glacé cherries | 2½ oz | 3 oz | 4 oz | 5 oz | 7 oz | 9 oz | 12 oz | 13 oz |
| plain flour | 6 oz | 7 oz | 9 oz | 11 oz | 1 lb | 1 lb 5 oz | 1 lb 10 oz | 1 lb 13 oz |
| currants | 5 oz | 6 oz | 8 oz | 10 oz | 14 oz | 1 lb 3 oz | 1½ lb | 1 lb 11 oz |
| sultanas | 7½ oz | 9 oz | 12 oz | 15 oz | 1 lb 5 oz | 1 lb 12 oz | 2 lb 4 oz | 2½ lb |
| raisins | 2½ oz | 3 oz | 4 oz | 5 oz | 7 oz | 10 oz | 12 oz | 14 oz |
| *mixed peel | 2 oz | 2 oz | 2 oz | 3 oz | 4 oz | 5 oz | 6 oz | 7 oz |
| *chopped nuts | 1 oz | 1 oz | 2 oz | 3 oz | 3 oz | 4 oz | 6 oz | 6 oz |
| butter | 5 oz | 6 oz | 8 oz | 10 oz | 14 oz | 1 lb 3 oz | 1½ lb | 1 lb 11 oz |
| caster sugar | 5 oz | 6 oz | 8 oz | 10 oz | 14 oz | 1 lb 3 oz | 1½ lb | 1 lb 11 oz |
| weight of eggs | 5 oz | 6 oz | 8 oz | 10 oz | 14 oz | 1 lb 3 oz | 1½ lb | 1 lb 11 oz |
| Cooking time (hrs) | 3¾ | 3¾ | 4 | 4½ | 4½ | 5 | 5 | 5 |
| No of slices | 25 | 35 | 45 | 60 | 80 | 100 | 120 | 140 |

* Optional: If one of these ingredients is not used, the weight can be made up by increasing any of the other fruits.

### Almond paste

Home-made almond paste or marzipan tastes especially good. Use the following guide to make enough almond paste to cover each cake in one layer.

| Size of Cake | Amount of Almond Paste Needed | Amount of Royal Icing Needed |
|---|---|---|
| 15 cm (6 in) round | 1 lb (450 g) | 1 lb (450 g) |
| 15 cm (6 in) square **or** 18 cm (7 in) round | 1¼ lb (550 g) | 1½ lb (700 g) |
| 18 cm (7 in) square **or** 20.5 cm(8 in) round | 1½ lb (675 g) | 1½ lb (700 g) |
| 20.5 cm(8 in) square **or** 23 cm (9 in) round | 1¾ lb (800 g) | 2 lb (900 g) |
| 23 cm (9 in) square **or** 25.5 cm (10 in) round | 2 lb (900 g) | 2¼ lb (1 kg) |
| 25.5 cm (10 in) square **or** 28 cm (11 in) round | 2¼ lb (1 kg) | 2½ lb (1.1 kg) |
| 28 cm (11 in) square **or** 30.5 cm (12 in) round | 2½ lb (1.1 kg) | 3 lb (1.4 kg) |
| 30.5 cm (12 in) square | 3 lb (1.4 kg) | 3½ lb (1.6 kg) |

To make 1 lb (450 g) almond paste the following ingredients are required:

1 lb (450 g) ground almond
8 oz (225 g) icing sugar
8 oz (225 g) caster sugar
2 standard eggs

Halve or double these ingredients as necessary for the cake you are covering.

### Royal Icing

To make 1 lb (450 g) of Royal Icing the following ingredients are required:

1 lb (450 g) icing sugar
2 egg whites

Halve or double these ingredients as required.

# 4

# SMALL COOKING EQUIPMENT

● ● ● ● ● ● ● ● ● ● ● ● ● ● ● ● ● ● ● ● ● ● ● ● ● ● ● ● ● ● ● ● ● ● ● ● ● ● ● ● ● ● ● ● ● ●

## BAKING TRAYS

Baking trays, sometimes called baking sheets, are used for baking biscuits, meringues, scones, Danish pastries or similar individual items of no fixed shape. Often no particular size tray is required, but all the items to be cooked should fit easily onto the tray, allowing space for them to spread and rise as necessary. It is better to use a tray that is a bit too big than one where the items spread and join together during cooking. Before using, check that the tins will fit into your cooker, allowing some space around so that the hot air can freely circulate and provide an even temperature during cooking. Items cooked together on one baking sheet should be the same size and thickness to enable them to cook and brown evenly.

In many recipes the recommended size of tray is given, sometimes in imperial and sometimes in metric measures.

These are the most popular sizes of tray made in metric and imperial measure equivalents.

| Metric Measurement | | | | Imperial Equivalent | | |
|---|---|---|---|---|---|---|
| cm wide | cm long | cm deep | | in wide | in long | in deep |
| 18 x | 30.5 x | 2 | or | 7 x | 12 x | ¾ |
| 20.5 x | 30.5 x | 2 | or | 8 x | 12 x | ¾ |
| 23 x | 33 x | 2 | or | 9 x | 13 x | ¾ |
| 25.5 x | 35.5 x | 2 | or | 10 x | 14 x | ¾ |

Larger trays are available but are only used commercially as they will not fit into the standard domestic cooker.

If you haven't a proper baking sheet do not make do with a tin with higher sides as this will prevent the hot air circulating around the items and cooking them. A flat underside of a shallow pan can be used.

## Swiss roll tins

If cooking a baked item such as a Swiss roll it is vital to use the correct sized tray. Buy a proper Swiss roll tin, do not make do with a baking tray. If the volume of mixture made is cooked in an incorrect sized tin then the finished product will either be too thin and overcooked or too thick and undercooked.

### Standard recipe
A standard Swiss roll is made using:
4 oz (100 g) caster sugar
4 oz (100 g) plain flour
3 eggs
It should be cooked in a lined Swiss roll tin measuring:
9 in x 13 in x ¾ in (22.5 cm x 33.6 cm x 2 cm)
(see page 76 for lining a tin)

This basic quantity of mixture should be baked at 425°F (220°C) (Gas Mark 7) for about 8 minutes until golden brown.

### To make a chocolate Swiss roll
Replace 1 tablespoon (15 ml) of the flour in the above recipe with 1 tablespoon (15 ml) cocoa powder

### Fillings for a Swiss roll

**For a cream filling use** ¼ pt (142 ml) double cream into which has been folded 2 teaspoons (10 ml) caster sugar and a few drops of vanilla essence.

**For a butter cream filling use** 4 oz (100 g) butter creamed with 8 oz (225 g) icing sugar plus a few drops of flavouring if desired.

## Cake tins

For a successful baked product it is essential to use the correct size tin for the job. Many tins aren't labelled at all by the manufacturers, while some are labelled in pints or litres to indicate their capacity. Others are measured in inches or centimetres, indicating the distance across the top of the tin, regardless of the depth or capacity. All this can be very confusing.

A good recipe will have been tested thoroughly and the size cake tin required written into the method. This is fine as long as the measure used is understood and the size of tins owned is known. Many recipes omit proper sizing information which can result in a cake which is out of proportion and undercooked or overcooked.

Too small a tin results in a cake which will rise higher than the edges of the tin and overflow. It will also look too deep. Too large a tin results in a cake being too thin and shallow, causing it to cook too quickly and being likely to burn.

The time the cake will take to cook will also vary according to the tin size used.

Every household cannot own a vast array of tins of all shapes and sizes. But if you know how to calculate the quantity of mixture you are making and how to calculate the size of a tin you own and wish to use, and how to adapt it, then there is no reason why a good result should not be achieved.

### Measuring of cake tins

An 8 in/20.5 cm **square** tin refers to the length of each side of the tin.
An 8 in/20.5 cm **round** tin refers to the diameter of the tin - the distance across the middle.

| Approximate Metric Equivalent of Various Tin Sizes | | | |
|---|---|---|---|
| 4 in | 10 cm | 8½ in | 21.5 cm |
| 4½ | 11.5 | 9 | 23 |
| 5 | 13 | 9½ | 24 |
| 5½ | 14 | 10 | 25.5 |
| 6 | 15 | 10½ | 26.5 |
| 6½ | 16.5 | 11 | 28 |
| 7 | 18 | 11½ | 29 |
| 7½ | 19 | 12 | 30.5 |
| 8 | 20.5 | | |

Cake tins in the shape of a number, a heart and so on are measured by their capacity.

### To find the capacity of a tin

Fill it right to the very top with water. Carefully tip the water into a measuring jug and read the capacity from the scale on the side. Convert this information into pints or litres using the conversion chart on page 21 if required.

If you have a tin in which you wish to bake a fruit cake but you don't know how much mixture to make, follow the directions below.

### To calculate how much cake mixture is required to fit in any given tin

• fill the tin with water to the depth you want
  the finished cake to be (loose bottomed tins
  should be lined with foil first)

- transfer the water into a measuring jug

- make 1½ lb (680 g) rich fruit cake mixture
  for every pint (½ litre) water measured

- add together the weight of all the ingredients
  in the desired recipe to check the total weight
  of mixture and that it will fit the tin.

A rich fruit cake is cooked at 300°F / 150°C / Gas Mark 2.

A fruit cake cooked at this temperature will require these approximate baking times for the various tin sizes.

| Square | | Round | | Capacity | | Cooking Time |
|--------|----|-------|----|----------|-------|--------------|
| in | cm | in | cm | pt | litre | (in hours) |
| | | 5 | 13 | 1 | ½ | 2 - 2½ |
| 5 | 13 | 6 | 15 | 1½ | ¾ | 2½ - 3 |
| 6 | 15 | 7 | 18 | 2 | 1 | 3 - 3½ |
| 7 | 18 | 8 | 20 | 3 | 1¾ | 3½ - 4 |
| 8 | 20 | 9 | 23 | 4 | 2¼ | 4 - 4½ |
| 9 | 23 | 10 | 25 | 6 | 3½ | 6 - 6½ |
| 10 | 25 | 11 | 28 | 8 | 4½ | 7 - 7½ |

The above quantities and times cannot be precise but are a good average guide. Test the cake to see if it is cooked half an hour before you expect it to be ready and then check it again every ten to fifteen minutes until a warm skewer or thin bladed knife inserted into the middle of the cake comes out clean.

## Lining Cake Tins

### Non-stick baking ware
Some baking tins now have a silicone finish and are advertised as non-stick. This means they should not require greasing or lining with paper. However, to obtain a good result it is usually necessary to grease and line a baking tin and it is essential if it is not coated with a non-stick finish. The appearance of a finished cake depends to a great extent on careful preparation of the tin.

### Greasing
Use oil or melted fat, lightly brushed on, making sure all surfaces are greased. Do not use too much or it will mix with the cake mixture and make the cake greasy. Tins may also be dredged with flour which will stick

onto the oil and can be an extra safeguard against sticking. Sprinkle a little flour into the tin and shake it around until all surfaces are covered.

## Lining

It is usual to grease the tin first before lining it with greaseproof or silicone paper. If greaseproof paper is used the surface which will be next to the food should then be greased, but this is not necessary if silicone paper is used. When baking sandwich cakes and sponges only the base of the tin need be lined. For speed and convenience, lining paper in strips and various diameter circles can be bought in packs ready to use.

Fruit cakes require a long cooking time and therefore it is recommended that the lining paper should be doubled to prevent the outside of the cake becoming too brown and drying out.

Extra rich fruit cakes for Christmas or for a wedding need protection against over cooking or over browning. It is advisable to wrap a double strip of brown paper around the outside of the tin and fix it with string or paper clips. Similarly a piece of brown paper can be placed on top of the cake towards the end of the cooking time to prevent the top becoming too brown.

### To line a round cake tin

Cut a strip of greaseproof paper as long as the circumference (around the outside edge) of the tin and 2 in (5 cm) wider than the depth of the tin. Make a fold about 1 in (2.5 cm) along one long edge of the strip. Cut this edge at ½ in (1.5 cm) intervals up to the fold making the cuts at a slight angle (see diagram below). Place the strip around the inside edge of the tin with the ends overlapping and with the cut edge lying on the base of the tin. Cut a circle of greaseproof paper slightly smaller than the base of the tin using the tin as a template and place this circle flat on the bottom of the tin. Grease the paper lining.

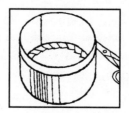

### To line a square or rectangular tin

Measure the length and width of the tin and add twice the depth of the tin onto these measurements. Cut a rectangle of paper to this size and place the tin in the centre. Mitre the corners by making a cut from the edge of the paper up to the corner of the tin (see diagram below). Place the paper in the tin, overlapping the paper at the corners to make a trim fit. Grease the paper.

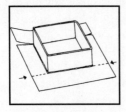 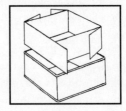

### To line a Swiss roll tin

Cut a piece of greaseproof paper or silicone paper 5 cm (2 in) larger all round than the tin. Place tin on it and cut from each corner of the paper to the corner of the tin as illustrated in diagram for lining a square tin. Grease the tin and put in the paper, overlapping it at the corners. Grease the paper.

## Loaf tins

Loaf tins and large shallow tins in which to cook batters are measured by volume.

### Small loaf

A standard small loaf weighs 1 lb or around 450 grams.
This is a liquid capacity of 900 ml or 1½ pt.
The approximate size of a small loaf tin is 8 x 4 x 2½ in (20.5 x 10 x 6.5 cm) measured across the top.

It is not usual to make one small loaf of bread on its own. Two small loaves can be produced from the quantities given below for making one large loaf.

### Large loaf

A standard large loaf weighs 2 lb or around 900 grams.

This requires a tin size of 1.75 (1¾) litre or 3 pints.

The approximate size of this tin is 9 x 5 x 3 in (23 x 13 x 7 cm) measured across the top. The amount of dough cooked in a tin of this size will be made from a standard recipe for a large loaf using:

700 g (1½ lb) strong plain flour
10 ml (2 level teaspoons) salt
15 g (½ oz fresh yeast)
400 ml (¾ pt) water

When making bread remember it is going to rise, so when the dough is placed in the tin it should not fill it or the bread will rise and spill over the edge. This is one reason why the capacity of the tin suitable for the recipe you are making should be known.

**Measuring a tin**

If you have a tin and are not sure what size it is, follow this simple procedure. Fill the tin to the brim with water, pour the water into a measuring jug and see how much liquid in pints or litres the tin will hold. Compare with the figures given above. This is useful to know even if you rarely make bread as many cakes are baked in a loaf shaped tin.

The same procedure of measuring can be carried out with cake tins, pie dishes or other irregular containers where capacity figures are required.

## Pudding basins

Pudding basins are measured by the liquid capacity they can hold, not by the width across the top or their depth.

They are still often referred to in recipes as 'transfer mixture to a 1 pint pudding basin', but they should now be made in metric measures and labelled in millilitre and litre capacities. Unfortunately manufacturers rarely mark the capacity on the basin, but it is easy to work out the capacity of the basins you already possess. In most homes there are one or two sizes of basin and one can probably be found to suit the recipe without having to buy new equipment. But do not be misled by thinking that the size of the basin is not important. If the correct size is not used the pudding will not cook so well, the timing may be wrong and the pudding can look very out of proportion when served. Space must also be allowed for the pudding to rise.

**To find the metric capacity of any basin** you have which is not labelled, fill it right to the brim with water, carefully transfer the water to a measuring jug with a scale of metric or imperial measures marked and read off how many litres, pints or parts of a litre or pint your basin holds. Convert this information as necessary using the chart below.

| ¼ | pt container holds | 150 ml |
|---|---|---|
| ½ | pt container holds | 300 ml |
| ¾ | pt container holds | 450 ml |
| 1 | pt container holds | 600 ml |
| 1¼ | pt container holds | 750 ml (¾ litre) |
| 1½ | pt container holds | 900 ml |
| 1¾ | pt container holds | 1 litre |
| 2 | pt container holds | 1.1 litre |
| 2¼ | pt container holds | 1.3 litre |
| 3 | pt container holds | 1.7 litre |
| 4 | pt container holds | 2.2 litre |
| 5 | pt container holds | 3 litre |
| 6 | pt container holds | 3½ litre |

NB - the volumes given are not exact conversions but are rounded up by the manufacturers.

**If you wish** to make a steamed pudding for four people from a
basic recipe using:
4 oz (100 g) margarine
4 oz (100 g) caster sugar
2 eggs
6 oz (175 g) self raising flour

This will require a pudding basin size 1½ pt or 900 ml. Using this as a guide
you can easily judge that you will require a 2 pt or 1.1 litre basin if the
ingredients are increased half as much again to make a pudding for six
people.

To steam a pudding of this size in a saucepan, you will need a large saucepan
with a capacity of around 9 pt (5 litres). The depth and diameter of the
saucepan is important to enable the pudding basin to fit in easily with
adequate water around it to create the steam. Before starting to mix the
pudding, check that you have a suitable large saucepan to accommodate the
basin you wish to use and that there is sufficient space around it to get the
basin in and out safely.

## Standard cup measures

Cups that are usually found around a home vary greatly in their capacities.
They are all shapes and sizes and may be sold as teacups, breakfast cups or
coffee cups and their capacity is not standard.

Therefore when using cup measures for cooking it is wise to buy a set of
standard measuring cups to use for all ingredients measured in cups. They
may be made of metal or plastic and are cheap to buy from a hardware shop
or household department of a large store. Plastic cups are useful as you can
use them in a microwave. Check that all measuring equipment is marked
with the BSI standard so they are really accurate. This is the only way you
can be sure that your cooking will be a success. Careful measuring of
ingredients is especially important when making baked goods.

This chart gives the standard capacities of British cups when measuring
liquids.

| | | | |
|---|---|---|---|
| one | measuring cup holds | 300 ml | |
| one half | measuring cup holds | 150 ml | (5 fl oz) |
| one third | measuring cup holds | 100 ml | (4 fl oz) |
| one quarter | measuring cup holds | 75 ml | |
| a cup is also available which holds | | 50 ml | (2 fl oz) |

This chart gives the standard capacities of British cups when measuring
dry ingredients.

| one | measuring cup holds | 200 g | (8 oz) |
| one half | measuring cup holds | 100 g | (4 oz) |
| one third | measuring cup holds | 75 g | (2½ oz) |
| one quarter | measuring cup holds | 50 g | (2 oz) |

## Standard spoon measures

For successful cooking, especially baking, careful measuring is required.

There are many spoons on sale which are not accurate. It is not a good idea to use just any spoons or some from a set or canteen of cutlery. Whether they are cheap or solid silver they are not made to any particular standard measurements and it is most unlikely that they will be accurate for cookery use. They are designed for their aesthetic appeal on a dining table not for cooking.

Sets of measuring spoons are available at low cost from the household department of large department stores and kitchen suppliers. They are usually made of plastic and each spoon should have its capacity stamped on the handle to avoid confusion.Look for spoons carrying the British Standard Institute mark so you can be sure they are really accurate.

### Sets of spoons

| 1 standard quarter | teaspoon | holds | 1.25 ml |
| 1 standard half | teaspoon | holds | 2.5 ml |
| 1 standard | teaspoon | holds | 5 ml |
| 1 standard | tablespoon | holds | 15 ml |

1 standard tablespoon is equivalent to 3 standard teaspoons.

All printed recipes use level spoons unless otherwise stated. This fact is usually stated at the front of the book or recipe.

To get a level spoonfull, fill the spoon and level off the top surface with a knife. (For standard American spoon capacities see page 37-38.)

## Level spoon capacities in millilitres

| | | | |
|---|---|---|---|
| ¼ | level teaspoon | 1.25 | ml |
| ½ | level teaspoon | 2.5 | ml |
| 1 | level teaspoon | 5 | ml |
| 2 | level teaspoons | 10 | ml |
| 3 | level teaspoons (1 level tablespoon) | 15 | ml |
| 1½ | level tablespoons | 25 | ml |
| 2 | level tablespoons | 30 | ml |
| 3 | level tablespoons | 45 | ml |
| 4 | level tablespoons (⅛ pt) | 60 | ml |
| 5 | level tablespoons | 75 | ml |
| 6 | level tablespoons | 90 | ml |
| 7 | level tablespoons | 105 | ml |
| 8 | level tablespoons (¼ pt) | 120 | ml |

As standard spoons are needed to measure many things around the home and garden it is advisable to buy at least two sets - one for the kitchen and one to measure possible hazardous substances such as weed killer in the garden.

### Cup and spoon replacements for ounces
The chart below is a great help when using American recipes.
't' represents a 5 ml teaspoon
'T' represents a 15 ml tablespoon
'C' represents an American Standard Cup.

### To use
Find the ingredient you are using in the recipe, e.g. caster sugar.
If the American recipe states ½ cup, look along the line until you come to ½ cup and the figure at the top of that column shows that this is the same as 4 oz caster sugar.

Similarly if using currants, 2T is the same as 1 oz currants.
These imperial measures can be converted to metric measures if desired by refering to page 33.

Those who prefer to work in American cups can use the chart the opposite way by finding the imperial weight the recipe states at the top of the chart and reading the spoon or cup equivalent below.

| INGREDIENT | ½oz | 1oz | 2oz | 3oz | 4oz | 5oz | 6oz | 7oz | 8oz |
|---|---|---|---|---|---|---|---|---|---|
| Almonds, ground | 2T | ¼C | ½C | ¾C | 1¼C | 1⅓C | 1⅔C | 2C | 2¼C |
| slivered | 6t | ¼C | ½C | ¾C | 1C | 1⅓C | 1⅔C | 2C | 2¼C |
| whole | 2T | ¼C | ⅓C | ½C | ¾C | 1C | 1¼C | 1⅓C | 1½C |
| Apples, dried whole | 3T | ½C | 1C | 1⅓C | 2C | 2⅓C | 2¾C | 3⅓C | 3¾C |
| Apricots, chopped | 2T | ¼C | ½C | ¾C | 1C | 1¼C | 1½C | 1¾C | 2C |
| whole | 2T | 3T | ½C | ⅔C | 1C | 1¼C | 1⅓C | 1½C | 1¾C |
| Arrowroot | 1T | 2T | ⅓C | ½C | ⅔C | ¾C | 1C | 1¼C | 1⅓C |
| Baking Powder | 1T | 2T | ⅓C | ½C | ⅔C | ¾C | 1C | 1C | 1¼C |
| Barley | 1T | 2T | ¼C | ½C | ⅔C | ¾C | 1C | 1C | 1¼C |
| Bicarbonate of Soda | 1T | 2T | ⅓C | ½C | ⅔C | ¾C | 1C | 1C | 1¼C |
| Breadcrumbs, dry | 2T | ¼C | ½C | ¾C | 1C | 1¼C | 1½C | 1¾C | 2C |
| soft | ¼C | ½C | 1C | 1½C | 2C | 2½C | 3C | 3⅔C | 4¼C |
| Biscuit crumbs | 2T | ¼C | ½C | ¾C | 1¼C | 1⅓C | 1⅔C | 2C | 2¼C |
| Butter | 3t | 6t | ¼C | ⅓C | ½C | ⅔C | ¾C | 1C | 1C |
| Cheese, grated, lightly packed | | | | | | | | | |
| natural cheddar | 6t | ¼C | ½C | ¾C | 1C | 1¼C | 1½C | 1¾C | 2C |
| processed cheddar | 5t | 2T | ⅓C | ⅔C | ¾C | 1C | 1¼C | 1½C | 1⅔C |
| parmesan, Romano | 6t | ¼C | ½C | ¾C | 1C | 1⅓C | 1⅔C | 2C | 2¼C |
| Cherries, glace chopped | 1T | 2T | ⅓C | ½C | ¾C | 1C | 1C | 1⅓C | 1½C |
| whole | 1T | 2T | ⅓C | ½C | ⅔C | ¾C | 1C | 1¼C | 1⅓C |
| Cocoa | 2T | ¼C | ½C | ¾C | 1¼C | 1⅓C | 1⅔C | 2C | 2¼C |
| Coconut, desiccated | 2T | ⅓C | ⅔C | 1C | 1⅓C | 1⅔C | 2C | 2⅓C | 2⅔C |
| shredded | ⅓C | ⅔C | 1¼C | 1¾C | 2½C | 3C | 3⅔C | 4⅓C | 5C |
| Cornflour | 6t | 3T | ½C | ⅔C | 1C | 1¼C | 1½C | 1⅔C | 2C |
| Coffee, ground | 2T | ⅓C | ⅔C | 1C | 1⅓C | 1⅔C | 2C | 2⅓C | 2⅔C |
| instant | 3T | ½C | 1C | 1⅓C | 1¾C | 2¼C | 2⅔C | 3C | 3½C |
| Cornflakes | ½C | 1C | 2C | 3C | 4¼C | 5¼C | 6¼C | 7⅓C | 8⅓C |
| Cream of Tartar | 1T | 2T | ⅓C | ½C | ⅔C | ¾C | 1C | 1C | 1¼C |
| Currants | 1T | 2T | ⅓C | ⅔C | ¾C | 1C | 1¼C | 1½C | 1⅔C |
| Custard powder | 6t | 3T | ½C | ⅔C | 1C | 1¼C | 1½C | 1⅔C | 2C |
| Dates, chopped | 1T | 2T | ⅓C | ⅔C | ¾C | 1C | 1¼C | 1½C | 1⅔C |
| whole, pitted | 1T | 2T | ⅓C | ½C | ¾C | 1C | 1¼C | 1⅓C | 1½C |
| Figs, chopped | 1T | 2T | ⅓C | ½C | ¾C | 1C | 1C | 1⅓C | 1½C |
| Flour, plain or self-raising | 6t | ¼C | ½C | ¾C | 1C | 1¼C | 1½C | 1¾C | 2C |
| wholemeal | 6t | 3T | ½C | ⅔C | 1C | 1¼C | 1⅓C | 1⅔C | 1¾C |
| Fruit, mixed | 1t | 2T | ⅓C | ½C | ¾C | 1C | 1¼C | 1⅓C | 1½C |
| Gelatine | 5T | 2T | ⅓C | ½C | ¾C | 1C | 1C | 1¼C | 1½C |
| Ginger, | | | | | | | | | |
| crystallised pieces | 1T | 2T | ⅓C | ½C | ¾C | 1C | 1¼C | 1⅓C | 1½C |
| ground | 6t | ⅓C | ½C | ¾C | 1¼C | 1½C | 1¾C | 2C | 2¼C |
| preserved, heavy syrup | 1T | 2T | ⅓C | ½C | ⅔C | ¾C | 1C | 1C | 1¼C |
| Glucose, liquid | 2t | 1T | 2T | ¼C | ⅓C | ½C | ½C | ⅔C | ⅔C |
| Golden syrup | 2t | 1T | 2T | ¼C | ⅓C | ½C | ½C | ⅔C | ⅔C |
| Haricot Beans | 1T | 2T | ⅓C | ½C | ⅔C | ¾C | 1C | 1C | 1¼C |

| INGREDIENT | ½oz | 1oz | 2oz | 3oz | 4oz | 5oz | 6oz | 7oz | 8oz |
|---|---|---|---|---|---|---|---|---|---|
| Honey | 2t | 1T | 2T | ¼C | ⅓C | ½C | ½C | ⅔C | ⅔C |
| Jam | 2t | 1T | 2T | ¼C | ⅓C | ½C | ½C | ⅔C | ¾C |
| Lentils | 1T | 2T | ⅓C | ½C | ⅔C | ¾C | 1C | 1C | 1¼C |
| Milk powder full cream | 2T | ¼C | ½C | ¾C | 1¼C | 1⅓C | 1⅔C | 2C | 2¼C |
| non fat | 2T | ⅓C | ¾C | 1¼C | 1½C | 2C | 2⅓C | 2¾C | 3¼C |
| Nutmeg | 6t | 3T | ½C | ⅔C | ¾C | 1C | 1¼C | 1½C | 1⅔C |
| Nuts chopped | 6t | ¼C | ½C | ¾C | 1C | 1¼C | 1½C | 1¾C | 2C |
| Oatmeal | 1T | 2T | ½C | ⅔C | ¾C | 1C | 1¼C | 1½C | 1⅔C |
| Olives,whole | 1T | 2T | ⅓C | ⅔C | ¾C | 1C | 1¼C | 1½C | 1⅔C |
| sliced | 1T | 2T | ⅓C | ⅔C | ¾C | 1C | 1¼C | 1½C | 1⅔C |
| Pasta,short (e.g. macaroni) | 1T | 2T | ⅓C | ⅔C | ¾C | 1C | 1¼C | 1½C | 1⅔C |
| Peaches, dried and whole | 1T | 2T | ⅓C | ⅔C | ¾C | 1C | 1¼C | 1½C | 1⅔C |
| chopped | 6t | ¼C | ½C | ¾C | 1C | 1¼C | 1½C | 1¾C | 2C |
| Peanuts,shelled, raw, whole | 1T | 2T | ⅓C | ½C | ¾C | 1C | 1¼C | 1⅓C | 1½C |
| roasted | 1T | 2T | ⅓C | ⅔C | ¾C | 1C | 1¼C | 1½C | 1⅔C |
| Peanut butter | 3t | 6t | 3T | ⅓C | ½C | ½C | ⅔C | ¾C | 1C |
| Peas,split | 1T | 2T | ⅓C | ½C | ⅔C | ¾C | 1C | 1C | 1¼C |
| Peel,mixed | 1T | 2T | ⅓C | ½C | ¾C | 1C | 1C | 1¼C | 1½C |
| Potato,powder | 1T | 2T | ¼C | ⅓C | ½C | ⅔C | ¾C | 1C | 1¼C |
| flakes | ¼C | ½C | 1C | 1⅓C | 2C | 2⅓C | 2¾C | 3⅓C | 3¾C |
| Prunes,chopped | 1T | 2T | ⅓C | ½C | ⅔C | ¾C | 1C | 1¼C | 1⅓C |
| whole pitted | 1T | 2T | ⅓C | ½C | ⅔C | ¾C | 1C | 1C | 1¼C |
| Raisins | 2T | ¼C | ⅓C | ½C | ¾C | 1C | 1C | 1⅓C | 1½C |
| Rice, short grain, raw | 1T | 2T | ¼C | ½C | ⅔C | ¾C | 1C | 1C | 1¼C |
| long grain,raw | 1T | 2T | ⅓C | ½C | ¾C | 1C | 1¼C | 1⅓C | 1½C |
| Rice bubbles | ⅔C | 1¼C | 2½C | 3⅔C | 5C | 6¼C | 7½C | 8¾C | 10C |
| Rolled oats | 2T | ⅓C | ⅔C | 1C | 1⅓C | 1¾C | 2C | 2½C | 2¾C |
| Sago | 2T | ¼C | ⅓C | ½C | ¾C | 1C | 1C | 1¼C | 1½C |
| Salt,common | 3t | 6t | ¼C | ⅓C | ½C | ⅔C | ¾C | 1C | 1C |
| Semolina | 1T | 2T | ⅓C | ½C | ¾C | 1C | 1C | 1⅓C | 1½C |
| Spices | 6t | 3T | ¼C | ⅓C | ½C | ½C | ⅔C | ¾C | 1C |
| Sugar, crystalline 1A | 3t | 6t | ¼C | ⅓C | ½C | ⅔C | ¾C | 1C | 1C |
| caster | 3t | 5t | ¼C | ⅓C | ½C | ⅔C | ¾C | 1C | 1¼C |
| icing | 1T | 2T | ⅓C | ½C | ¾C | 1C | 1C | 1¼C | 1½C |
| moist brown | 1T | 2T | ⅓C | ½C | ¾C | 1C | 1C | 1⅓C | 1½C |
| Sultanas | 1T | 2T | ⅓C | ½C | ¾C | 1C | 1C | 1¼C | 1½C |
| Tapioca | 1T | 2T | ⅓C | ½C | ⅔C | ¾C | 1C | 1¼C | 1⅓C |
| Treacle | 2t | 1T | 2T | ¼C | ⅓C | ½C | ½C | ⅔C | ⅔C |
| Walnuts,chopped | 2T | ¼C | ½C | ¾C | 1C | 1¼C | 1½C | 1¾C | 2C |
| halved | 2T | ⅓C | ⅔C | 1C | 1¼C | 1½C | 1¾C | 2¼C | 2½C |
| Yeast,dried | 6t | 3T | ½C | ⅔C | 1C | 1¼C | 1⅓C | 1⅔C | 1⅔C |
| compressed | 3t | 6t | 3T | ⅓C | ½C | ½C | ⅔C | ⅔C | 1C |

# 5

# LARGE KITCHEN EQUIPMENT

The range of large kitchen equipment available is changing all the time, as advances occur in design and efficiency.

There is a gradual change from the Fahrenheit scale to the Centigrade scale of temperatures and therefore these and gas cooker equivalents need to be known to successfully cook any recipes regardless of the type of equipment available. Labels on food indicating its storage life, how it should be stored and at what temperature, leads to safer and enhanced flavoured foods. The latest labels on convenience meals prepared for cooking in the microwave make it quite clear how long and at what setting the dish requires cooking in order that the centre is well cooked and/or adequately heated through.

Thermometers for the oven, freezer and refrigerator should be considered essential pieces of equipment in the home so that at any time the temperature can be checked and adjusted as necessary.

Many companies around the country will design a kitchen, but this can only be really successfully done by the person who spends most time working in it. Measurements given here will enable everyone to check the best way to lay out the kitchen and place equipment for greatest ease and efficiency of time and effort.

### Conversion temperatures for cookers
Four equivalent temperatures are given on this chart; three for electric cookers and one for the gas mark equivalent. The temperature of some electric cookers is marked in degrees Fahrenheit and some in degrees Centigrade.

### Circotherm cookers
The temperature of Circotherm cookers is marked on the centigrade scale. These cookers are more economical to use than other electric cookers as they cook to the same standard but at a lower temperature and a bit quicker. Therefore if a recipe gives the temperature at which an item should be cooked as 350°F, (180°C), (Gas Mark 4), those using a Circotherm cooker should set the dial at 160°C to cook the same item as can be seen from the chart on page 84.

| Equivalent Temperature Settings | | | | |
|---|---|---|---|---|
| **ELECTRIC COOKER** Degrees Fahrenheit | **ELECTRIC COOKER** Degrees Centigrade | **CIRCOTHERM COOKER** Degrees Centigrade | **GAS COOKER** Gas Mark | **Heat of Cooker** |
| 200 | 100 | 100 | ¼ | very cool |
| 225 | 110 | 110 | ½ | very cool |
| 250 | 130 | 120 | ½ | very cool |
| 275 | 140 | 130 | 1 | cool |
| 300 | 150 | 140 | 2 | cool |
| 325 | 160 | 150 | 3 | moderate |
| 350 | 180 | 160 | 4 | moderate |
| 375 | 190 | 160 | 5 | fairly hot |
| 400 | 200 | 170 | 6 | fairly hot |
| 425 | 220 | 180 | 7 | hot |
| 450 | 230 | 190 | 8 | very hot |
| 500 | 240 | 190 | 9 | very hot |

The temperatures shown are equivalent settings rather than exact conversions of degrees of heat.

Cookers are checked by the manufacturers before leaving the factory, but for good results it is wise to check the temperature of your cooker regulary using an oven thermometer to make sure that it has remained accurate. They can be bought at hardware stores or the kitchen department of large department stores. Just place them in the oven on one of the shelves, not the bottom, and check that it reads the same as the oven dial just as the heat cuts out.

For the best cooked results, always consult the manufacturer's instruction book that comes with your cooker.

This is a guide to the dishes which are cooked at the various temperatures shown below.

| **Very cool** | | meringues |
|---|---|---|
| **Cool** | - lower setting | meringues, stewed fruit |
| | - higher setting | rich fruit cakes, milk puddings, baked egg custards |
| **Moderate** | - lower setting | casseroles, milk puddings, egg custards |
| | - higher setting | slow pot roasts, sponge cakes, Victoria sandwich cakes |

| **Fairly hot** | - lower setting | baked fish, baked fruit and vegetables, biscuits |
| | - higher setting | shortcrust pastry, flans, quiches, roast meat, souffles |
| **Hot** | | flaky pastry pies, Yorkshire pudding, Swiss rolls roast vegetables |
| **Very hot** | | puff pastry, bread, and to brown foods quickly |

## Microwave ovens

Microwave ovens vary in design, size and shape but more importantly they differ a great deal in wattage or power output. They are tested to an internationally agreed standard method called the International Electrotechnical Commission specification number 705 (IEC 705).

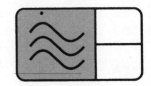

## Power of microwave ovens

Wattages available are 420, 450, 480, 500, 550, 600, 650, 700, 720, 740, 750, 800, 850 and 1000. The wattage of each oven is always in its accompanying manual, but its power is now also stated on a label attached to the front of the machine (see diagram). People with older microwave ovens should check the wattage of their model and stick a note of it onto their machine to remind themselves into which category their cooker falls.

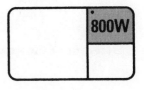

It is very important to know the power of your oven for successful cooking results. The higher the wattage the quicker the heating process. If your oven is rated 700 watts it will heat food faster than one of 600 watts but not as fast as an 800 watt oven. (see page 87 re cooking times chart) (see diagram).

oven power rating

| 500W | 600W | 700W | 800W |

◄ more heating time    less heating time ►

If packs of ready prepared food from the freezer or chill cabinet are to be cooked it is important that each is cooked through or heated through sufficiently to make it safe to eat. Until recently it has been difficult to know just how long each dish will need to be in the microwave at each power level. To overcome this problem a labelling system has been developed.

### Labelling of foods which may be cooked/reheated in a microwave

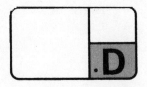

Every oven is categorised with a letter from A to E (see diagram )

Pre-packed food suitable for microwaving and weighing up to 500 g (just over 1 lb) is also marked with a letter between A and E (see diagram)

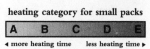

heating category for small packs

◄ more heating time     less heating time ►

By matching the information and symbols on your oven to the information given on packs of food, the food can be heated through exactly the right amount for its size and density.

For instance if your oven is category E it will heat through small portions of food quicker than a category A oven. If the category letter on your oven is different to that written on the pack of food then you need to adjust the timing a little. For instance if your oven is category C and a pack of food you buy gives the timing for category B and D then you need to heat the food for the time midway between the two times suggested. Similarly if your oven is category E you need to give the pack a shorter heating time than that given for D ovens. This system is now used on numerous packs of food and ready prepared meals manufactured by the major retailers. This makes the use of the microwave far less of a hit and miss procedure.

### Diagram of the new labelling system

There are thousands of microwave ovens in existence which are not labelled in this way. So tables are available showing the IEC 705 power output of every model and the heating category, the letter of the alphabet which applies to each model. The tables are in a 'Food Sense' booklet called 'The New Microwave Labels'. The booklets can be found in some supermarkets or are available from the Ministry of Agriculture, Fisheries and Food (MAFF).

## Converting recipes for the microwave

Many conventional recipes can be totally converted for cooking in a microwave or certain processes during the preparation of dishes can be carried out.

## Preparation

Read the recipe carefully and note which processes such as lightly frying off onions at the start of a dish or stewing ingredients at some stage, fit the processes easily carried out in the microwave. Foods and processes involving moist methods of cooking such as boiling, poaching and steaming are most suitably adapted for the microwave.

Sauces, soups and gravies are excellent prepared in the microwave. Check that all the ingredients used are suitable to be cooked in a microwave.

## Timings

Try to find a similar recipe in a microwave recipe book to get an idea of the necessary timings. If this is not possible, underestimate the cooking times and then check very frequently to see when the food is ready. This also gives a chance to rearrange or stir the food so it cooks evenly. Microwave cooking times are usually around one-third to one quarter of conventional cooking times. Remember that if you double the contents of the recipe the cooking time needs to be increased by around 75%.

If you halve the ingredients you need to halve the cooking time and add a fraction more.

## Adapting the recipe

Meat and vegetables should be cut into smallish even-sized pieces so they cook more quickly and evenly than large pieces.

The amount of liquid in, for instance, a casserole, can be cut by at least one quarter as there is much less evaporation in microwave cooking. Vegetables can be cooked in a few tablespoons of water instead of in a large amount of liquid in a saucepan. Use less spices than in conventional recipes and season at the end of cooking time rather than during preparation.

Switching to cooking in the microwave saves a lot of time and washing up. To enjoy recipes previously cooked in a conventional oven is not difficult but takes some thought, and is best carried out after one is completely familiar with using the microwave and has some experience of timings and methods. It is well worth any effort.

## Settings for various dishes cooked in a microwave

This chart indicates the various settings on a microwave and for which use each is best.

| This Example is Based on a 600W Oven | | |
|---|---|---|
| **POWER** | **OUTPUT** | **USE** |
| High | 100% | Cooking small to medium-sized poultry Cooking fresh fruit and vegetables Cooking fish, Browning minced beef Roasting small joints of meat |
| Medium | 70-80% | Roasting meat, Reheating leftovers Heating milk for drinks, Cooking rice |
| Low | 50-60% | Cooking pot roasts, Fast defrosting Simmering, Defrosting and reheating frozen casseroles |
| Defrost | 30-40% | All defrosting and thawing Slow cooking less tender joints Softening butter and margarine |
| Warm | 15-30 % | Very slow defrosting Keeping foods warm |

(See page 86 for microwave labelling)

## Cooking times

The charts below are produced by microwave manufacturers and indicate how much extra time should be allowed if it is decided to cook a dish on medium or low power instead of high power or vice versa.

For instance some dishes like casseroles often benefit from being cooked on a lower power for longer instead of on high power for a shorter time.

| 600 - 700 Watt Machines | | | |
|---|---|---|---|
| **HIGH 100%** | **MEDIUM HIGH 70%** | **MEDIUM 50%** | **LOW 30%** |
| 1 min | 1½ min | 2 min | 2½ min |
| 2 min | 3 min | 4 min | 5 min |
| 3 min | 4½ min | 6 min | 7½ min |
| 4 min | 6 min | 8 min | 10 min |
| 5 min | 7½ min | 10 min | 12½ min |
| 6 min | 9 min | 12 min | 15 min |
| 7 min | 10½ min | 14 min | 17½ min |
| 8 min | 12 min | 16 min | 20 min |
| 9 min | 13½ min | 18 min | 22½ min |
| 10 min | 15 min | 20 min | 25 min |
| 12 min | 18 min | 24 min | 30 min |

| 450 - 550 Watt Machines | | | |
|---|---|---|---|
| **HIGH**<br>**100%** | **MEDIUM HIGH**<br>**70%** | **MEDIUM**<br>**50%** | **LOW**<br>**30%** |
| 1¼ min | 1¾ min | 2½ min | 3 min |
| 2½ min | 3½ min | 4¾ min | 6 min |
| 3½ min | 5¼ min | 7¼ min | 9 min |
| 4¾ min | 7¼ min | 9½ min | 12 min |
| 6 min | 9 min | 12 min | 15 min |
| 7¼ min | 10¾ min | 14½ min | 18 min |
| 8½ min | 12½ min | 16¾ min | 21 min |
| 9½ min | 14½ min | 19 min | 24 min |
| 10¾ min | 16 min | 21½ min | 27 min |
| 12 min | 18 min | 24 min | 30 min |
| 14½ min | 21½ min | 29 min | 36 min |

## Refrigeration in the home

The widespread use of freezers and refrigerators would seem to be a blessing in preventing food poisoning. But in order to be effective against bacteria multiplying and food poisoning occuring, the food has to be packed correctly, stored in the correct area of the refrigerator and at the correct temperature according to its type.

Food manufacturers and retailers take a lot of time and trouble to ensure that our food is prepared under hygienic conditions and that correct temperature control is enforced throughout the food chain. Environmental health officers and trading standards officers check to ensure that all food is sold according to strict codes of hygiene and safety practice.

If chilled or fresh food is transfered from a shop quickly and then placed correctly into a refrigerator at the correct temperature in the home, then it will stay in good condition to cook and serve later.

### Refrigerator temperatures

A refrigerator needs to be in the kitchen readily to hand at all times of the day. This means that it can sometimes be difficult to keep it cool enough especially as every time the door is opened warm air rushes in and the temperature rises. Open the door as little as possible and always close it as quickly as possible. The temperature of a refrigerator at home should be less than 4°C at all times. If your kitchen is hot then set the dial a little lower than this. Each home should have a refrigerator and freezer thermometer because it is important to check that items are being stored at the recommended temperature.

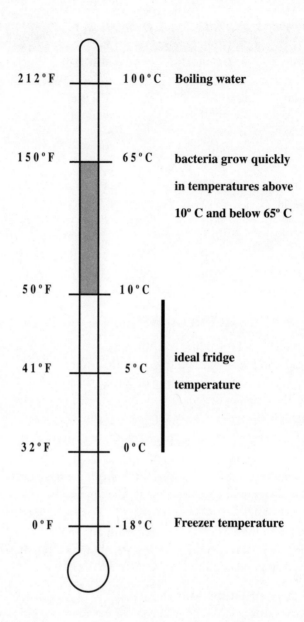

| | |
|---|---|
| 212°F — 100°C | **Boiling water** |
| 150°F — 65°C | **bacteria grow quickly** |
| | **in temperatures above** |
| | **10° C and below 65° C** |
| 50°F — 10°C | |
| 41°F — 5°C | **ideal fridge** |
| | **temperature** |
| 32°F — 0°C | |
| 0°F — -18°C | **Freezer temperature** |

## Choosing the size of your refrigerator

The capacity is sometimes measured in cubic feet but may also be in litres.
30 litres is approximately equivalent to 1 cubic foot.

| | |
|---|---|
| 100 litres = 3.5 cubic feet | 280 litres = 10.0 cubic feet |
| 140 litres = 5.0 cubic feet | 340 litres = 12.0 cubic feet |
| 180 litres = 6.5 cubic feet | 400 litres = 14.0 cubic feet |

### The correct size for you

As a guide allow 1 cubic foot of space for each person in the family and then add one cubic foot more. The shape or size finally chosen will depend on the size of the family and their lifestyle, whether a lot of entertaining is done, the size and shape of the kitchen and of course the cost involved.

### Positioning of the refrigerator

Measure the space available in your kitchen and then allow about 2 in (50 mm) at the back of the refrigerator for the heat generated by it to escape. Place it in as cool a place as possible and certainly away from the cooker.

### Packing the refrigerator correctly

Remember that the quality of food taken from a refrigerator or freezer is only as good as its quality when it went in. It is only sensible to preserve food that is good and uncontaminated.

Food poisoning organisms will not grow if they are colder than 5°C (41°F) for a short while in a refrigerator, or at -15°C (5°F) or colder in a freezer. Bacteria multiply quickly above these temperatures.

### Positioning food in a refrigerator

Cold temperatures will not kill bacteria so it is important to stop them spreading from one food to another.

Cover all food, but especially fresh, juicy foods and liquids. This will avoid contamination and transfer of smells.

### Raw food

Place on the lower shelf on a covered plate, all food such as raw meat or fish which might drip. Then if drips occur, no contamination is passed to foods placed below which may not be cooked before eating.

### Cooked items and baked products

Place on the top and centre shelves.

### Eggs

These are best not stored in a refrigerator but may be stored in a rack in the door if desired.

### Cheese, butter and margarine

Place in a plastic container in the back of the door.

### Salad items

Store in the salad compartment at the bottom of the refrigerator.

(See page 93 for maximum safe storage times in the refrigerator)

Once food is removed from a refrigerator care must be taken to prepare it and cook it in hygienic conditions. Once food reaches room temperature bacteria become very active again and deterioration of the food starts (see below). Keep raw and cooked food apart on chopping boards and work surfaces.

## How food poisoning bacteria react to different temperatures

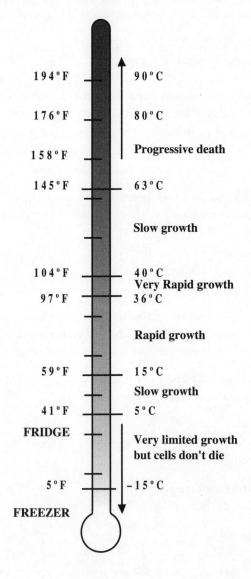

| | |
|---|---|
| 194°F | 90°C |
| 176°F | 80°C |
| 158°F | **Progressive death** |
| 145°F | 63°C |
| | **Slow growth** |
| 104°F | 40°C **Very Rapid growth** |
| 97°F | 36°C |
| | **Rapid growth** |
| 59°F | 15°C |
| | **Slow growth** |
| 41°F | 5°C |
| **FRIDGE** | **Very limited growth but cells don't die** |
| 5°F | –15°C |
| **FREEZER** | |

## Maximum Safe Storage Time for Foods in the Refrigerator

The following safe storage times presume that the refrigerator is at the recommended temperature of not higher than 4°C (40°F) and that the food is fresh and within its 'use by' date before storing.

### Dairy Foods

| | | |
|---|---|---|
| Fresh milk | in a bottle or carton | 3-4 days |
| Yogurt | as bought in a carton | follow 'use by' date |
| | if homemade | 2-3 days |
| Butter and margarine | in their original wrappers | 2-4 weeks |
| Cheese | in covered container | 1-2 weeks |
| | cheese does not have to be stored in a fridge but if it is it should be removed from there half an hour before eating. | |
| Cream cheese | keep in covered container | 5-7 days |

### Poultry

| | | |
|---|---|---|
| Fresh | washed and wrapped in polythene | 2-3 days |
| Cooked | cooled, wrapped, covered on a plate | 2-3 days |
| Frozen | wrapped well and stored in the frozen food compartment unless it is to be defrosted and eaten within | 2-3 days |

### Fish

| | | |
|---|---|---|
| Raw | covered in a container or foil to prevent flavours transfering | 1-2 days |
| Cooked | in a container or covered with foil | 1-2 days |
| Frozen | leave in shop packaging and place in frozen food compartment  following star rating | |

### Meat

| | | |
|---|---|---|
| Raw -all kinds | remove shop wrapping, place in foil or a dish and cover. Store on lower shelves of refrigerator | |
| joints | | 3 days |
| small items like chops | | 3 days |
| mince and offal | | 1 day |
| bacon | wrapped well | 7 -9 days |

### Meats

| | | |
|---|---|---|
| Cooked | wrap well or place in covered dish | 3-4 days |

### Eggs

| | | |
|---|---|---|
| | best bought in small quantities as needed and used within a week. | |
| whole yolks | cover with water in a cup | 3 days |
| whites | store in covered container | 3-4 days |
| hard boiled | leave in shell | 7 days |

# Freezers

It is often forgotten that the quality and safety of food placed in a home freezer is only as good as the quality and safety of it when it was put in. Never freeze produce that is not really fresh or suitably frozen by a frozen food manufacturer.

### Buying frozen food

Always buy frozen food from a shop with a good regular turn-over of goods, where the freezers are clean, kept at the correct temperature and where frozen food is not stored above the storage line level marked on the equipment.

Frozen food should be the last items collected and placed in the shopping trolley and then should ideally be placed directly into a cool bag for transportation home. Do not leave frozen foods in a shopping basket or boot of a car while remaining shopping is done or a coffee stop made.

Immediately on reaching home, place the frozen food in the freezer before doing anything else and if you know that a lot of food is going to be bought, turn the freezer to a colder setting before going shopping. This prevents the temperature of the freezer rising too high when cooler items are placed in it.

Certain foods such as ice-cream **must** stay frozen. Do not refreeze melted ice-cream. If meat defrosts then it should be cooked, before placing it in the freezer as a ready to eat dish such as a casserole. The home freezer should be minus 18°C or below all the time.

### Choosing the size of your freezer

It is always recommended that one should buy the largest one can afford and accommodate correctly into the home. The capacity required will depend on whether the freezer is needed to store a lot of fresh produce from the garden or pick your own farms, or perhaps needs to accommodate lots of ready - made frozen meals.

### Capacity

A rough guide is that every cubic foot of volume in the freezer will store 20 lb (9 kg) of frozen food. More neat square packets or boxes of food can be stored as they can be packed closely together; odd - shaped bundles like joints of meat, or decorated cakes in large boxes can take up a great deal of space.

### Home freezing of food

The amount of food that can be home frozen at any one time varies from model to model so check the manufacturer's instructions for this. A rough guide is that 2 lb (1 kg) of fresh food per cubic foot of freezer capacity can be frozen during any 24 hour period.

This is an important factor if you freeze your own produce, use 'pick your own' farms or if you enjoy large baking sessions. It is very important that the unfrozen food which is put into the cabinet doesn't raise the temperature so much that the food already in the freezer rises in temperature and deteriorates.

## Positioning of the freezer

A freezer must have space around it for warm air to escape from the condenser. It should be between 1 and 4 in (25 to 100 mm) away from the wall. Unlike a frig which needs to be to hand for frequent use, a freezer can be placed virtually anywhere. A dry, cool utility room or a well ventilated garage is ideal. It can be placed in a spare bedroom, but this will probably be warm, and remember that often the motor of a freezer can make quite a disturbing noise if someone is sleeping nearby.

## Electricity supply

A freezer must always have its own fused 13 or 15 amp power supply and ideally its own fuse box at the consumer unit. This enables it to be left on during holiday time so the other electricity supply in the house can be switched off.

## The effect of power cuts on frozen food

Frozen food should keep in good condition for at least eight hours, longer if the weather is cold and if the door of the freezer is not opened. Try not to open the door for at least two hours after the power has been turned back on.

## Star codes

To simplify correct storage, all modern refrigeration appliances have a star code system which will correspond to the stars printed on packets of frozen foods. The stars represent a temperature.

| | | |
|---|---|---|
| ★ | -6°C | Stores frozen food safely for up to one week in a frozen food compartment. Eat within one week of purchase. |
| ★★ | -12° C | Stores frozen food safely for up to one month in a frozen food compartment. Eat within one month of purchase. |
| ★★★ | -18°C | Stores frozen food safely for up to three months in a frozen food compartment. Eat within three months of purchase. |
| ★★★★ | -18°C | A food freezer capable of freezing down fresh food to -24°C. Stores frozen food safely for up to three months. Available as a fast freeze facility on selected models. Eat food within three months of purchase. |

Once food is removed from a freezer then care must be taken to defrost it, prepare it and cook it in hygienic conditions. Once food reaches room temperature, bacteria become very active again and deterioration of the food starts.

### Storage times for food in a freezer

Commercially prepared foods and convenience dishes bought frozen and transferred to the home freezer, should have a date on the packaging indicating where it should be stored and a 'Best Before' date. Always buy food well within its 'Best Before' or 'Use By' dates. Alternatively there may be a panel on the package giving clear storage instructions along with nutritional information etc.

This information makes storage easy. But if you buy fresh food and freeze it yourself, or prepare a cooked dish, how long can it be safely frozen?

## Maximum Safe Storage Time for Foods in the Freezer

The following give times for freezing food providing that it is in a good, clean state when put in the freezer, is wrapped correctly and when the temperature of the freezer is -18°C.

| | | | |
|---|---|---|---|
| Cooked meat - sliced | 1 month | Shortcrust pastry raw | 4 months |
| Casseroles | 2 months | Shortcrust pastry - cooked | 6 months |
| Cooked fish | 2 months | | |
| Shellfish | 1 month | Pancakes - cooked | 2 months |
| White fish | 6 months | Sponge pudding - cooked | 3 months |
| Oily or smoked fish | 3 months | Vegetables - average - *depending on type* | 6 -12 months |
| Raw bacon | 1 month | | |
| Uncooked beef and lamb | 12 months | Soft fruit | 8 months |
| Uncooked pork | 9 months | Stoned fruit | 12 months |
| Mince and sausages | 6 weeks | Egg whites and yolks - separately | 10 months |
| Chicken and turkey | 9 months | Ice cream | 3 months |
| Bread | 1 month | Hard cheese | 6 months |
| Small cakes and sponges | 6 months | Butter | 12 months |
| Rich fruit cake | 12 months | | |

All packages in the freezer should be clearly labelled with the contents and the date they were placed in the freezer.

Just because something has been in the freezer longer than the time stated above doesn't necessarily mean that it shouldn't be eaten, but the flavour and texture of the goods may well have deteriorated.
Never refreeze thawed items unless they are cooked first, e.g. frozen mince removed from the freezer, made into a sauce and then refrozen.

# Measuring a kitchen

Kitchens vary greatly in size and shape so it is impossible to cater for all measuring requirements here.

However for a kitchen to be efficient and an attractive place to work in it is essential to do some careful planning and measuring and think carefully just how you want it arranged. This is important even if you intend to employ a kitchen manufacturer to make it for you. The measuring and planning is best done initially by the person who is going to be working in the kitchen, as only he/she knows the type of meals they wish to cook, how many they usually cook for and what equipment they need and can afford to put in the kitchen.

### Height of counter/worktops
Work surfaces are usually built 900 mm (35 ½ in) high, the most comfortable height for most people to work at. To check the ideal height for you, stand with your arms bent, and 75 mm (3 in) below elbow level is the correct height for the work surface for you. If you have to perform a certain task very often which involves putting pressure down on the surface such as rolling pastry, you could have the counter top at 750 mm (29 ½ in). This will avoid back and arm strain occuring. Remember though that if you are very short, the counter cannot be lower than 850 mm (33 ½ in) or equipment such as a refrigerator or dishwasher won't fit underneath.

### Depth or width of counter/worktops
The depth of working surfaces should be a minimum of 600 mm so that electrical appliances can be fitted underneath if desired.

### Length of worktops and equipment
From left to right these are in multiples of 100 mm (4 in). Any gaps left by equipment being placed in certain positions can be filled in with filler pieces or put to practical use to house a wine rack, towel rail or similar.
Counter tops come in very long lengths so that joins do not have to be made. They can also be cut in 'L' shapes to go around corners without a join.

### Placing of equipment

When measuring where to place items it is important to remember that space is required around equipment. Cooker tops and hobs should have 300 mm each side to allow for space for saucepans and for cooks to gain easy access to the oven.

Cookers and refrigerators which have opening doors require space each side to allow the door to open back fully. (See page 91 for sizes of refrigerators).

### Equipment

Collect as many brochures as possible which give measurements of equipment. Small models are made by many manufacturers for those with limited space. (See page 94 or sizes of refrigerators and freezers).

Ideally you don't buy a certain piece of equipment just because it happens to fit into your plans, but this is the only thing to do in some instances. All kitchen equipment is now made and sold in metric measures so it is preferable to work completely in metric measures. If imperial measures are prefered then translate these into metric measures following the table on page 23.

### Sinks

There is a huge range of sinks and what is fitted depends on individual taste. Measurements worth remembering are that a sink size 500 x 350 mm (20 x 14 in) and 175 - 200 mm (7 - 8 in) deep will accommodate oven and refrigerator shelves for washing. A minimum depth of 250 mm (10 in) is required if the sink is to be used for washing clothes. If you have or wish to buy a waste disposal unit then make sure the sink outlet is adequate size.

### Storage space

You can never have too much storage space. Shelves between 760 mm and 1520 mm are within comfortable reach for most people but this depends on the height of the person using the kitchen. Some space which can only be reached by using steps can still be useful for storage of items that are not used often.

### Extractor fans

To remove smells and moisture from a kitchen it is wise to fit an extractor fan or extractor cooker hood. An extractor fan should remove 60 litres per second of air from the room and a cooker hood 30 litres per second from just the cooker area.

# 6

# THE UTILITY ROOM

Decisions made within the European Union have necessitated many alterations to the way things are measured and labelled in the utility room. The lobbying of consumer groups for improved safety measures and clearer marking has also had effect.

The care procedures for clothes and fabrics should now be easier for everyone to understand once they know the International Care Labelling System now in use. Those with older equipment can use the information in this chapter to convert the new symbols to the equipment they use.

Ignorance regarding electrical wiring and changing plugs and fuses can be very dangerous. It is vital to know what each coloured wire represents and how it should be fitted into plugs. Lack of knowledge about which fuse to use in equipment around the home can lead to the incorrect fuse being fitted, damage to the equipment and the safety of the user.

It is always wise to keep a check on how much energy is being used around the home. Learn how to read the gas and electricity meter so that bills can be checked.

## Electrical wiring

Until recently, different countries used different colours to distinguish the live, neutral and earth wires in their electrical wiring. As a result, the colours used in flexes attached to imported appliances differed from those normally used in Britain. Old British equipment will also have flexes containing the old coloured wires.

### Colour coding of wires

There is now an agreed international standard for the colours of the wires in a flex so that the danger in this area is greatly reduced, providing everyone knows the new colour codes. The international agreement also benefits manufacturers as they can now use one standard flex for appliances made for home use and for export.

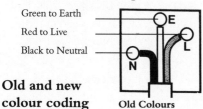

Green to Earth
Red to Live
Black to Neutral

**Old and new colour coding**

Old Colours

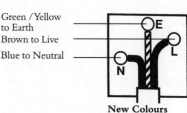

Green / Yellow to Earth
Brown to Live
Blue to Neutral

New Colours

## Types of electric plugs

In European countries the two-pin round plug is favoured while plugs in Britain have three square pins. This leads to the danger of wires being incorrectly connected to a plug or a two-pin plug being pushed into a three - pin socket in the wall. This is dangerous. The plug should be changed if the appliance is to be continually used in one country or a plug adaptor used for short time use, such as on a hair dryer when on holiday abroad. The European Commission are attempting to replace the traditional British rectangular three-pin plug and socket with round two-pin and three-pin plugs and sockets.

This move could cost billions of pounds for the British consumer and British industry as all plugs and sockets in all homes and businessess would need replacing. It could cause extremely dangerous hazards to everyone using electrical equipment. Fires and electric shocks could result from all the non-compatable equipment and plugs, so it seems likely that Britain may opt out of this European move and the safe, reliable, electrical system we have will remain.

## Hints for connecting plugs

### General rules

**Never** use a two-pin plug to connect a three-wire flex.

**Do not** use the earth terminal when connecting a two wire flex to a three pin plug.

**Make sure** all the screws are tight when connected so the wires are firmly secured in place and cannot pull free.

If your appliance has a metal case always use a three-wire flex and a three - pin plug unless the appliance is marked to show it is double insulated.

If your flex has wires with any strange colours, you should consult a qualified electrician or your local electrical shop. If you buy a second hand appliance it should be checked by a qualified electrician before use.

A few manufacturers are now selling appliances with a plug firmly fixed to the end of the flex so no wiring by the purchaser is required. However these are in the minority and there are still millions of electrical items throughout the country requiring plugs to be wired on by the consumer. When the flex to an appliance wears thin or needs to be extended then understanding how to attach a plug is still essential. Plastic plug covers crack if dropped and then need replacing. If a plug is going to get rough wear then replace it with a rubber plug which cannot crack.

Wires in a plug can work loose, fray or pull out. A quite simple occurence such as an iron slipping off an ironing board can cause a great tug on the flex and cause the wires to pull away. Keep a regular check on them before the appliance becomes dangerous or stops working.

A new type of electrical plug is just appearing in a few shops. Called the **Rotaplug** it is a 13 amp plug which can be fitted to a flex without using a screwdriver. By twisting the pins and the inner section of the plug anti-clockwise three colour coded channels are revealed. Each wire can be pressed into its appropriate channel before the inner section is twisted back to complete the wiring.

The plug cannot be pushed into a socket unless the rotation step has been completed and the fuse is firmly in position, so making it very safe. In years to come maybe these plugs will supercede the millions of plugs which at present requiring wiring.

## Electric fuses

Plugs are fused to prevent too much electricity passing through the wiring so causing damage to the appliance. If more current flows through the wiring circuit than it is designed to carry, the flex or cable could get dangerously hot. The fuse is made of weaker material so that it 'blows' or melts when overloading occurs. It does this by interrupting the flow of electricity.

It is very important that the fuse in the plug on each appliance is the correct one for that appliance. If the appliance requires a 3 amp fuse and a 13 amp fuse is fitted, the appliance will work perfectly well, but if a fault develops, the appliance and the flex could be damaged. So never replace a fuse with one of a higher rating and never substitute another piece of metal if you haven't a suitable fuse to hand.

When buying fuses for use in plugs look for the British Standard 1362 marked on them.

### Which fuse to use
Each fuse is colour coded as well as having the number written on it. The most common are:

3 amp fuses are RED and suitable for appliances rated up to 720 watts.

13 amp fuses are BROWN and suitable for appliances with a rating of 720 to 3,000 watts.

1 or 2 amp fuses are available for electric clocks.

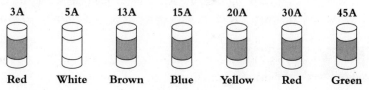

| 3A | 5A | 13A | 15A | 20A | 30A | 45A |
|---|---|---|---|---|---|---|
| Red | White | Brown | Blue | Yellow | Red | Green |

### Which fuse rating for which plug

Always double check by reading the label on the appliance indicating the wattage or the size fuse to use.

| Fuse rating | Appliance |
| --- | --- |
| Colour television | 13 amp |
| Washing machine | 13 amp |
| Dishwasher | 13 amp |
| Vaccuum cleaner | 13 amp |
| Tumbledrier | 13 amp |
| Electric kettle | 13 amp |
| 3 kW fire | 13 amp |
| Black and white television | 3 amp |
| Electric blanket | 3 amp |
| Record player | 3 amp |
| Radio | 3 amp |
| Extractor fan | 3 amp |
| Food mixer | 3 amp |
| Standard or table lamp | 3 amp |
| Power tools | 3 amp |
| Electric clocks | 1 or 2 amp |

### Circuit breakers

Some houses are fitted with circuit breakers instead of fuses. They automatically switch themselves off if any electrical circuit is over-loaded or if a fault in an appliance fails to 'blow' the fuse. The fault should be corrected and the switch can then be flicked on again. Miniature circuit breakers in the home are made in any combination of 5,10,15,20,30 and 45 amp.

## Reading the electricity meter

There are two kinds of meter, the digital and the dial. Both record the total number of units used since the meter was installed. To check how much electricity has been used since the last reading, subtract the previous reading which is recorded on the account from the new reading.

### Digital meter

A digital meter shows the units used as a row of figures. A special White Meter shows two rows of figures, one for lower priced electricity used at night time and the other the electricity that has been used in the day time.

### To read it
Read the figures from left to right.

### Dial meter
The dial meter has six dials and each pointer on each dial moves around in the opposite direction to the one next to it. From left to right it records units in ten thousands, thousands, hundreds, tens and single units.

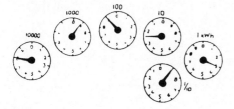

### To read it
Read from left to right. If the pointer is between two figures write down the lowest figure. If the pointer is on a figure, for instance 7, look at the next dial to the right of the 7 and if the number is between 9 and 0, write down 6. If it is between 0 and 1, write down 7.

### Lowering of voltages
The British Government adopted the European standard for low voltage supplies on 1st January 1995. This means that in England, Scotland and Wales the nominal voltage is 230 volts. The current mainland UK voltage is 240 volts.

At the same time other countries within the EC and EFTA will change their existing 220 volt supplies to 230 volts.

For those living in Great Britain the adoption of a European Standard will require no change to any equipment or to the electricity supply received.

The change will not lead to any reduction in quality, safety or reliability of the supply.

The change should help in the design and testing of low voltage appliances and provide consumers with greater choice.

## Gas in the home

Every house which is connected to the mains gas supply has a meter to measure the flow of gas into the house.

Modern metres are the digital kind indicating a row of easy-to-read figures.

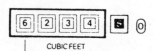

CUBIC FEET

Older meters have a series of dials which measure the gas consumption in hundreds of cubic feet. The amount of heat used is measured in therms and it is necessary to know the amount of energy that is generated when a given amount of gas burns. A typical value is about 1035 British

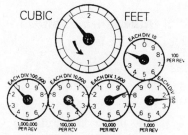

thermal units per cubic foot of gas burned. The actual calorific value of the gas supplied is stated on the gas bill.

To convert the cubic feet used to therms it is necessary to first muliply the figure by the quoted calorific value.

This gives the number of British thermal units used.

1 therm is equivalent to 100,000 Btu.

### Here is an example of how to work out your gas bill

| | |
|---|---|
| Present meter reading | 7519 |
| Previous meter reading | 7491 |
| Amount of gas burnt in hundred cubic feet | 28 |
| Quoted calorific value | 1035 |

$$\frac{\text{Calorific value} \times \text{hundreds of cubic feet}}{1000} = \text{Therms}$$

$$\frac{1035 \times 28}{1000} = 29\,\text{Therms}$$

Multiply the cost per therm by 29 to find the cost of the gas you have used.

### Cooking by gas
To check the temperature of your gas cooker settings and to learn which dishes are best cooked on each setting see page 84.

## International care labelling symbols

Care labels in garments, diagrams on washing machines and information on detergent packets, need to conform in order for a successful wash or clean to be achieved.

Over the years, symbols and numbers have been developed to indicate the treatment and temperatures required for varying fabrics.

The International Textile Care Labelling Code consists of five symbols -

for washing     for bleaching     for ironing     for dry cleaning     for drying
(by hand or machine)

The symbols are always presented in the same sequence. In the UK they are mainly found arranged vertically in other European countries they are more usually arranged horizontally.

## Symbols and labels

Until recently each washing machine programme was designated a number and many machines still have these. But in newer models the signs have been changed. Research has shown that most people prefer to read the recommended temperatures on garment labels when sorting washing, rather than a programme number. Temperatures are universal so everyone can understand them, whereas knowing what temperature a number on the machine cycle means can be confusing.

### Washing temperature

| | | |
|---|---|---|
| 100°C | Boil | Self-explanatory |
| 95°C | Very Hot | Water heated to near boiling temperature |
| 60°C | Hot | Hotter than the hand can bear. The temperature of water coming from many domestic hot taps. |
| 50°C | Hand-hot | As hot as the hand can bear. |
| 40°C | Warm | Pleasantly warm to the hand. |
| 30°C | Cool | Feels cool to the touch. |

**Old  New  Examples of application**

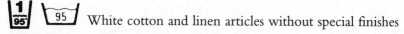

White cotton and linen articles without special finishes

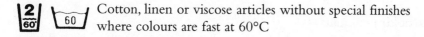

Cotton, linen or viscose articles without special finishes where colours are fast at 60°C

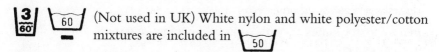

(Not used in UK) White nylon and white polyester/cotton mixtures are included in

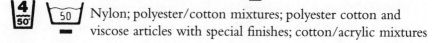

Nylon; polyester/cotton mixtures; polyester cotton and viscose articles with special finishes; cotton/acrylic mixtures

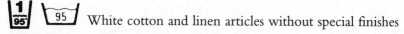

Cotton, linen or viscose articles where colours are fast at 40°C but not at 60°C

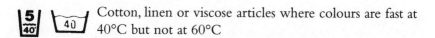

Acrylics, acetate and triacetate, including mixtures with wool; polyester/wool blends

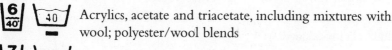

Wool, wool mixed with other fibres; silk

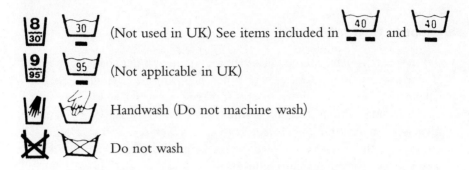

There are still thousands of machines in use with old symbols and temperatures. There are eleven possible variations covering the whole range of known washable fabrics. The chart below explains how to relate them to the labels now seen in garments.

**The wash tub number** shows the most effective water temperature for the various categories and types of material.

### The significance of the bar beneath the wash tub

If there is no bar then the normal maximum machine action will take place.

If there is a bar then reduced (medium) machine action will occur.

A broken bar means much reduced (minimum) machine action
(see diagram)

### Mixed wash loads

As a general guide, you can combine all items without a bar and wash them at the lowest quoted temperature.

Items with the same bar symbol can be combined and washed at the lowest quoted temperature.

Mixed wash loads with and without a bar can be carried out providing that the wash is carried out at the lowest temperature and also reduce the washing action.

### Sorting washing

Always carefully read labels on the article to be washed and follow any special instructions indicated such as washing dark coloured items separately.

Heavily soiled washing should be washed according to its care label but not included in mixed loads.

Refer to the instructions for your specific machine if you have any problems.

## Approximate weight of laundry items

When using a washing machine it is important not to overload it. If the items to be washed weigh more than the recommended weight given for that machine, a great strain is placed on the motor.

The chart below gives a guide to the approximate weight of common articles so that the weight of the total wash can be calculated.

|  | Imperial | Metric |
|---|---|---|
| Ladies underwear - each piece | 1 - 2 oz | 25 - 50 g |
| Mens underwear - each piece | 3 - 5 oz | 75 - 125 g |
| Nightdress | 4 - 7 oz | 100 - 200 g |
| Pyjamas | 10 - 12 oz | 300 - 400 g |
| Dressing gown | 1¼ - 1¾ lb | 600 - 800 g |
| T shirt | 4 - 6 oz | 100 - 150 g |
| Sweater | 7 - 12 oz | 200 - 400 g |
| Shirt | 7 - 9 oz | 200 - 250 g |
| Blouse | 6 - 11 oz | 150 - 300 g |
| Dress | 11oz - 1 lb | 300 - 500 g |
| Skirt | 6 - 12 oz | 150 - 400 g |
| Single sheet | 1 - 1¾ lb | 500 - 750 g |
| Double sheet | 1½- 2 lb | 700g - 1 kg |
| Pillow case | 5 - 7 oz | 125 - 200 g |
| Single blanket | 2 - 3½ lb | 1 - 1.5 kg |
| Double blanket | 3½- 4½ lb | 1.5- 2 kg |
| Duvet cover | 2 - 3½ lb | 1 - 1.5 kg |
| Hand towel | 6 - 9 oz | 150 - 250 g |
| Bath towel | 1 - 1½ lb | 500 - 700 g |
| Tea towel | 2½- 3½ oz | 75 - 100 g |
| Table cloth | ¾ - 1½ lb | 400 - 700 g |

# Other International Care Labelling Symbols

## Bleaching

 The bleaching symbol is the triangle

 This symbol indicates that houshold (chlorine) bleach could be used. Care must be taken to follow the manufacturer's instructions

 When this symbol appears on a label household bleach must not be used

## Drying

The drying symbol is the square

Tumble dry at high heat setting

Tumble dry at low heat setting

Do not tumble dry

Drip dry

Hang/line dry

Dry flat

## Ironing

The ironing symbol is in a flat iron

Hot Iron - Cotton, Linen, Viscose

Warm Iron - Polyester mixtures

Cool Iron - Acrylic, Nylon, Polyester

## Dry Cleaning

The dry cleaning symbol is the circle

Normal goods dry cleanable in all solvents

Normal goods dry cleanable in perchloroethylene, white spirit, Solvent 113 and Solvent 11

Normal goods dry cleanable in white spirit and Solvent 113

Do not dry clean. The cross must be of the shape shown overlaying the circle

In some countries two extra symbols are advocated, as follows:

Goods sensitive to dry cleaning which may be cleaned with the same solvents shown for ⓟ but with a strict limitation on the addition of water during cleaning and/or certain restrictions concerning mechanical action or drying temperature or both.

Goods sensitive to dry cleaning which may be cleaned with the same solvents shown for Ⓕ but with a strict limitation on the addition of water during cleaning and/or certain restrictions concerning mechanical action or drying temperature or both.

If labels employing these "underlined" symbols are used, care should be taken not to hide the underline, as in a stitched seam.

A X through any symbol means **DO NOT**

# 7

# THE BATHROOM

Placing furniture in most rooms is no problem as it can be moved around as desired and items added or removed as the need arises.

Bathrooms however need to be carefully measured and planned and the limitations of the plumbing system have to be considered. It is most important to allow the recommended space around each piece of equipment and it is recommended that a plan to scale is drawn on graph paper rather than just rough sketches made on a piece of paper.

The bathroom section of this book will facilitate planning, design and layout and should save considerable time when shopping for bathroom furniture.

## BATHS

**BS 4305 Part 1 1989**
**EN 198  1987**

Baths vary greatly in quality and price and it is important to choose one which is made to the British Standard of quality.

The European standard which specifies the requirements for domestic baths made from acrylic materials ensures the product when installed is satisfactory. It will be free of sharp edges, be neither cracked or chipped, uneven colour or anything which will impair the appearance or performance of the bath.

### British standard bath

The size of a basic bath in Britain is 1.65 metres (5 ft 6 in) long x 75 cm (2 ft 5 in) wide x 50 cm (1 ft 8 in) high. However there are many variations on this and generally speaking it is wise to buy the biggest bath that will fit into the space available if you can. This does mean using more hot water which can add to the expense of a bath.

If there is a shower over the bath you need to choose a bath with a flat bottom.

#### Showers
A separate shower will need about 1 m (3 ft) square floor space and a similar area just outside it for a drying area.

There are standard recommendations for space required around each item in the bathroom and cloakroom and while it is good to draw up plans yourself it is sensible to ask a bathroom fitter to check that what you have planned will really fit and work. (see page 111)

### Bath tap holes

### British Standard BS 4305 part 2 1989
Bath tap holes have a British Standard which is important to look for if you wish to fit old taps to new baths or new taps in old baths and expect them to fit well.

The hole diameter should be 36 mm (+2 or -0). The distance between the hole centres should be 180 mm (+2 or -0 ).

### Waste hole
### BS 3380
Waste hole fittings should comply with BS 3380 which gives the specification for waste and bath overflows.

### BS EN 232 1992
### Connecting dimensions for baths
These are important if you are fitting a new bath with metric measurements, into a bathroom with old piping.

The diameter of a waste hole is 52 mm (+3 or -2).

The diameter of an overflow hole should be 52 mm (+3 or -2). It is important to leave the correct space between the bottom of the bath wastehole and the ground, for the installation of the trap which should be 130 mm minimum.

## Design and layout of the bathroom or cloakroom

Before actually buying fittings for a bathroom or cloakroom it is wise to call in a plumber and get his expert advice on where it is possible to place items in this room. Or design it and then have it checked out before ordering. Many measurements are involved in placing equipment correctly and careful measuring is essential.

Bathroom furniture and fittings are now sold in metric sizes, so even if you are not familiar with centimetres and millimetres, it is wise to buy a good measuring tape and place metric measures on your plan. Draw a plan of the room on squared paper to as large a scale as possible, the squares representing feet and inches or metres and centimetres. Then draw in major permanent fixtures such as alcoves, recesses, windows and doors. Draw an arc in front of the door as shown in the diagram to indicate the space occupied by the door as it opens and shuts. That is if it opens into the room which is the most usual.

Pick up leaflets which illustrate the style and sizes of the bathroom items you like and following the measurements on these leaflets draw these onto the plan. Or better still cut out scale shapes of the equipment and place them in varying positions on the plan of the room to see how they look.

## Measuring the bathroom

It is at this stage that the following information is vital. In the bathroom it is essential that the recommended areas of space around each piece of equipment is allowed for activity in that area. For instance it is no use having the lavatory so near the wash basin that when it is used your head hits the basin. Sufficient space must be allowed for a person to dry himself when getting out of the bath. Shower trays must be a certain depth. Leave suitable space for stepping out of them and a shower door to open and shut.

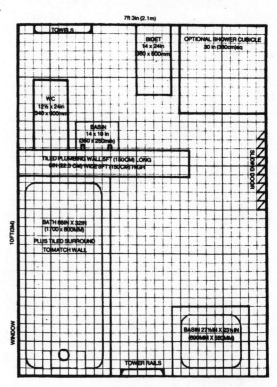

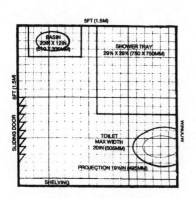

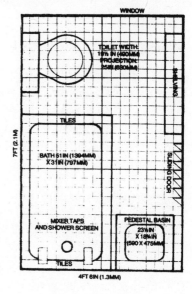

### Recommended allowances

Allow 1100 x 700 mm (43 x 28 in) alongside baths.

Allow 200 mm (8 in) on either side of a wash basin and 700 mm (28 in) in front of the basin.

Allow 200 mm (8 in) either side of a lavatory and bidet and 600 mm (24 in) in front of each.

Allow 900 mm x 400 mm (35 x 16 in) by the side of an enclosed shower.

Allow 900 x 700 mm (35 x 28 in) alongside a shower enclosed on three sides.

Although these measurements make it seem as if a great deal of space is required, in fact the areas left for comfortable movement overlap, as more than one piece of equipment is rarely in use at any one time.

Storage space for toiletries, towels etc can usually be easily positioned between pieces of equipment or on shelves above. Before fixing shelves be sure to ensure that there is a headroom 2200 mm (86 in) is required above a bath or shower.

Place the appropriate spaces on your plan when designing your layout. Then get in a professional to check that what you have planned will really work in design and with the plumbing system in your house.

As drains, pipe work and generally all plumbing is now produced in metric dimensions, it is essential that new pipes and bathroom furniture will link in successfully with any old imperial measure plumbing that is already in the house. (see page 110)

## Towels

Towel sizes can vary a little from make to make but average sizes for a set are as shown in this list.

| | | |
|---|---|---|
| Face cloth | 30 x 30 cm | (12 x 12 in) |
| Guest towel | 36 x 56 cm | (14 x 22 in) |
| Hand towel | 48 x 90 cm | (19 x 35 in) |
| Bath towel | 66 x 122 cm | (26 x 48 in) |
| Bath sheet | 107 x 152 cm | (42 x 60 in) |

All sizes are rounded off to the nearest inch

### Other bathroom accessories

| | | |
|---|---|---|
| Bath mat | 48 x 81 cm | (19 x 32 in) |
| Pedestal mat | 48 x 56 cm | (19 x 22 in) |

# 8

# THE BEDROOM

● ● ● ● ● ● ● ● ● ● ● ● ● ● ● ● ● ● ● ● ● ● ● ● ● ● ● ● ● ● ● ● ● ● ● ● ● ● ● ● ● ●

Sizes and styles of bedrooms vary tremendously, depending on the age and design of the house, the personal preferences of the occupants for layout and decorations and whether the room has to double as a sitting room, nursery or even a study. Childrens' nurseries or bedrooms will have to accommodate toys and need to be flexible enough to change as the child's requirements change, such as when homework needs to be done in the bedroom. Unit furniture made to metric measurements are usually 1000 mm (1 m)(39 ½ in)wide. Three units, for instance a wardrobe, chest of drawers and desk, will not fit along a 9 foot wall which is the measurement to be found in many bedrooms. There will be space for two items of furniture and 10 inches 'over' which is not a lot of use for anything and is unslightly.

It is essential that furniture such as baby's cots and bunk beds meet the stringent size and safety regulations in place in this country, so the British Standard Institution (BSI) numbers are given in the text where applicable.

But perhaps the most common major problem in bedrooms is the sizes of beds and bed linen. Numerous people have suffered expense and disappointment because of the disparity between imperial and metric measured beds and bed linen, especially bed linen imported from Europe.

This chapter concentrates on helping to overcome all these measuring and sizing problems.

## BEDS

The sizes of British beds remained the same for many, many years until recently when there have been changes. A wider variety of lengths and widths of bed have been introduced; some are still manufactured in imperial sizes and some are now manufactured in metric sizes. An increasing number are imported from abroad. There are so many varieties from which to choose that it is important to know the exact size of bed you need to purchase before going shopping. Just asking for a single or double bed is not really sufficient.

Whichever method of measuring is preferred, each size of bed now has a specific name and this should be used to describe the bed you want to buy.

## Bed names and sizes

| | Metric measurements | Imperial measurements |
|---|---|---|
| Compact Single (new designation) | 75 x 190 cm | 2 ft 6 in x 6 ft 3 in |
| Popular Single (formerly called small single) | 90 x 190 cm | 3 ft x 6 ft 3 in |
| Compact Double (new designation) | 120 x 190 cm | 4 ft x 6 ft 3 in |
| Popular Double (formerly called small double) | 135 x 190 cm | 4 ft 6 in x 6 ft 3 in |
| Queen Size (formerly called standard double) | 150 x 200 cm | 5 ft x 6 ft 6 in |
| King Size (new designation) | 180 x 200 cm | 6 ft x 6 ft 6in |

The metric and imperial sizes are not exact conversions.

### European bed sizes

Bed sizes around Europe vary from country to country. A bed that is even just 10 cm (4 in) larger in size than a bed made in Britain can cause a number of difficulties. A larger Continental bed may not fit so well in a room and will not fit between fixed bedside tables or in front of a British made bedhead. Some European bed linen will not fit British beds.

**French** beds are -   single    180 cm (6 ft wide)
double   240 cm (8 ft wide)
kingsize 270 cm (9 ft wide)

**Belgian** beds are -    90 x 190 cm (3 ft x 6 ft 3 in)
140 x 190 cm (4 ft 10 in x 6 ft 3in)

**Luxembourg** beds are -      90 cm (3 ft) wide
                                140 cm (4 ft 8 in) wide
                                150 cm (5 ft) wide
                                160 cm (5 ft 4 in) wide
                                180 cm (6 ft) wide

All these beds are 200 cm (6 ft 6 in) long.

It is a common procedure on the Continent to place two small (90 cm x 200 cm) ( 3 ft x 6 ft 6 in) beds alongside one another or zip them together to form one large bed. It can be difficult finding suitable bed linen for the latter.

### Choosing the correct size bed
For comfort and a good sleep it is important to buy a bed of the correct size for your requirements.

### It should be -

At least 15 cm (6 in) longer than your height but ideally nearer 20 cm (8 in) longer than you are tall.

At least 90 cm (3 ft) wide if used for one person.

At least 150 cm (5 ft) wide if it is to be used for two people.

The former British standard double bed was 135 cm (4 ft 6in) wide which allows 68 cm (2 ft 3 in) for each person, about the same width as a baby's cot! Buy as wide a bed as you can afford which will fit into your bedroom.

Always lie on a bed in the shop to check for comfort as well as size before buying.

### To check for width
You *and* your partner should lie on the bed with your hands behind your head, elbows outstretched. You shouldn't be touching elbows with your partner or hanging over the side. It is important to do this however silly you feel.

### To check for length
If you are tall and need a longer bed, then you will need to buy the Queen size bed which is 10 cm (3 in) longer - these three inches will make all the difference to a good night's sleep. The standard length of a British bed is 190 cm (6 ft 3 in) but there are a few British manufacturers who will make beds 200 cm (6 ft 6 in) long. You may need to go to a large store for these and may not have so many varieties from which to choose. If you buy a continental bed which will be 200 cm (6 ft 6 in) long remember that standard British bed linen will not fit it.

### Height of beds

There is no British Standard bed height.

Bed heights can vary by as much as 20 cm (8 in) and new divan bases are often deeper than those of a decade ago. Some with drawers in the base are particularly deep. This presents problems when buying valances (see page 128).

### Unusual beds

Some manufacturers will make beds to any unusual shape or size desired such as round or oval, but a custom made bed is usually expensive unless you make it yourself. Care must be taken that a suitable sized mattress and bed linen are available for any bed varying from the standard measurements. There are manufacturers who will make bed linen to individual requirements and specifications.

### Starter beds

These are small in size about 75 x 165 cm (2 ft 6 in x 5 ft 5 in) and are useful when a child is ready to move out of its cot. Some have safety rails each side which can later be removed.

The size will suit a child for many years before the recommended sizes for adult beds will become necessary.

### Bed heads

Bed heads should be the same width as the bed *when made up*. Many bed heads incorporate small units such as bed side cabinets or shelves at each side, leaving just a fixed space for the bed to fit between. Before buying a bed head it is essential to measure the width of the bed with the mattress, bed linen and duvet or eiderdown on. These can add at least 46 cm (18 in) onto the width of the bed and could mean the bed will not fit between two fixed points. Manufacturers allow a bit of space for this, but often it is a tight squeeze to get the bed in once the covers are on, especially if the bed and mattress are metric sizes and the duvet is thick. If you are buying a new bed head to place behind an old bed, or buying a new bed to put between old bedside tables, check the width carefully before shopping.

A bed is quite high when it has pillows and a duvet on. The height of bed heads is usually ajustable to allow for this, but it is wise to check, otherwise you will not be able to see the bed head once the bed is made. Besides not looking right it will not be comfortable for anyone sitting up in the bed and leaning against it.

# Mattresses

A bed is only as good as its mattress. While it is pleasant to have an attractive bed head and colourful duvet it is the mattress placed on a good suitable base which will determine whether you have a good, relaxing night's sleep.

### Choosing a mattress

There are many variations of mattresses comprised of a combination of various springs, upholstery, fillings and covers. To a great extent you get what you pay for and as such a large percentage of time is spent in bed it is important to get the best that you can afford and make sure you buy one that suits your needs.

The mattress and bed base should always be bought in conjunction with one another as it is important they are compatible.

### Types of mattresses

The three main types are sprung interior, non-sprung such as latex, foam or futon, and flotation, commonly called water beds.

### Sprung interior

The number of springs, the gauge of wire used and the size and type of springs, controls the firmness of the bed. The springs may be open or open coil and the degree of firmness of the mattress depends on the different gauges (thickness and strength) of wire used and the number of springs formed.

If you want a firm, hard spring, look for a mattress with springs made of 12.5 or 13 gauge wire, while a 14 or 15 gauge wire is soft. The minimum number of springs for a 5 ft (150 cm) mattress is 325 springs.

### Construction of spring units

The shapes and construction of springs within mattresses vary considerably from one manufacturer to another and they also vary a great deal in price. Generally it is wise to buy the best mattress you can afford and to discuss your needs and what you are prepared to spend with the salesman. One thing to look for is a bed where stronger springs are placed in the parts of the bed which take the most weight such as the central area where the hips need supporting and also around the edge where people may sit.

### Pocket springs

The springs are each placed in individual fabric pockets which ensures that each spring remains parallel when compressed. The wire gauge will be 16 gram and the diameter of each spring varies from around 2½ in (6.5 cm) for mattresses with between 800 and 1,000 springs and 2 in (5 cm) springs for those mattresses with more than 1,200 springs in the 5 ft (150 cm) size mattresses.

In the clipped pocketed type spring a mattress of similar size would contain between 500 and 600 springs in the 5 ft (150 cm) size bed.

The measuring, sizing and types of spring are useful to know when choosing a bed base and mattress. When choosing a foam mattress there is little measuring involved as long as it is the same as the bed base.

## Water beds

There are two main kinds of water bed.

**The hard sided bed** has a rigid frame, inside which the water bed is supported. The frames are about 7 ft (215 cm ) long, so care must be taken to ensure it will fit into the bedroom. The depth of water is 9 in (23 cm).

**The soft sided beds** have mattresses varying from 2 in (5 cm) up to 7 in (17 cm) deep with a cushioned foam edge.

## Bunk beds

### British Standard 6998
Since 1988, new laws have been in force regarding the sizes of bunk beds. Look for BS 6998 to ensure that your purchase conforms to the sizing and very important safety regulations. Check the following measurements carefully when buying second hand bunks or those in kit form. Those who choose to make their own bunk beds should make them to conform to the same recommended measurements to ensure the safety of the occupants.

### British standard measurements
The law states that no gap anywhere in the structure of bunk beds should be more than 7.5 cm (3 in) wide except for access to the top bunk which should be no less than 30 cm (12 in) and no more than 40 cm (16 in) wide.

The space between the upper and lower beds should be no more than 75 cm (2 ft 6 in).

Any bunk which is more than 80 cm (2 ft 8in) off the ground must conform to BS 6998.

### Mattresses
When buying mattresses be sure to allow for the variations that occur between metric and imperial measures. As sizes of bunks and mattresses may vary from country to country, check carefully that the one you choose will fit correctly in the bunks you buy. The thickness or depth of a mattress is also very important. When in place, the top of the mattress should be at least 10

cm (4 in) below the guard rail. On beds which conform to BS 6998 this level should be marked on the frame.

### Ladders
The ladder to the top bunk should have treads less than 30 cm (12 in) wide and 20 cm (8 in) apart.

## Carry cots

### British Standard 3881
Carry cots must be at least 19 cm (7.5 in) deep and carry the British Standard label to be sure they comply with all the safety regulations.

It is especially important to check imported carry cots for dimensions and safety.

Care must be exercised in checking that if the carry cot is placed on wheels or a frame of any kind, it is stable, firmly attached and will not slip off or tip up.

Travel cots are also subject to size regulations. British Standard 7423 states that a mattress sold as part of a cot should not be more than 40 mm shorter or narrower, so avoiding a gap between the mattress and the sides.

To avoid the child climbing out, the mattress base to the top of the cot should not be less than 595 mm.

## Cots

### British Standard 1743

### Sizes
Childrens' cots made in Britain are usually 120 cm long and 60 cm wide (4 ft x 2 ft). Continental cots are larger, about 130 or 140 cm (4 ft 2 in or 4 ft 6 in) long and 70 cm (2 ft 4 in) wide. If you buy an imported cot, check the measurements carefully to make sure the mattress and bed linen you choose will fit.

### Safety
For safety there should be at least 495 mm (1 ft 8 in) between the top of the mattress and the top of the cot.

The spaces between the bars should be between 25 mm and 60 mm (1 in to 2.5 in) so that a baby cannot trap its head between them.

A mattress for a child's cot must fit properly and not leave a gap more than 4 cm (1.5 in) anywhere between the mattress and the frame where a child's head, leg or arm could be trapped.

Measure any cot carefully before using it. Relatives often keep old cots to be used on fairly rare occasions when children visit. Second hand cots may also not conform to the recommended safety measurements if they are more than four years old.

### Cot beds
A cot bed is a large cot with sides which can be removed to convert it into a bed when the child is old enough.

## Bed linen

### British Standard 5815
Until recently it has been quite easy to buy bed sheets without paying much attention to the exact measurements of each item. One could simply read on the packet, 'One single sheet', and know that the contents would be one flat sheet which would fit a single bed.

Bed linen is now imported from various countries and very few make items especially for the British market. So care needs to be taken when choosing sheets, as for instance a fitted bottom sheet that has been made in France will not fit properly over a British mattress.

Manufacturers of bed linen will in due course be adopting the new names and sizes as described for beds. Meanwhile it is advisable always to take the measurements of your bed with you to the shops to check that what you are buying is suitable for your needs.

### Fitted sheets
These can cause problems as the depths of mattresses vary so much that the gusset allowance may not fit. A well fitting bottom sheet should cover the sides of the mattress and then tuck well under it so that the side of the mattress material does not show at all. Before shopping, measure the depth of your mattress and allow a bit extra to accommodate any piping around the edges of the mattress and to allow for ease of getting the sheet on and off.

Sizes of bed linen vary from make to make and country to country.

Most common metric measurements for fitted sheets are the following -

### Fitted sheets to fit

| | |
|---|---|
| A Popular single bed - | 90 x 190 cm <br> (3 ft x 6 ft 3 in) |
| A Popular double bed - | 135 x 190 cm <br> (4 ft 6in x 6 ft 3in) |
| A Queen size bed - | 150 x 200 cm <br> (5 ft x 6 ft 6 in) |
| AKing size bed - | 175 x 200 cm <br> (6 ft x 6ft 6in) |

Even if your mattress is only an inch or two different to one of these sizes you may find it difficult to buy a fitted sheet of suitable size and will have to use a flat sheet tucked in instead. Check on the depth of your mattress before going shopping for a fitted bottom sheet.

### Flat sheets

Flat sheets for use on top of the bed must be large enough to allow for the size of the body in the bed as well as sufficient material to tuck in.

Most common measurements for flat sheets are the following -

### Flat sheets to fit

| | |
|---|---|
| A Popular single bed - | 180 x 260 cm <br> (6 ft x 8 ft 6 in) |
| A Popular double bed - | 230 x 260 cm <br> (7 ft 6 in x 8 ft 6 in) |
| A Queen size bed - | 275 x 275 cm <br> (9 ft x 9 ft) |

If there is no flat sheet specifically for your bed size then buy the next size up.

Packs of bed linen should have the sizes written on. Sometimes the measures are in imperial and sometimes in metric measures or they may be labelled with the new system of nomenclature for beds.

## Continental quilts

### British Standard 5335
An International Committee is at present working on the harmonisation of sizes and quality of continental quilts throughout Europe.

### Choosing a continental quilt or duvet
It is essential that a duvet is the correct size for the person and bed it is intended to cover. Do not buy something that is labelled just 'double duvet', or 'single duvet', without checking that it is really suitable for your requirements.

### Length of duvet
Beds are made in different lengths. Check the length of your bed. It will almost certainly be either 6 ft 3 in (190 cm) or 6 ft 6 in (200 cm) long. A good duvet should be at least 6 ft 6 in (200 cm) long, but if you have a longer bed or are tall, you will need to buy a longer duvet. This can occasionally mean placing a special order.

### Width of duvet
To feel the full benefit of a quilt it should mould around the body to eliminate draughts. To do this it must be at least 24 in (61 cm) wider than a large bed being used by two people and 18 in (46 cm) wider than a bed for single use.

Before shopping, measure the width of your bed carefully and add the appropriate amount, i.e. 24 or 18 in, or 61 or 46 cm to check the size duvet you should buy.

Look for the measurements on the label sewn into the duvet as well as the measurements written on the box. If there is any doubt, always buy a larger duvet, it will be money well spent.

### Non-standard beds
Dimensions of quilts for non-standard beds should be at least 35 cm (1 ft 2 in) wider than a bed used by one person and 65 cm (2 ft 1in) wider than any bed used by two people. The length of the quilt should never be less than the length of the bed.

### Standard size duvets on sale
Following the above recommendations, decide which duvet size will suit you best from these commonly available sizes.

54 x 78 in (135 x 200 cm) for a Popular Single bed measuring
90 x 190 cm

54 x 87 in (135 x 220 cm) for an extra long single bed measuring
100 x 200 cm

79 x 79 in (200 x 200 cm) for a Popular Double bed measuring
135 x 190 cm

79 x 87 in (200 x 220 cm) for a Queen size bed measuring
135 x 190 cm

89 x 87 in (225 x 220 cm) for a King size bed measuring
150 x 200 cm.

Many duvets on sale do not meet these measurements so may well not be
the bargain they seem.

## The filling in duvets

### British Standard 1425

The filling is probably the most important part of any duvet so decide what
is the best for your needs and pocket.

Fillings in new quilts must be new, waterfowl and comply with the
appropriate requirements of BS 1425.

There are two main types of filling - natural and synthetic fibres.

**Natural** fillings are pure down or a mixture of down and feather. Pure
down forms the softest, warmest and lightest filling but is the most
expensive and is not suitable for all needs.

**Down** filling should be all down, but because of the difficulty of removing
all the feathers the law states that up to 15 per cent by weight of small, fluffy
feathers may remain amongst the down.

**Feather** filled duvets are rarely sold but many people have made their own
from old feather beds which were a great favourite with grandparents.

**Down and feather** mixture combines the luxury of down with the more
economical feather. Down and feather duvets should have at least 51 per
cent down and 49 per cent feather by weight. Feather and down usually has
about 85 per cent feather and 15 per cent down by weight.

**Synthetic fillings** are mostly terylene, Dacron, Trevira and polyester. They
are cheaper to buy and are ideal for those people who are allergic to feathers
of any kind. They can be washed in the washing machine so are ideal for
childrens' use.

When buying any duvet it is really essential to read the label carefully to make sure the filling meets all your requirements. Fillings can be very inadequate, so look for BS 5335 to be certain that what you are buying is good quality in every way. It is wise to buy the best duvet you can afford as it will last longer and be more efficient.

The better and more expensive duvets have the filling in 'tunnels' and these provide more warmth without cold areas on the surface.

### Measuring the warmth of a continental quilt

In Britain the measurement of warmth obtained from a duvet is given in togs. There is no British Standard for the tog value of a continental quilt. Togs are the rate at which body heat escapes through the duvet. The higher the tog rating the less heat escapes so the warmer you will be. There is a wide range of togs - from 4.5 for light summer use, to 15.0 for use in the coldest temperatures. The choice of togs is 4.5 tog, 6.0 tog, 7.5 tog, 9.0 tog, 10.5 tog, 12.0 tog, 13.5 tog and 15 tog.

If you live in a well heated house, a 10.5 tog or 12 tog duvet should be suitable for all year round use.

If your home isn't centrally heated or it is cold where you live, you will probably need a 13.5 tog. A 15 tog is very warm and most people find it too hot for use in Britain.

Always buy a duvet which is clearly labelled with its tog value. If it isn't labelled it probably does not conform to any recommendation, is very thin and will not provide the required warmth.

### Dual duvets

These consist of a low tog duvet for use in warm weather and a medium tog duvet which can be joined to the low tog duvet with velcro or press studs when the weather is very cold.

If two people like a different tog rating, i.e. one partner prefers a higher tog rating than the other, then two single differing tog duvets can be used over a large bed instead of one large duvet being bought.

### Electric duvets

You may decide to invest in an electric duvet which is like an electric blanket inside a duvet. This should be serviced frequently in the same way as an electric blanket.

### Duvet covers

Many duvet covers are the same size as duvets. The better ones are made a little larger, leaving space for the filling to be looser and enabling them to curve around the body more and provide more warmth.

The sizes of the better covers are -

| | |
|---|---|
| Popular Single size | 140 x 225 cm (55 x 89 in) |
| Popular Double | 200 x 225 cm (79 x 89 in) |
| King size | 230 x 254 cm (91 x 100 in) |

### Cleaning of continental quilts

### British Standard 5742

All duvets should be used with a cover on to protect them so they do not require cleaning very often. If they are given a really good shake and a regular airing, cleaning is rarely required. However washing and dry cleaning instructions should be on a label sewn into one seam.

There are many things to consider before you shop for a continental quilt, but the time taken in the initial measuring and thinking about your needs is time well spent and could save you a lot of money.

## Bedspreads and throwovers

### Throwovers

A bedspread or throwover which is just a large piece of fabric, needs to be large enough to just reach the floor at each side and the bottom end of the bed.

### Width

Measure the total width required by taking the measure from the floor on one side of the bed, loosely over all covers of the *made* bed to the floor the other side of the bed.

### Length

Measure the length from just over the top of the pillows by the bed head, following loosely over the curve of the pillows, then down the length of the bed over the covers to the floor at the bottom of the bed.

Both these measurements will vary a lot from bed to bed depending on the height the bed is from the ground, the height of the pillows and the thickness of the duvet or eiderdown and blankets, so it is important to measure carefully before you leave home and take these measurements with you when going shopping.

### Fitted bedspreads

If you want a bedspread with a smooth top and a frill or pleats all around the sides, then first measure carefully in imperial and metric measures the length and width of the *top flat* surface of the bed when all the covers are on. This will ensure a good fit around the top edge. Then measure the height of this top edge from the floor to find the depth of frill or pleats required. As beds are not yet made to a standard height it is easy to buy a fitted bedspread which doesn't hang correctly, is too short so it doesn't reach the floor or drapes on the floor as it is too long.

Allow at least 5 cm (2 in) everywhere for hems if you are making your own bedspread.

## Blankets

### British Standard 5129 : 1982
### EN:14

There are six British standard sizes for blankets within three categories.

| | | |
|---|---|---|
| Single | 180 x 230 cm | (6 ft x 7 ft 6 in) |
| | 180 x 250 cm | (6 ft x 8 ft 2 in) |
| Double | 200 x 250 cm | (6 ft 6 in x 8 ft 2 in) |
| | 230 x 250 cm | (7 ft 6 in x 8 ft 2 in) |
| King size | 280 x 250 cm | (9 ft 2 in x 8 ft 2 in) |
| | 300 x 250 cm | (9 ft 10 in x 8ft 2in) |

Continental and American blankets vary in size.

This chart indicates sizes available in various countries.

| Standard Sizes of Blankets Available in European Countries | | | | | | | | |
|---|---|---|---|---|---|---|---|---|
| Dimensions in cm | Germany | Austria | Belgium | Spain | France | Italy | Portugal | UK |
| 90 x 120 | | | | | | ★ | | |
| 110 x 150 | | | | | | ★ | | |
| 130 x 150 | | ★ | | | | | | |
| 130 x 180 | | ★ | | | ★ | | | |
| 130 x 190 | | ★ | | | | | ★ | |
| 140 x 190 | ★ | ★ | | | | ★ | | |
| 140 x 200 | | ★ | | | | | ★ | |
| 150 x 220 | ★ | | ★ | | | | | |
| 160 x 210 | | | | | | ★ | ★ | |
| 160 x 220 | | | | ★ | | | | |
| 170 x 210 | | ★ | | | | | | |
| 180 x 220 | ★ | ★ | | | ★ | ★ | ★ | |
| 180 x 230 | | | | | | | ★ | ★ |
| 180 x 250 | | | | | | | | ★ |
| 190 x 230 | | | ★ | | | | | |
| 200 x 210 | | | | ★ | | | | |
| 200 x 220 | ★ | | | | | | | |
| 200 x 250 | | | | | | | | ★ |
| 210 x 250 | | | | | | ★ | | |
| 230 x 250 | | | | | | | | ★ |
| 230 x 270 | | | | | | ★ | | |
| 260 x 240 | | | ★ | | ★ | ★ | | |
| 280 x 250 | | | | | | | | ★ |
| 300 x 250 | | | | | | | | ★ |

For comfort and warmth, the correct sized blankets should be chosen for each bed. However because they are not fitted, the size does not have to be too accurate.

Each blanket should have a label securely attached showing its dimensions in centimetres. It is comforting to know that blankets used in the public sector are subject to tight regulations regarding flame retardation under BS 5866.

# Pillows

### British pillows
Pillow dimensions and fillings vary a great deal but there is a range of standard sizes.

British pillows are rectangular and are either

74 cm (29 in) long and 48 cm (19 in) wide **or**
69 cm (27 in) long and 46 cm (18 in) wide.

British pillow cases are made to fit these sized pillows and measure 74 x 48 cm (29 x 19 in).

### Continental pillows
Continental style pillows are becoming more popular in Britain and are 65 x 65 cm (26 in square).

Continental pillow cases are therefore made slightly bigger. They are 70 - 71 cm x 70 - 71 cm (27 - 28 in) square.

There are some German pillows which are slightly larger at 80 x 80 cm (31½x 31½in) square.

Another variation to the Continental standard pillow is in Austria where some are 70 x 90 cm (27 x 35½in).

### Pillow fillings
Fillings must comply to BS 1425 for cleanliness.

A wide range of British standards are in force for the wide range of fillings. Always look for the BSI label. The weight of fillings in any pillow is also important and should conform to regulations. The most comfortable pillows are filled with feathers or down or a mixture of both.

Pillows are also available with synthetic fillings and these are ideal for those suffering from asthma or similar allergies, or in situations where they might require washing fairly often in a washing machine.

Pillows with a network of holes through them are available for use as first pillows for toddlers who might suffocate if they bury their face in a feather pillow.

### Pillow ticking

To prevent the feathers poking through the material of a pillow case they need to be encased in a ticking case made of strong twill material.

Look for British Standard 2036.

Tickings can be home made or bought ready to fill. To prevent these becoming dirty, a pillow ideally has an under pillow case which can be of cheap material or an old pillow case which has become rather thin or faded. On top of this is placed the pretty top pillow case.

### Cot and pram pillows

Fillings must comply to British Standard 4578 for safety and for depth of filling.

## Valances

As beds are not made to any standard height it can be difficult to buy a valance which is exactly right. Beds with drawers in the base or a second bed stored underneath, are often particularly deep. This is an important fact to remember, whether you are buying a bed and already own a valance you wish to continue using, or if you are buying new bed linen to put on a bed you already own.

### Measuring for a valance

Because of the lack of standardisation of valance depths it is important to measure the height of your bed from the ground before going shopping and then compare this with what is written on the packets in the shops. Measure the height in imperial and metric measures as the packet may have either of the measurements on.

The two measurements to take with you are:

- from the top edge of the bed base to the floor if you are buying just a valance;

- from the top edge of the mattress to the floor if you are buying a valance and bottom sheet combined.

### Types of valance

Valances may be frilly, pleated or plain. If plain, then check that there is sufficient material to stretch around the corner of the base of your bed. If the valance has been made on the Continent it is very unlikely that it will fit a British bed base properly, it will be pulled around the corners and not hang correctly. This creates an unsightly gap at the corners and reveals the bed base.

Some valances just cover the bed base, others have the bottom sheet incorporated.

If you buy a valance incorporating the bottom sheet, remember that the sheet area must be the correct size for the mattress in the same way as described for a fitted bottom sheet (see page 121).

Also consider that you will have to wash the whole thing every time you change the bottom sheet which can be an unnecessary nuisance.

Some manufacturers will make valances to specific individual requirements for those who have odd shaped beds.

## Travel rugs

Once used for warmth when travelling in open carriages these rugs are still ideal for older people, for babies and toddlers to sit and play on and for students to throw over their beds in chilly student houses.

There are two main sizes -

48 in x 67 in (122 cm x 70 cm)
54 in x 72 in (137 cm x 182 cm)

### Knee rugs
Knee rugs which are smaller just to cover the lap and knees measure -

31 in x 51 in (80 cm x 130 cm).

# 9

# CLOTHES

The measurements and sizing of clothes vary tremendously from country to country and manufacturer to manufacturer. The labels can also vary, causing great confusion amongst consumers. There is sometimes a difference in actual size between garments labelled the same but made by two different manufacturers in the same country. Some manufacturers in Britain now print both Imperial and metric sizes on the labels.

Some just use metric measures as well as a general sizing code such as 'Size 14'. But clothes from other countries are sized in a different way. If 'Size 14' is written on a label it will mean something different to a shopper in Britain than to a shopper in America and something different again for those shopping in other countries throughout Europe. Imported clothes usually have sizing labels relevant to their own country and should not be confused with British sizing.

Shoes are often labelled on the sole with European measures but shoe shops still label the racks 'size 5' or 'size 6' etc.

Children's clothes were until recently bought by age, but are now based on weight or height.

This chapter should solve the many sizing problems to be found in this area.

## MEN'S CLOTHES (BRITISH STANDARD 6185)

### Men's suits

Men's suits should be bought for a well fitting jacket and trouser waist fit and then the leg and arm length can be altered as required.

| Men's Coats, Jackets and Suits Sizes | | | | | |
|---|---|---|---|---|---|
| British | 34 | 36 | 38 | 40 | 42 | 44 |
| American | 34 | 36 | 38 | 40 | 42 | 44 |
| Continental | 44 | 46 | 48 | 50 | 52 | 54 |

**A typical label on a man's jacket would be:**

| | |
|---|---|
| CHEST GIRTH | 96 (38 in) |
| WAIST GIRTH | 64 (25 in) |
| HEIGHT | 152 (60 in) |

## Trousers

Casual trousers are usually available in a combination of sizes, e.g. a larger waist and a shorter leg or an average waist and longer leg.

**A typical label would read**

| | |
|---|---|
| WAIST | 97 cm/38 in |
| INSIDE LEG | 81 cm/32 in |

**or**

| | |
|---|---|
| WAIST GIRTH | 92 |
| HIP GIRTH | 108 |
| INSIDE LEG LENGTH | 84 |
| BOTTOMS | 55 |

## Men's shirts

As most men have neck size and chest in proportion, a shirt is bought for its neck size and the rest should be a good fit. Collar sizes are given in the table below.

| Men's shirt sizes | | | | | | | | | |
|---|---|---|---|---|---|---|---|---|---|
| British | (in) | 14 | 14½ | 15 | 15½ | 16 | 16½ | 17 | 17½ |
| American | (in) | 14 | 14½ | 15 | 15½ | 16 | 16½ | 17 | 17½ |
| Continental | (cm) | 36 | 37 | 38 | 39 | 40 | 41 | 42 | 43 |

There are some labels now being produced which give the arm length of the shirt as well as the neck size.

The metric label of this kind on a size 16 inch neck shirt in Britain would read:

| | |
|---|---|
| NECK GIRTH   40 | (meaning 40 cm) |
| ARM LENGTH  74 | (meaning 74 cm or 29 in) |

## Men's sweaters and cardigans

These may be labelled as:

| | |
|---|---|
| CHEST GIRTH | 92 - 100 |
| HEIGHT | 164 - 170 |

## To measure a man's body correctly

**Chest**
Measure around the fullest part.

**Waist**
Measure around the point where the waistband of the trousers normally lies in a comfortable wearing position.

**Hips**
Measure around the fullest part.

**Neck**
Measure around the neck at the Adams apple.

**Wrist**
Measure for cuff length around arms 3 in (7.5 cm) above wrist bones.

**Shirt length**
Measure from nape of neck to finished length. Other measurements are taken in the same way as for women (see page 135).

# WOMEN'S CLOTHES

## Measuring and labelling

The measurements and sizing of women's clothes vary tremendously from country to country and manufacturer to manufacturer. The style of labels also varies, causing confusion amongst consumers. There is also sometimes a difference in actual size between garments labelled the same but made by two different manufacturers in the same country. Sales people are often heard to remark that a certain manufacturer's clothes are 'cut big'.

## Understanding labels

Some manufacturers in Britain now print both Imperial and metric sizes on clothes labels. Some use just metric measures as well as a general sizing code such as 'Size 14', but clothes from other countries are sized in a different way. If 'Size 14' is written on a label it will mean something different to a shopper in Britain than to a shopper in America and something different again for those shopping in other countries thoughout Europe. Imported clothes may well carry sizing labels of another country. So it can be very confusing and this chart is a good starting point to guide you when shopping for women's clothes.

| Equivalent Clothing Sizes | | | | | | |
|---|---|---|---|---|---|---|
| **WOMEN'S COATS, SUITS, DRESSES AND BLOUSES** | | | | | | |
| British | 10 | 12 | 14 | 16 | 18 | 20 |
| American | 8 | 10 | 12 | 14 | 16 | 18 |
| Italian | 44 | 46 | 48 | 50 | 52 | 54 |
| French | 40 | 42 | 44 | 46 | 48 | 50 |

**British Standard BS 3666** gives the size codes relating to standard body measurements in Britain.

| British Standard Size Codes | | | | | | | | |
|---|---|---|---|---|---|---|---|---|
| SIZE CODE | HIPS | | | | BUST | | | |
| | CM | IN – | CM | IN | CM | IN – | CM | IN |
| 8 | 83 | (33) | 87 | (34) | 78 | (31) | 82 | (32) |
| 10 | 87 | (34) | 91 | (36) | 82 | (32) | 86 | (34) |
| 12 | 91 | (36) | 95 | (37½) | 86 | (34) | 90 | (35½) |
| 14 | 95 | (37½) | 99 | (39) | 90 | (35½) | 94 | (37) |
| 16 | 100 | (39½) | 104 | (41) | 95 | (37½) | 99 | (39) |
| 18 | 105 | (41½) | 109 | (43) | 100 | (39½) | 104 | (41) |
| 20 | 110 | (43½) | 114 | (45) | 105 | (41½) | 109 | (43) |
| 22 | 115 | (45) | 119 | (47) | 110 | (43½) | 114 | (45) |
| 24 | 120 | (47) | 124 | (49) | 115 | (45) | 119 | (47) |
| 26 | 125 | (49) | 129 | (51) | 120 | (47) | 124 | (49) |
| 28 | 130 | (51) | 134 | (53) | 125 | (49) | 129 | (51) |
| 30 | 135 | (53) | 139 | (55) | 130 | (51) | 134 | (53) |
| 32 | 140 | (55) | 144 | (57) | 135 | (53) | 139 | (55) |

Although the above size codes should relate to the measurements shown, it is always better to follow the actual measurements on the garment if they are given, rather than presume that a Size 14 or whatever size you think you are, will fit. Also very few people are an exact size. Hip size may fall into one size category and bust size in another, so it may be necessary to buy the larger size. Depending on the style of the garment the waist size and length are also important for a good fit.

Shops specialising in clothes for the larger lady may stock sizes larger than this, or place special orders for goods to be made.

## How to measure the body correctly for women's clothes

For clothes to fit well, whether bought from a shop, by mail order, made by a dressmaker or home made, careful sizing and measuring is essential. Just where the tape measure is placed on the body to take measurements can also make or mar the way the garment fits. To be accurate, measuring must be done correctly.

When measuring your body it is best to get someone to help you as it is not easy to do it correctly on your own.

Wear good fitting underclothes.

Do not have the tape too tight, just comfortably touching the body. Place the tape measure around your body as illustrated below.

Measure in metric or imperial measures, whichever you prefer, or write both down. Most tape measures have inches on one side and centimetres on the other.

### Bust
Measure around the fullest part of the bust and back, under the arms and over bust point. Measure the depth from centre of shoulder down to bust point.

Measuring for a brassiere is different - see page 138.

### Waist
Measure around the natural curve of the waistline. Do not hold breath in while doing this. Use this point as a reference point from which to measure outside leg measurement and length of back.

### Hips
Measure around the fullest part of your hips which are usually about 7 - 8 in (18 - 20 cm) below the waistline.

For some garments, the upper hip measurement about 3 in (7.5 cm) below the waist is required.

### Upper arms
Measure around the fullest part of the top muscle when arm is bent.

### Arm length
Measure from the top shoulder bone down the arm to the wrist. Have the elbow bent.

### Wrist
Measure around the arm about 2 in (5 cm) above wrist bone.

### Shoulder width
Measure from side of neck to point of shoulder.

### Neck
Measure around base of neck.

## To measure lengths of garments

### Dresses and coats
Measure from the nape of the neck to the finished length required. This tends to depend on the fashion at the time.

### For length of back of neck to waist
Measure from nape of neck straight down the back.

## Trousers

### Outside leg
Measure straight down the outside leg from waist to floor while wearing the shoes you will normally wear with the trousers.

### Inside leg
Measure from crutch straight down inside leg to required length.

**Crutch length**

Measure from the side of the waist when sitting down, to the seat of the chair. Take another measurement from the back waistline through the crutch to front waist.

**Thigh**

Measure the widest part when sitting down.

# UNDERSTANDING GARMENT LABELS

The law states that each garment should have a label, or a swing ticket or both, on which must be clearly indicated the size and designation of the garment. Any drawings and numbers used must be easy to read and understand.

**A typical dress label may look like this:**

| | |
|---|---|
| SIZE | 14 |
| HIPS | 97/38 |
| BUST | 92/36 |

**If Imperial measures are omitted and the national size code incorporated, a typical label on a woman's coat or dress would look like this:**

| | |
|---|---|
| SIZE | 16 |
| BUST GIRTH | 96 |
| HIP GIRTH | 104 |
| HEIGHT | 164 |

**A typical label on a woman's jacket would look like this:**

| | |
|---|---|
| SIZE | 16 |
| BUST GIRTH | 96 |
| HIP GIRTH | 104 |
| HEIGHT | 164 |

**A typical label on a pair of women's slacks would look like this:**

| | |
|---|---|
| HIP GIRTH | 124 |
| WAIST GIRTH | 96 |
| OUTSIDE LEG LENGTH | 104 |

# Blouses

Blouses are labelled in a similar way to dresses except that of course they are shorter. They and similar items such as sports tops may be marked 10, 12, 14, 16, 18, 20, 22, 24 and/or the bust measurement may be given in inches and/or centimetres.

# Bras

## To measure correctly when buying a bra

An over-bust measurement can only be a guide to the size bra you need to buy. The distance around the bust gives the *total* chest measurement but makes no allowance for those who have a very broad back but smaller bust or those with a large bust and narrow back. Two people could measure 36 in (92 cm) around, but be a completely different shape.

At present AA (very small), A, B, C, D, DD, E, F, FF, G, GG, H and HH(very large) are used to denote cup sizes for small, average or large size busts. There is talk that this system may be replaced by numbers at a future date. Some swimwear is sized by the same system. Not all makes are made in the very large sizes.

## How to find your size in metric measures

First take the under-bust measurement in centimetres as shown below.

| International Over Bust Measurement in cm | | | | | | |
|---|---|---|---|---|---|---|
| Underbust | Size | AA | A | B | C | D |
| 63-76 | 65 | 75-77 | 77-79 | 79-81 | 81-83 | 83-85 |
| 68-72 | 70 | 80-82 | 82-84 | 86-88 | 86-88 | 88-90 |
| 73-77 | 75 | 85-87 | 87-89 | 89-91 | 91-93 | 93-95 |
| 78-82 | 80 | 90-92 | 92-94 | 94-96 | 96-98 | 98-100 |
| 83-87 | 85 | 95-97 | 97-99 | 99-101 | 101-103 | 103-105 |
| 88-92 | 90 | - | 102-104 | 104-106 | 106-108 | 108-110 |
| 93-97 | 95 | - | 107-109 | 109-111 | 111-113 | 113-115 |
| 98-102 | 100 | - | 112-114 | 114-116 | 116-118 | 118-120 |
| 103-107 | 105 | - | 117-119 | 119-121 | 121-123 | 123-125 |
| 108-112 | 110 | - | 122-124 | 124-126 | 126-128 | 128-130 |
| 113-117 | 115 | - | - | 129-131 | 131-133 | 133-135 |
| 118-122 | 120 | - | - | 134-136 | 136-138 | 138-140 |

Find this measurement in the first column in table

The figure in the second column on the same horizontal line shows the size of bra needed. E.g. if the measurement under the bust equals 86 cm you will find this in the range of the fifth line down.

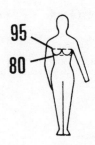

Look along the same horizontal line and you will see that 85 comes in the next column so you will need an 85 International size bra.

Now measure over the fullest part of your bust and following along the same horizontal line as before on the chart, note the column in which your measurement appears. The letter at the top of this column will give you your cup size.

E.g. if over-bust measurement equals 100 you will need a B cup size bra. To measure in imperial measures is rather different although the measurements taken need to be the same.

### Example

Measure around the body just under the bust and add 5 onto this figure. E.g measurement 31 inches add 5 equals 36. You should need a 36 inch bra.

Then measure the over-bust measurement.

If the measurement is the same as the under-bust measurement then an A cup will be needed. For every inch the over-bust measurement is more than the under-bust measurement add one letter on.

For instance if the under bust measurement is 34 inches and the over bust measurement is 36 inches then a C cup will be required. The same principle is used to measure all sizes.

The above information gives a very helpful starting point when shopping. However it is recommended that every bra should be tried on to check the fit before purchase.

## Measuring for a skirt

Measure for waist and hip size as illustrated using imperial or metric measures as prefered. It is wise to make a note of both measures before shopping.

### For the length

Measure from the centre of the natural waistline to the length of hemline desired but do not include the width of the waistband.

**A typical label on a woman's skirt would be:**

```
HIP GIRTH       124
WAIST GIRTH      96
SKIRT LENGTH     66
```

To provide suitable garments for people of the same body size but different height, garments such as skirts are labelled short or longer length. Some companies state the length of a garment in inches or centimetres as a measure which their designers consider is longer or shorter than what they call 'average' at that time. Fashion plays a part in this so no definite measure can be given.

## Measuring for a slip

To buy a slip of suitable length to wear under your clothes, you need to make a note of your dress or skirt lengths and take these with you when shopping. A full length slip must fit your bust size correctly as well as the waist and hip measurements. Then choose a slip about two or three inches (five to eight centimetres) shorter than the skirts you wish to wear it under.

**The label on a full length slip would read:**

```
SIZE 16
BUST 97 cm/38 in
```

**The label on an waist slip would read:**

```
SIZE 12/14
WAIST 61/66 cm/24/26 in
```

## Nightwear

Buying a nightdress requires similar measurements to buying a dress.

## Pyjamas

Buying pyjamas is similar to buying a blouse and a pair of trousers.

All nightwear should be a loose fit to be comfortable and some manufacturers make generous allowances for this. Yet many people like to buy nightwear a size larger than the size they would choose when buying daywear. Unfortunately it is often impossible to try nightwear on in a shop before buying.

## Hats

Hat sizes are based on the size of the circumference of the head measured just above the eyebrows. Hair thickness and styles can cause a great variation in size so the only reliable way to buy a hat that fits and looks good is to try it on.

## Cardigans and sweaters

These are often marked S for small, M for medium, L for large and then sometimes an accompanying sales board in the store may give an indication of the range of bust size these letters indicate.

Many give no indication, leaving the customer to judge the size by holding the garment up or if possible trying it on.

It would be helpful if some indication was given about just what 'small', 'medium', or 'large' means. At present it is up to each manufacturing company to decide on what it thinks is small, medium or large.

## Adult shoes

It is very important that shoes should fit correctly. Paying a lot of money does not necessarily mean that shoes will fit any better; it is the correct size and shape that is so important.

Shoes seen in an advertisement or bought by your best friend may not be right for *your* feet. Similarly do not buy the incorrect size just because the shop hasn't your size in stock. Having shoes stretched, or filling the extra space with an inner sole is not good for the feet. You may be prepared to put up with a bit of discomfort, but long term damage can be done. Remember the width of the shoe is as important as the length. Shoes mould themselves to the feet after a little wear. Everyone's feet are such a different shape that shoes should never be bought second hand or handed on from a friend.

Shoes that are worn every day for work should be especially suitable for the job, and shoes for sports such as running, should be fitted by someone at a good sports shop.

All good shoe shops have special equipment for measuring feet and are happy to check your feet for size before you buy.

### Shopping for shoes

When you shop for shoes what size do you look for? Some are labelled in British sizes, some American and some Continental. Many are marked in Continental sizes, yet are put on racks labelled in British sizes.

It is a good idea to make a note of the equivalent sizes and widths around the size you think you will need and take this with you to the shops. This information is also invaluable when shopping abroad.

The length of shoe required will vary according to the toe shape, so remember this size guide is only a starting point; get measured correctly before buying.

### British sizes

The British sizing system is based on inches.

One British size equals one third of an inch, that is 3 sizes per inch.

### Continental sizes

Continental sizing is based on centimetres.

One Continental size equals two thirds of a centimetre, that is 3 sizes per 2 centimetres.

**Conversion** from British to Continental and Continental to British sizes can be worked out using a mathematical formula, but for general use they have been calculated for us and the answer given to the nearest half size.

| Adult Shoe Sizes | | | | | |
|---|---|---|---|---|---|
| **BRITISH** | | **CONTINENTAL** | | **USA** | |
| **Women** | **Men** | **Women** | **Men** | **Women** | **Men** |
| 1 | 1 | 33 | 33 | 2½ | 1½ |
| 1½ | 1½ | 33½ | 34 | 3 | 2 |
| 2 | 2 | 34 | 34½ | 3½ | 2½ |
| 2½ | 2½ | 34½ | 35 | 4 | 3 |
| 3 | 3 | 35 | 35½ | 4½ | 3½ |
| 3½ | 3½ | 35½ | 36 | 5 | 4 |
| 4 | 4 | 36½ | 37 | 5½ | 4½ |
| 4½ | 4½ | 37 | 37½ | 6 | 5 |
| 5 | 5 | 37½ | 38 | 6½ | 5½ |
| 5½ | 5½ | 38½ | 38½ | 7 | 6 |
| 6 | 6 | 39 | 39½ | 7½ | 6½ |
| 6½ | 6½ | 39½ | 40 | 8 | 7 |
| 7 | 7 | 40½ | 40½ | 8½ | 7½ |
| 7½ | 7½ | 41 | 41 | 9 | 8 |
| 8 | 8 | 41½ | 42 | 9½ | 8½ |
| 8½ | 8½ | 42½ | 42½ | 10 | 9 |
| 9 | 9 | 43 | 43 | 10½ | 9½ |
| 9½ | 9½ | 44 | 43½ | 11 | 10 |
| 10 | 10 | 44½ | 44 | 11½ | 10½ |
| 10½ | 10½ | 45 | 44½ | 12 | 11 |
| | 11 | | 45 | | 11½ |
| | 11½ | | 45½ | | 12 |

# CHILDRENS CLOTHES

**Sizes and labels are based on British Standard 7231.**

Children's clothes are difficult to measure and label as they vary so widely. Until a few years ago they were bought according to the age of the child. But babies and children vary so widely in size that age is not a good indication. So although the age is still included on many labels it is there as a rough guide rather than to indicate an exact measure on which to base one's purchase.

**Baby clothes are usually based on weight, so a typical label on a baby's dress would be:**

| | |
|---|---|
| WEIGHT | 8 kg |
| APPROXIMATE AGE | 6 months |

As a child gets older and can stand, then clothes can be bought according to height as well as chest measurement.

**A label on a child's jumper would be:**

| | |
|---|---|
| HEIGHT | 128 cm |
| CHEST GIRTH | 60-65 cm |
| APPROXIMATE AGE | 8 - 9 years |

For some clothes an indication of the waist measurement is required.

**A label on a skirt or shorts would be:**

| | |
|---|---|
| HEIGHT | 116 cm |
| CHEST GIRTH | 50-55 cm |
| APPROXIMATE AGE | 6 years |

Numerous body dimensions of children were taken to arrive at detailed charts of measurements of children at different ages.

There are many variables, but if you know the age of the child and his or her height, the other measurements should be around those shown.

Chest and waist measurements given on labels are actual body measurements not garment measurements, so a jumper marked 66 cm/ 26 in chest is made to fit a girl about 8 years old with that size chest.

This chart shows the average height children are for their age. If you always keep a note of their height, clothes shopping will be much easier, although it is still preferable to have the child with you in the shop to try the garment on.

As can be seen in the examples of labels after 12 months the labels show the height of the child and approximate age.

| Children's Age and Height | | | | | |
|---|---|---|---|---|---|
| AGE | TOTAL HEIGHT WITHOUT SHOES | | AGE | TOTAL HEIGHT WITHOUT SHOES | |
| | cm | in | | cm | in |
| Baby | 76 | 30 | 6 | 114 | 45 |
| " | 79 | 31 | | 117 | 46 |
| " | 81 | 32 | 7 | 119 | 47 |
| " | 84 | 33 | | 122 | 48 |
| Infant | 86 | 34 | 8 | 124 | 49 |
| | 89 | 35 | | 127 | 50 |
| 2 | 91 | 36 | | 130 | 51 |
| | 94 | 37 | | 132 | 52 |
| 3 | 96.5 | 38 | 9 | 135 | 53 |
| | 99 | 39 | | 137 | 54 |
| 4 | 102 | 40 | 10 | 140 | 55 |
| | 104 | 41 | | 142 | 56 |
| 5 | 107 | 42 | | 145 | 57 |
| | 109 | 43 | 11 | 147 | 58 |
| | 112 | 44 | | | |

## Measuring a child's body for garments

When measuring a child's body before making clothes or knitting a garment follow these guidelines.

Measure children in their underwear, including nappies if worn.

Measure without shoes.

### Chest
Measure around the widest part of the chest under the shoulder blades.

### Waist
Little children do not have much of a waist, but if there is a natural indented line then measure around this.

### Hips
Measure around the fullest part of the buttocks.

### Back of neck to waist
Measure from nape of neck to waist down centre of back.

### Shoulder width
Measure from side of neck to point of shoulder.

### Neck
Measure around base of neck.

### Length of arm
Measure from point of shoulder over bent elbow to wrist.

### Dress length
Measure from nape of neck to desired finished length.

### Skirt length
Measure from waist to finished length.

### Trousers
Measure from back waist under the crutch to front waist.

Measure outside leg from waist to ankle and inside leg from crutch to ankle with shoes on.

Taking as many measurements as possible before starting to make a garment will ensure a good fit. Allow for growth in height when making items for children.

### Children's nightwear
When buying nightwear for children it is important to buy that made from flameproof material. This will be shown on a label attached to the garment.

### Children's shoes
Children's feet are changing shape and growing all the time and there are times when they grow particularly fast. So it is very important that their shoes are bought specially for them and fitted by a trained sales assistant at a reputable shop. Have children's feet checked regularly - about every three months - just to make sure that the feet have not got too big for the shoes. Shops do not mind measuring a child's feet and then not selling you shoes because the previous pair are still the correct size. They know that you are likely to return to their shop when new shoes are required. Checking on footwear such as wellingtons and football boots which are not worn all the time and are soon outgrown is important. Use hand-me-downs for any other clothes items but try never to do this for shoes.

**British sizes** for children's shoes start at 0 which is 4 inches long. Children's sizes go up to 13 (8½ inches) and then they move on to the adult size 1.

**Continental sizes** for children's shoes start at 15. They go up to 32½ and then they move on to the adult size 33.

Shoe sizes cannot be worked out by measuring the foot in inches and converting it to centimetres or converting centimetres to inches. The sizes are worked out by shoe manufacturers.

**Always** take your child with you to buy shoes and don't buy them in a hurry. If possible try to shop when the shop isn't too busy - avoid Saturday mornings just before term starts.

If you buy shoes from chain stores or by mail order you will need to check their suitability yourself.

### Here are some guidelines

* is the shoe too loose so the foot slops around in it

* does the shoe fit firmly at the heel when the child stands on tip toe

* are the toes too near the end of the shoe so they have to curl up instead of lying flat

* have they suitable fastenings across the instep to prevent the shoes falling off or the foot moving forward so crushing the toes

* are they too narrow so that part of the sole of the foot is in fact walking on the upper of the shoe preventing the toes moving correctly

* does the shoe bend with the foot and in the correct place as the child walks

* does the shape of the shoe fit the natural shape of the foot?

### To check the length of your child's feet

* cut two thin strips of cardboard longer than the feet

* stand your child on them with bare feet, one  foot on each strip

* draw a mark on the cardboard at the back of each heel

* draw another mark at the end of the longest toe on each foot

* mark the strips left or right feet

* cut the cardboard at the marks

* place a strip in each shoe - the one marked left in the left shoe and the one marked right in the right shoe so the ends touch the toes of the shoes.

If the shoe is the correct length there should be about ½ in (1.3 cm) of growing room gap between the end of the strip and the heel end of the shoe. If there is less than a ½ in(1.3 cm) gap or if the piece of cardboard touches the heel or if it doesn't lie flat then the shoe is too short.

This is only a rough guide as it doesn't take the width of the foot into account, but it does help if no proper fitting service is available.

## Socks

A lot of damage can be done to children's feet even before they start to wear shoes. Babies' feet are soft and pliable and the toes are quite curled up when they are born. If they are then put into all-in-one suits, booties or socks which are a bit tight and constricting, the toes have no opportunity to straighten out and develop.

### Points to note

* babies should go barefoot as long as possible but if the weather is cold then large soft roomy socks can be worn
* check regularly that the socks are big enough and if the feet of an all-in-one suit become too small then cut the feet off at the ankle and put socks on baby instead
* socks should be big enough without being stretched
* choose wool, cotton or a mixture of natural and man-made fibres
* check regularly that socks haven't shrunk and therefore become too tight
* all socks should be long enough in the foot to be able to be pulled away making spare room at the end
* stretch socks should not be used for small children and should not be tight on older children.

| Children's Shoe Sizes | | | | | | | | | | | | |
|---|---|---|---|---|---|---|---|---|---|---|---|---|
| British | 2 | 3 | 4 | 5 | 6 | 7 | 8 | 9 | 10 | 11 | 12 | 13 |
| USA | 1 | 2 | 3 | 4 | 5 | 6 | 7 | 8 | 9 | 10 | 11 | 12 |
| Continental | 18 | 20 | 22 | 23 | 24 | 25 | 26 | 28 | 29 | 30 | 31 | 32 |

## Buying socks

Some socks can be bought by using the same sizing as shoes. However unlike shoes they can easily shrink in the wash so check regularly that this hasn't occured.

Measure your child's feet in inches or centimetres and take a measure with you when shopping to check the socks will be suitable.

# 10

# *HOME AND HOBBIES*

Most measuring problems occur in the kitchen followed closely by activities in the home.

The measuring of carpets and other flooring is another situation where people should be encouraged to 'think metric' as a step towards complete metrication. Large carpet retailers work out their prices in pounds per metre, but because this is not understood by the majority of the public and makes the price appear larger, they transcribe the information into price per square yard which most people can understand and more easily compare.

Deciding on how many rolls of wallpaper to buy is not easy until it is explained; a situation not helped by the fact that wallpaper is still manufactured 22 in wide or 5.6 cm.

Even age old hobbies like knitting and crochet have their problems. Thousands of people already possess good knitting needles and favourite patterns in the old sizing. There is no need to rush out and buy more in new sizes, if reference is made to the enclosed charts to see the equivalent metric size or American size as required by the pattern.

To look attractive, curtains require fullness whichever measurements are used. How much extra material to allow in the width if pencil pleat heading is desired in thick fabric or lots of gathers in fine net is explained so that the final results are successful.

## CARPETS

It is now usual for builders to build houses to metric measurements so the sizes of finished rooms are actually in metric sizes. However because most people do not yet 'think metric' and relate and compare sizes of rooms and furniture in imperial sizes with which they are more familiar, estate agents still give imperial sizes in their literature.

**What happens when these rooms need carpeting?**
**Carpets made to imperial measurements**

The best quality British carpets are made in imperial measurements and may be:

3 foot, 9 foot, 12 foot and 15 foot wide. Pattern repeats are usually every 3 feet.

If these are to be fitted in a room measuring 4 metres wide by 5 metres long (20 square metres), what does one buy? The area of the floor is found by multiplying the length by the width of the room and the answer is always square metres, yards or feet.

The table below converts square metres to square feet.

| Square Metre | | Square Feet | Square Metre | | Square Feet |
|---|---|---|---|---|---|
| 1 | equals | 10.764 | 20 | equals | 215.278 |
| 2 | equals | 21.528 | 30 | equals | 322.917 |
| 3 | equals | 32.292 | 40 | equals | 430.556 |
| 4 | equals | 43.056 | 50 | equals | 538.196 |
| 5 | equals | 53.820 | 60 | equals | 645.835 |
| 6 | equals | 64.583 | 70 | equals | 753.474 |
| 7 | equals | 75.347 | 80 | equals | 861.113 |
| 8 | equals | 86.111 | 90 | equals | 968.752 |
| 9 | equals | 96.875 | 100 | equals | 1076.391 |
| 10 | equals | 107.639 | | | |

To change square feet to square yards divide by 9 as there are nine square feet in 1 square yard.

In the example of the room given above, i.e. a room with a floor area of 20 square metres - this is the same as saying the room is 215.278 square feet or ÷9 is 23.9 square yards which rounded up is 24 square yards of carpet needs to be bought.

### Carpets made to metric measurements

Carpets made in Europe and imported into Britain are made on metric looms. They may be:

1 metre, 2 metres, 3 metres, 4 metres or 5 metres wide.

To lay carpet made to metric measures in a room which is 12 feet wide by 16 feet long (192 square feet) or (21.3 square yards) refer to the table overleaf.

| Square Feet | | Square Metre | Square Feet | | Square Metre |
|---|---|---|---|---|---|
| 1 | equals | 0.093 | 20 | equals | 1.858 |
| 2 | equals | 0.186 | 30 | equals | 2.787 |
| 3 | equals | 0.279 | 40 | equals | 3.716 |
| 4 | equals | 0.372 | 50 | equals | 4.645 |
| 5 | equals | 0.465 | 60 | equals | 5.574 |
| 6 | equals | 0.557 | 70 | equals | 6.503 |
| 7 | equals | 0.650 | 80 | equals | 7.432 |
| 8 | equals | 0.743 | 90 | equals | 8.361 |
| 9 | equals | 0.836 | 100 | equals | 9.290 |
| 10 | equals | 0.929 | | | |

Most large carpet retailers price their carpets in square yards but will convert this cost to the price per metre if you wish.

### Matching patterns and awkward shaped rooms

If a pattern needs to be matched, remember to allow for this in the same way as measuring for wallpaper (see page 154).

It is also necessary to consider which way the pile is going to lay; it should lie away from you as you enter the room. This can make a difference to the amount of patterned carpet you need.

If your room has difficult-shaped alcoves and fireplaces then it may be wise to ask the shop where you are buying your carpet to send a man to your home to check exactly how much carpet you need. This may save you making an expensive mistake.

## Stair carpet

The area of the stairs are not needed, only the width and the length. Most stairs are not more than 1 metre or 3 feet 3 inches wide, so a strip of 3 feet or (1 metre) wide carpet can be bought.

## Underlay

Underlay can be measured for in the same way as carpets but may be sold in varying widths.

## Vinyl flooring

The area of the floor can be measured in the same way as for carpet to find the number of square yards or metres that are needed. It is made in varying widths and once the area to be covered is known then the nearest suitable size can be chosen. This will prevent unsightly and dangerous joins having to be made.

## CURTAINS

Some of the best curtain materials, like carpets, are still made and sold in imperial measurements.

Whether metric or imperial measures are preferred, it is important to measure the window correctly in order to achieve a good well finished result. To convert feet and yards to centimetres and metres and vice versa see page 23.

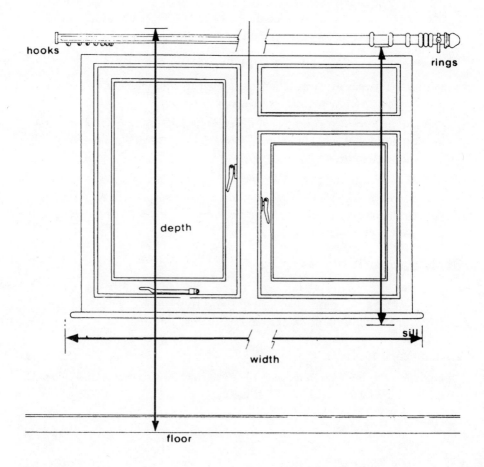

**Measuring the length**

The first thing to consider is which variety of track and heading is desired as this will affect the length of material required for each curtain. There is a wide variety of tracks and poles from which to choose. They may be hung from the wall or from the ceiling or bent around a bay window. It is important to have the track firmly fixed in position before you start to measure, it is no use imagining where the top of the curtain might come.

Decide where you wish the top edge of the curtain to be. If you want the curtains to cover the curtain track when they are closed then measure from just above the track. If the track is to be exposed, as occurs when curtains are suspended from rings on a pole, then the top measure will start from the bottom of the ring, the top of the hook (see diagram).

Next decide where you wish the bottom edge of the curtain to be; just skimming the window sill, just below the window sill or to the floor. Allow half an inch, just over one centimetre, extra clearance if the curtains are to go to the floor.

**Heading allowance**

If the curtains are just thin cotton or net gathered onto a wire then 2 in (5 cm) is all that is needed for the heading. Heavy fabrics require more and at least 3 in (7.5 cm) heading should be allowed.

**Hem allowance**

Allow 6 in (15 cm) for the bottom hem. If material is being used that will be washed at home, check that it will not shrink. If this is likely make the hem deeper. Heavy curtains will require dry cleaning so should not shrink.

**Measuring for width**

Measure from one end of the curtain track to the other.

When the window is very wide and if the curtains are heavy, the curtain track is often divided in the centre and fixed to overlap. This also prevents any gap in the curtains when they are drawn. It does mean that the overlap measurement has to be counted in as in effect you are covering that part of the window with double curtains.

**Allowance for fullness**

Each curtain for a small window may only require one width of fabric, but usually two or more widths of fabric need to be joined together to create sufficient fullness.

**Decide on the fullness and effect desired and follow the guide below.**

For **simple gathers** allow 1½ to 2 times the width of the track.

**Pinch pleats** require twice the width of the track.

**Pencil pleats** formed in thin curtains require three times the width for full effect.

**Pencil pleats** in medium weight fabric require 2½ times the width.

**Pencil pleats** in heavy fabrics like velvet should be made with 2¼ times fullness.

While it looks good to have plenty of fullness, regard has to be taken of the thickness of the material. If there is too much fullness it can bunch up at the track. Also very full curtains can be difficult to pull back and so cover the glass and keep light from the room. For this reason the curtain track is often extended beyond the sides of the actual window and is why the track length is measured and not the width of the window itself.

**For example**

If the curtain track is 6 ft (180 cm) long, when multiplied by 1½ times to allow for fullness the total width of fabric needed will be 9 ft (270 cm), each curtain will need to be 4½ ft (135 cm) wide.

Then add 2½ in (6 cm) x four for the four edge seams.

The same window curtained with thicker fabric in pleats will require 6 x 2½ = 15 ft or 180 x 2½ = 450 cm or 4.5 metres.

Wide windows will need to have several lengths of fabric joined together to provide sufficient fullness. If the fabric chosen has a pattern, then extra allowance must be made for matching across the widths and where the two curtains meet at the centre of the window.

**How much material to buy**

Multiply the number of fabric widths required by the length including hem allowances, and add any extra required for matching to get the total material required.

**Measuring for curtain heading tape**

The tape is sewn across all the widths of fabric before the pleats or gathers are formed, so count up the final number of widths of material used, multiply this by the width of the material used and that is the length of tape required.

**For example**

If each curtain requires two widths of fabric for the desired fullness and the

fabric is 54 in (137 cm) wide, then 54 x 4 = 216 in = 18 ft = 6 yards tape.
OR 135 x 4 = 540 cm = 5.4 metres tape.

To convert feet and yards to metres and centimetres and vice versa see page 23.

# PAINTING

There are numerous painting jobs around the home each requiring measuring and thought before progressing.

### To decide how much paint you need to buy

First calculate the area to be covered by muliplying the height by the width of each wall and add all the totals together.

To calculate the paint needed for moulded window or door frames, multiply the height by the width of the frames and consider it as a solid surface. If the frames are smooth and flat then calculate as above and take off one quarter of the total.

To paint a moulded door multiply the height of the door by the width and add one quarter as much again to allow for the increased surface area.

### Extra considerations

Surfaces vary and require different paints. Paints specially prepared for outside use on pipes, gutterings, cement and timber are available. Ask your local DIY store for advice.

Some paints are more porous than others. If the surface is textured more paint may be required. Also if you are painting over a dark colour you may need an extra top coat as well as two or three undercoats. This should be considered before the paint is bought.

### How to buy paint

Different types of paint cover different areas (see chart).

Paint is generally sold in litre cans, each litre covering a stated surface area. It is best to buy all the paint you need before you start the job and always be generous in your calculations.

For a guide to the amount to buy, use the following table.

### Surface area which one litre of paint will cover:

| | | | |
|---|---|---|---|
| Emulsion | 12 m² | or | 130 ft² |
| Non-drip gloss | 12 m² | or | 130 ft² |
| Gloss | 14 m² | or | 150 ft² |
| Undercoat | 16 m² | or | 170 ft² |
| Primer | 12 m² | or | 130 ft² |

## WALLPAPER

### Rolls of wallpaper are made:

33 ft (11 yards) (10.5 metres) long
20½in (526 mm) wide.

### Borders of wallpaper are made:

33 ft (11 yards) (10.5 metres) long
and some are 16 ft (5⅓ yards) (5 metres) long.

As borders are a design feature they are made in a wide variety of widths, but the most common is 4 in (10 cm) wide.

### To find how much wallpaper you need to buy

Measure the height of the room from the top edge of the skirting board to the ceiling.

Measure the distance around the room taking the measure right into every corner of any alcoves.

It is usual to ignore the size of doors or windows when calculating, as wallpaper is usually required above and below them. However if your room has huge patio doors, then their width can be deducted from the measurement taken around the room.

### Example

If a room is 10 ft (3.5 m) high you will get three lengths of paper from one roll e.g. 33 ft ÷ 10 ft = 3 or (10.5 m ÷ 3.5 m = 3).

Then multiply the number of lengths by the width of the paper, in this example 3 lengths x 20½ in = 61½ in = 5 ft 1½ in or (3 lengths x 526 mm = 1578 mm = nearly 160 cm).

Then divide the distance around the room by 5 ft 1½ in (160 cm) and you have the number of rolls needed.

If the room is 54 ft (16.5 m) around, then 54 ÷ 5 = 10 rolls or 16.5 ÷160 = 10 rolls.

In practice of course you cannot work so exactly, it is wise to always allow a few inches or centimetres extra whenever you measure. Also as you cannot buy parts of a roll you will have to buy up to the next whole roll. Many people prefer to buy an extra roll to the number calculated anyway just to make sure they have sufficient of the same batch number for matching all patterns or in case of accidents.

It is preferable to measure the room and do the calculations yourself, to check on the chart below, and as an extra safeguard take all the measurements to the shop with you and ask the assistant to check your workings if you are not 100% sure or if you choose a difficult repeat pattern.

### Patterned paper

Patterned paper always has a repeated pattern and allowance needs to be made for this. It means that you will always have to allow for wastage when cutting each length of paper.

The bigger the pattern repeat the more paper you are likely to have to waste by trimming a lot from each end of each length. This can work out quite expensive, so if economy is important choose a paper with a very small repeated pattern. Sizes of pattern repeats vary widely and are given with the details on each roll of paper.

### Buying

Always buy paper with the same batch number on the roll label to ensure colour consistency.

For a quick calculation or to check your own workings, refer to the chart below for the number of rolls of paper you need to buy. It does not allow for pattern matching.

| Distance Around the Room in Metres and Feet | | | | | | | |
|---|---|---|---|---|---|---|---|
| Metres | 9-12 | 13-15 | 17-18 | 20-21 | 22-24 | 26-27 | 29-30 |
| Feet | 30-40 | 42-50 | 55-60 | 65-70 | 75-80 | 85-90 | 95-100 |
| Number of Rolls | 2 | 3 | 4 | 6 | 7 | 9 | 10 |

### To calculate the number of rolls required to paper a ceiling

Measure the perimeter of the room, that is the distance all around the edge. Include the doors and windows in this calculation.

Then refer to the chart.

## Paper hanging

Some papers are ready pasted and just require wetting for a stated time in a trough of water before hanging. Other papers need to be pasted just before hanging. As a general rule the thicker and heavier the paper the thicker the paste needs to be (see below.) If you have paste of any kind, but especially one containing fungicide, in a bucket keep it well away from children.

## Pasting wallpaper

### Ready pasted

Many papers are ready pasted with an adhesive and these may contain a fungicide to inhibit mould growth. The piece to be hung is immersed in a trough of water or an automatic papering machine before hanging.

Borders are usually self adhesive.

Other papers require suitable paste to be spread on them before hanging.

**Standard paste** for lining paper and standard wallpaper.

Use 4.5 litres (1 gallon) for about every 6 rolls.

**Heavy duty paste** for heavy wallpapers such as imitation wood, tiling or brick or those with strong relief patterns.

Use 4.5 litres (1 gallon) for every 4-6 rolls.

**All purpose paste** for all general wallpapers.

Follow instructions on the packet regarding the dilution of the paste powder to suit the wallpaper you are hanging.

### Cold water paste

This could be called the original wallpaper paste suitable for most weights of wallpaper. It is mixed with cold water, 4.5 litres (1 gallon) per pack, for hanging 5-6 rolls of medium weight paper.

**Vinyl paper** is best hung using a paste with a fungicide content. 4.5 litres (1 gallon) will be needed to hang about 4 rolls.

### Ready mixed paste

Instead of mixing the paste yourself it comes in a tub. A 2.5 kilogram pack is sufficient for hanging 3-4 rolls. It works out more expensive than other pastes.

### Size

Before hanging paper the walls may be sized which means brushing them over with size which is like a glue. It makes the wall a bit slippery so that the paper can be manipulated into place easily when being hung.

5 litres (1 gallon) of made up size will cover the wall under 8 rolls of paper.

## Tiling walls

Measure the height and width of the area to be tiled and multiply the two figures together to get the area to be covered in square metres or square yards. Divide this by the size of the tiles to get the number required. Some manufacturers indicate on the box of tiles the area that will be covered from the contents. If bought singly, a guide is that a wall 8 ft x 10 ft (80 ft²) will be covered with 320 x 6 in square tiles. Tiles are still made in Imperial measures. If patterned tiles are to be inserted amongst plain for decoration it is wise to work out the design on graph paper.

Buy a few more tiles than needed to allow for breakages.

# LIGHTING

### Total light required

For general lighting a good guide is to allow 20 watts per square metre or 2 watts per square foot of floor space for filament lamps and 10 watts per square metre or 1 watt per square foot for fluorescent lamps. So for a room which has 100 square foot, or 225 square metres of floor space, a total of 200 watts of lighting from filament lamps is required.

### Spread and positioning of light

The above is the recommended *total* amount of light for general use. When placing lamps and deciding which light bulb to use it is important to consider what activities are being carried out in each particular room and adjust the source of light accordingly. So often the lighting in a room is limited to one light bulb hanging from a fixture in the centre of the room. This rarely looks good and can affect the sight of those living in the room. More concentrated light is required in areas where a lot of reading, embroidery or similar hobbies are enjoyed and in kitchens and staircases the light should be good to prevent accidents occuring. More subdued lower wattage lighting may be placed in an area where people are sitting talking or watching television.

Lamp shades and refection of light from surfaces all play an important part in the amount of light actually gained from each light bulb and can be used with advantage.

Decorative lighting giving special effects such as spotlighting pictures, ornaments or flower arrangements can greatly enhance an area as can lamp shades of various colours and types.

So plan where you need light then decide what sort and how much.

### How much light

As a rough guide a 60 watt bulb is suitable for general, low light requirements such as a centre light in a room, a 100 watt bulb gives more light in a table lamp near to where specific tasks are done and 150 watt bulb is good for over stairways and in bathrooms where light is needed for safety purposes more than effect. A 150 watt bulb in an angle-poise lamp, shining light over one shoulder, is good for close work. A 'daylight' bulb can be less stressful on the eyes and be useful where colours are being used.

## Lampshades

Check that any lampshade used is suitable for the wattage bulb you desire at that point. Many lampshade materials are inflammable and a maximum level of wattage bulb is often recommended.

## FABRICS

Material is woven in various widths according to the type of material and the manufacturer weaving it.

The chart below shows the most common widths of material in metric and Imperial measures. They are not exact conversion measures but are taken to the nearest inch or centimetre.

| Width of Material | | | |
|---|---|---|---|
| IMPERIAL (in) | METRIC (cm) | IMPERIAL (in) | METRIC (cm) |
| 36 | 90 | 56 | 140 |
| 45 | 115 | 60 | 150 |
| 48 | 120 | 68 | 170 |
| 54 | 135 | 72 | 180 |

Cotton, gingham, lawn, seersucker, cotton satin, muslin, organdie, silk, satin, voile, chiffon, denim, taffeta, nylon and georgette are sold either 90 cm (36 in) wide or 113 cm (45 in) wide.

Wool, crepe, wool flannel, wool gabardine, serge, worsted, thicker velvets and jersey are usually 135 cm (45 in) wide or 150 cm (60 in) wide.

Furnishing fabrics are 150 cm (60 in) wide or more.

While some items can be made out of any width fabric it can often be a disaster if the wrong width fabric is bought. At the very least it can lead to a lot of wastage of fabric and therefore money. If it is found to be necessary to join two smaller pieces of fabric together to make a larger piece, the join may well mar the look of the finished product, especially if it is difficult to match the pattern correctly.

## How much fabric to buy

Paper patterns for dressmaking suggest the lengths of material that need to be bought for each size of each design depending on the width of material used. Many paper patterns, especially older favourites which people use over and over again because they like them, will have body measurements, widths of material and amount of material needed to make the garment in imperial measures. Some new patterns will have both imperial and metric measures, others especially any foreign designs will be in metric measures only, so sizes and measurements often have to be converted one way or the other.

Quantities of required material suggested on the pattern envelope should be followed. This is especially important if patterns on the material need to be matched, for instance flowers, checks or stripes.

To check your body measurements to find out which pattern size you need to make up, refer to page 134-135.

## Buying fabric

Shopkeepers will cut lengths of fabric to the nearest 10 cm which is a fraction under 4 inches.

| | |
|---|---|
| 4 in = 10cm | ⅓ yard = 30cm |
| 8 in = 20cm | ½ yd = 46cm |
| ¼ yd = 23cm | ¾ yd = 70cm |
| 1 ft = 30cm | 1 yd = 90cm |

If you want to buy the *exact* metric equivalent of 4 yards of material you work it out this way:

4 yds x 91.44 cm = 365.76 cm

Divide by 100 to find out how many metres this is = 3 m 66 cm

Rounded up to the nearest 10 means you would buy 3 m 70 cm of material.

If you wanted to buy 2½ yards of material this is how you could work out how many centimetres you should buy using the above information.

1 yd = 91.44 cm so 2 yd = 182.88 cm

half a yard = 45.72 cm

Add the 2 yard and half yard figures together = 228.6 cm

Divide the 228.6 cm by 100 to turn it into metres and centimeters = 2 m 29 cm of material.

Rounded up to the nearest 10 cm you will actually buy 2 m 30 cm of material.

Paper patterns usually allow for a seam allowance, which should be followed carefully in order for the garment to fit correctly and for sufficient material to be available for neatening the seams.

Seam allowances vary from one make of pattern to another but the most usual measurements given in patterns are:

| | |
|---|---|
| ¼ in = 6 mm | ¾ in = 20 mm |
| ½ in = 13 mm | 1 in = 25 mm |

If you want to be really accurate it is a good idea to cut a length of card the width of the seam allowance, place this against the edge of the material and pin, tack or mark with tailors chalk along the inside edge of this card. Some patterns have the seam allowances drawn on them.

## CROCHET HOOKS

### Sizing

There used to be a numbering system for crochet hook sizes in Britain which distinguished between suitable sizes for wool and very fine threads.

Hooks are now numbered according to an international metric standard. Their thickness is measured by the diameter of the hook, the larger the number the larger the hook.

The length of the crochet hook is a standard length, they do not need to be long or short like a knitting needle.

### USA and metric equivalent sizes

In the United States there is a lettering and numbering system.

| Metric | United States | Metric | United States |
|---|---|---|---|
| 7.50 | - | 3.00 | C |
| 7.00 | K | - | C |
| - | J | 2.50 | B |
| 6.00 | I | 2.00 | 1 |
| 5.50 | H | 1.75 | 4 |
| 5.00 | H | 1.50 | 7 |
| 4.50 | G | 1.00 | 10 |
| 4.00 | F | 0.75 | 12 |
| 3.50 | E | 0.60 | 14 |
| - | D | | |

### Recommended suitable hook sizes for use with certain yarns.

The following list can only be a guide to what hook is normally recommended. Sometimes by using what could be called the 'wrong size' hook, interesting textures and effects can be achieved.

Use 0.6 - 1.00 size hooks when using very fine threads.

Use 1.25 - 1.75 sizes when using fairly fine yarn.

Use 2.00 - 3.50 sizes for cotton and wool mixtures up to 4 ply wool.

Use 3.50 - 4.50 sizes for thick cotton and double knitting wool

Above this thickness a special pattern recommending certain hooks will be needed unless you wish to experiment.

## KNITTING NEEDLES

### Sizes

All knitting needles were formerly given a size number which was not related to any particular measurement.

The sizes are now expressed in mm and relate to their diameter.

The United States have a completely different method of sizing.

The table below shows the new equivalent sizing, so if you have a knitting pattern which suggests using size 10 needles then this will mean you need to use size 3.25 mm needles in the new sizing.

Similarly if you wish to knit a garment from a new pattern which states you should use 5.00 mm needles and you wish to use perfectly good old needles you already possess, then you need to look out a pair of size 6.

| Knitting Needles | | | | | |
|---|---|---|---|---|---|
| OLD SIZE SIZE | NEW SIZE (in mm) | US | OLD SIZE SIZE | NEW SIZE (in mm) | US |
| - | 1.75 | 000 | 7 | 4.50 | 7 |
| 14 | 2.00 | 00 | 6 | 5.00 | 8 |
| 13 | 2.25 | 0 | 5 | 5.50 | 9 |
| - | 2.50 | 1 | 4 | 6.00 | 10 |
| 12 | 2.75 | 2 | 3 | 6.50 | - |
| 11 | 3.00 | 3 | 2 | 7.00 | 10 ½ |
| 10 | 3.25 | - | 1 | 7.50 | - |
| - | 3.50 | 4 | 0 | 8.00 | 11 |
| 9 | 3.75 | - | 00 | 9.00 | - |
| 8 | 4.00 | 5 | 000 | 10.00 | 13 |
| - | 4.25 | 6 | | | |

The larger the number in the old sizing the thinner and finer the needles. The smaller the number in the new sizing the thinner and finer the needles.

To cater for the variation in the number of stitches held on needles they can be bought in varying sizes from 25 cm to 40 cm long.

Sets of 4 needles for knitting gloves and socks without seams are obtainable in the same sizes as indicated on the chart.

### Buying wool

Wool used to be sold in ounce balls or hanks. In line with many other areas which have taken the 25 g as equivalent to one ounce, yarns are also now mostly sold in 25 g or 50 g amounts.

## Buying the correct size zip

The actual size of the opening on a zip is about ½ in(10 cm) shorter than the zipper tape into which the teeth are set. In order not to strain the teeth on the zip as you open and close it, it is wise to be able to get the garment on and off without opening the zip to quite its full extent. Take this into account when deciding which zip to buy and do not stint on the length zip you choose even if it costs a little more.

| Zipper Lengths | | | |
|---|---|---|---|
| in | cm | in | cm |
| 4 | 10 | 16 | 40 |
| 5 | 13 | 18 | 45 |
| 6 | 15 | 20 | 50 |
| 8 | 20 | 22 | 55 |
| 9 | 23 | 24 | 60 |
| 10 | 25 | 26 | 66 |
| 12 | 30 | 28 | 70 |
| 14 | 35 | 30 | 76 |

Measure carefully the actual size of the opening on the item or garment that needs a zip before going shopping.

If the length does not correspond to one of the measurements listed above, you need to decide whether to sew up a little of the gap and buy the shorter length zip or unpick a little of the seam and buy a longer length of zip to fit. If you choose to buy a shorter zip, make sure you will still be able to get the garment on when the opening is smaller.

## Colour matching the zip

Always take a piece of the fabric in which the zip is to be inserted so that you buy the correct shade. If the item is too big to carry to the shops then find a reel of thread, some embroidery thread, a sweater or something the same colour to which you can match the zip in the shop. A zip which is not quite the right colour looks awful, and however well the zip is sewn in place it will show.

Buy some matching thread at the same time as buying the zip. When it is sewn into place the stitches usually show on the front of the garment and it is preferable if these show as little as possible.

## A zip as a fashion feature

Alternatively you can buy an attractive contrasting thread so that the stiches show and make a fashion feature of the zip. This can be very effective, especially when inserting a decorative zip down the front of a garment. When inserting a zip this way the stitching must be perfect tension as every stitch will show.

## Types of zips

The label attached to the zip should indicate the weight of fabric or type of garment for which it is most suitable.

**Medium weight** closed-end zip with metal teeth on cotton tape for woollen garments such as skirts or dresses. The colour tape should be matched to the fabric.

**Lightweight** closed-end zip with coloured metal teeth on cotton tape for use with cotton materials. Its colour should be matched to the dress fabric.

**Polyester** closed-end zip, very light weight, coloured teeth for use with man-made and light fabrics, usually drip dry and shrink resistant.

**Invisible zip** - teeth on the zipper are turned in by the runner and so conceal the opening. More difficult to fit but the finished appearance is excellent and professional.

**Open-ended zip** - used for jackets, cardigans and anoraks so that the garment can easily be put on and removed without pulling it over the head.

**Curved zip** - necessary for the front crotch of all trousers. Never use a straight zip for this.

**Fashion zip** - often over-large, making it a feature of the design of the garment. May also have decorative coloured teeth, plain or patterned tape and fancy ring pulls.

# MAKING HOMES SUITABLE FOR DISABLED PEOPLE

**BS 5619 1978**

In recent years everyone has become more aware of the needs of disabled people. There are recommended measures for their many requirements and these are worth keeping in mind whenever alterations are being considered in a home. They can make all the difference to enable the disabled person to retain his or her independence.

## Getting in and out of a building

### Approach ramps

These should be not less than 1.2 m (4 ft) wide with a slip resistant surface. Ramps should be not less than 1 in 2, approximately 5°. For gradients of between 1 in 15 and 1 in 12; (between approximately 4° and 5°), the maximum unbroken length of ramp should be 10 m (33 ft). There should be rest areas between each section. A very slight gradient is necessary on all surfaces to allow for water to drain off.

**Garden paths** should be no less than 1 m (3¼ ft) wide and should be of lose material such as gravel to avoid slipping.

**Doors** can be a problem, especially for those in wheelchairs. There should be a minimum clear opening of 800 mm (2 ft 7½ in) except where there is a right angle turn immediately inside the door in which case the opening should be increased to a minimum of 850 mm (2 ft 9½ in). Many door frames measuring 900 mm (2 ft 11½ in) and 1 m (39½ in) are on sale and can be used; there should be no need to have a door frame made specially.

**Raised threshholds** to entrance doors can be a problem and should not be higher than 25 mm (1 in). Recessed mats are preferable to loose mats to prevent tripping or catching on wheels. To allow someone in a wheelchair to reach a door handle a clear space of 300 mm (12 in) up to the door handle is necessary.

**Internal doors** need a minimum clear opening of 770 mm (30½ in) and door handles should be set at 1040 mm (3 ft 5 in) (British Standard 4787 Part 1). Sliding doors are usually best for entrance of a wheelchair to a lavatory but they must slide easily.

### Windows

A disabled person may spend a lot of time sitting in a wheelchair or armchair and looking out of a window. Windows should ideally be at a lower level than usual to enable the seated person to see out with ease. Transoms get in the line of vision so should be avoided at eye level, about 1,100 to 1,200 mm (3 ft 7 in to 3 ft 8 in).

For general wheelchair manoeuvre a minimum clear space of 1.4 x 1.4 m (4 ft 7 in x 4 ft 7 in) is desirable.

Some areas within a building have their own specific British Standard such as BS 5395 - Code of practice for stairs.

Some people may like to work out the measurements for themselves and have items such as kitchen units made specially for them, especially if they are particularly handicapped in some way. Any deviations from standard can be expensive.

As a general guide these are recommended measurements for rooms and items in a house that is used by disabled people.

## Kitchens

Worktops should be 900 mm (2 ft 11 in) above floor level. Pull out boards from below a fixed work surface are a good idea especially if it is desirable for someone in a wheelchair to be able to work at them.

Storage shelves should not be higher than 1.6 m (5 ft 3 in) above floor level.

Sink bowls should be shallow with a bowl depth of 150 mm (6 in).

## Bathrooms

**Showers** need to be thermostatic and have an easily accessible hand nozzle as well as a fixed position.

**WC fixtures**. The fixing height needs to be 400 mm (1 ft 4 in) to 425 mm (1 ft 5 in) to the bowl rim, giving a seat height of about 425 mm (1 ft 5 in) to 450 mm (1 ft 6 in) above floor level.

**Washbasins** should be approximately 850 mm (2 ft 9½ in) above floor level and should be placed so they don't impede wheelchair access.

**Baths** should have a flat bottom with the rim 500 mm (1 ft 8 in) above floor level. Prefered bath lengths are 1.6 m or 1.7 m. Support rails and handles can be fitted when the exact requirements of the people using the facilities are known.

# 11

# THE STUDY

Many items are kept in a study or office causing numerous problems to occur over sizes, numbers and types of paper, envelopes and other stationery.

Stationery comes in all shapes, sizes and weights. Sorting out the correct one for each job is confusing if all the alternatives are not known. There are also now Post Office Preferred (POP) sizes.

Do you know what to use if adverts state that one should send an A5 envelope to an address for more information? Or a reply for a competition states that one should write one side of an A4 page.

Do you know what Bank or Conqueror paper are or how many sheets of paper form a ream?

Some more general information needed in a study situation is also included.

For example, you need to telephone a client in Sydney - what time is it there?

Do you know all the members of the European Union, units of European currency and Roman numerals?

This section of the book has all these answers and many more.

## Abbreviations and terms used in the computer world

The use of capital letters indicates an acronym - the first letter of each word is used.

**ASCI**          American Standard Code for Information Technology. This codes and lists all capital letters followed by lower case letters. The code can change letters into numbers when data is sent from one machine to another

**Applications package**      Means a programme or set of programmes together with instructions for use when carrying out a specific job such as accounts

**Backup**      As the name implies this indicates a copy of a disc to be used in the event of the original being lost or damaged

**BASIC**      Beginers All Purpose Symbolic Instruction Code

**BIT**      Binary DigIT

**BYTE**      A set of eight binary digits which represent one character and one unit on a computer

**CD-I**      Compact Disc Interactive - a disc which allows the user

| | |
|---|---|
| | to read and write and therefore interact with it |
| **CD-Rom** | Compact Disc Read Only Memory - a disc on which a great amount of information can be stored and retrieved |
| **Data** | A general term for information stored and processed on a computer |
| **Database** | A store of data stored on files for easy access |
| **Decoder** | Used to change data from one coded form to another so it can be accesssed |
| **DOS** | Disk Operating System |
| **DTP** | Desk Top Publishing - an integrated system allowing a variety of print and graphics to be processed into reports and magazines |
| **Floppy disc** | A flexible magnetic disc on which data is stored for use in a computer |
| **Hardware** | All the electronic equipment that makes up the computer system |
| **HZ** | Hertz - a standard unit of frequency. The basic unit is one cycle per second. 1,000 hertz equal one kilohertz. One million hertz equal one megahertz |
| **IAS** | Immediate Access Store |
| **IBM** | International Business Machines Inc |
| **ICL** | International Computers Limited |
| **IT** | Information Technology - the use of computers in the production, storage and communication of information |
| **Kbytes** | Kilobytes |
| **LCD** | Liquid Crystal Display |
| **Mainframe** | A large central computer which has many terminals |
| **MB** | Megabyte - taken to mean one million bytes although it actually equals 1,048,576 bytes |
| **MODEM** | Modulator Demodulator connects two computers by a telephone line |
| **MS-DOS** | Microsoft Disk Operating System |
| **PC** | Personal Computer |
| **PC-Dos** | Personal Computer Disk Operating System |
| **RAM** | Random Access Memory |
| **ROM** | Read Only Memory - a memory that holds data and instructions permanently |
| **VDU** | Visual Display Unit - the screen on which information is displayed on the computer |
| **WP** | Word Processor |

## Member Countries of the European Union

| | |
|---|---|
| Belgium | Italy |
| Denmark | Luxembourg |
| Finland | Netherlands |
| France | Portugal |
| Germany | Spain |
| Greece | Sweden |
| Republic of Ireland | United Kingdom |

# PAPER

European Standard sizes for paper were accepted by CEN on 12th March 1990. They are identical to Independent Standards Organisation 216:1975.

Sizes of Paper and Board are covered by BS 4000 Part 2 1983.

Paper sizes are divided into series; an 'A' series and a 'B' series. All sizes are based on the metric system of measures. Each size is achieved by dividing the size immediately above it into 2 equal parts, the division being parallel to the shorter side.

## 'A' series

The original sheet of paper called AO is nearly 3 ft x 4 ft (841 mm x 1189 mm) which is equivalent to one square metre. Smaller sizes of paper are derived from AO by progressive halving. The smallest piece is about 2 in by 3 in (50 mm x 75 mm). There is a ratio of 2:1 between areas of 2 successive sizes.

**The diagram below shows the relationship of the A series to the B series.**

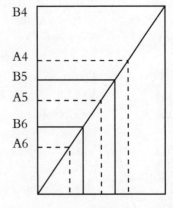

| International Paper Sizes | | | 'A' Series - Trimmed Sizes | | |
|---|---|---|---|---|---|
| | **mm** | | | **in** | |
| A0 | 841 | x 1189 | 33.11 | x | 46.81 |
| A1 | 594 | x 841 | 23.39 | x | 33.11 |
| A2 | 420 | x 594 | 16.54 | x | 23.39 |
| A3 | 297 | x 420 | 11.69 | x | 16.54 |
| A4 | 210 | x 297 | 8.27 | x | 11.69 |
| A5 | 148 | x 210 | 5.83 | x | 8.27 |
| A6 | 105 | x 148 | 4.13 | x | 5.83 |
| A7 | 74 | x 105 | 2.91 | x | 4.13 |
| A8 | 52 | x 74 | 2.05 | x | 2.91 |
| A9 | 37 | x 52 | 1.45 | x | 2.05 |
| A10 | 26 | x 37 | 1.05 | x | 1.45 |

In practice these sizes are often rounded up or down to the nearest whole number, but if someone asks for a sheet of A4 paper it means the same to everyone in any country.

## 'B' series

The 'B' series is intended primarily for posters, wall charts and similar items where the difference in size of the larger sheets in the 'A' series represents too large a jump.

| International Paper Sizes | | | B Series - Trimmed Sizes | | |
|---|---|---|---|---|---|
| | **mm** | | | **in** | |
| B0 | 1000 | x 1414 | 397.0 | x | 556.0 |
| B1 | 707 | x 1000 | 278.0 | x | 397.0 |
| B2 | 500 | x 707 | 198.5 | x | 278.0 |
| B3 | 353 | x 500 | 139.0 | x | 198.5 |
| B4 | 250 | x 353 | 99.2 | x | 139.0 |
| B5 | 176 | x 250 | 69.5 | x | 99.2 |
| B6 | 125 | x 176 | 49.6 | x | 69.5 |
| B7 | 88 | x 125 | 34.7 | x | 49.6 |
| B8 | 62 | x 88 | 24.8 | x | 34.7 |
| B9 | 44 | x 62 | 17.3 | x | 24.8 |
| B10 | 31 | x 44 | 12.4 | x | 17.3 |

## 'C' series

There is a 'C' series of paper sizes but unlike 'A' and 'B' series this is not an ISO series. It is a series of dimensions based on the same principle but each size falling midway between an adjacent A and B size. It tends to be used only for special use such as envelopes.

## ISO long series

There is an ISO long series cut from the ISO 'A' series used for labels and tickets.

| Designation | Sizes in mm |
|---|---|
| ⅓ A4 | 99 x 210 |
| ¼ A4 | 74 x 210 |
| ⅛ A7 | 13 x 74 |

There is another series of paper sizes which have names rather than numbers to describe them.

| Paper Sizes | | | | | |
|---|---|---|---|---|---|
| | mm | | | in | |
| Imperial | 559 | x 762 | 22.00 | x | 30.00 |
| Elephant | 508 | x 686 | 20.00 | x | 27.00 |
| Royal | 508 | x 635 | 20.00 | x | 25.00 |
| Medium | 457 | x 584 | 18.00 | x | 23.00 |
| Demy | 445 | x 572 | 17.50 | x | 22.50 |
| Large post | 419 | x 533 | 16.50 | x | 21.00 |
| Crown | 381 | x 508 | 15.00 | x | 20.00 |
| Foolscap | 343 | x 432 | 13.50 | x | 17.00 |
| B4 | 250 | x 353 | 9.84 | x | 13.90 |
| B5 | 176 | x 250 | 6.93 | x | 9.84 |

## Weight of paper

The quality of paper depends to a great extent on its grammage (weight). These are the weights in most common use.

**Bank** paper is the thinest and lightest A4 paper at 45 gm. This is usually used for second or third copies when typing.

**Conqueror** paper may be 80 gm or 100 gm. It is thicker and smoother and gives a good looking finish to correspondence. It will also have the distinctive Conqueror watermark.

**80 gm** paper is the weight used for most paper advertised as being most suitable for use with laser printers where a smooth surface which will not curl or be affected by any high temperature is required.

**90 gm** gives an even better quality for use with laser printers or for use with ink jet printers.

The chart below shows the wide range of preferred grammages which are all in multiples of $5g/m^2$.

| | |
|---|---|
| Bank and Bond | 30 45 60 70 80 85 95 100 115 |
| Blotting | 55 100 140 300 450 |
| Book Publishing | 60 70 80 90 100 |
| Metalic coated | 80 90 |
| Duplicator | 70 80 85 |
| Leatherette | 95 |
| Gummed surface | 100 |
| Printing and writing | 60 70 85 100 105 115 135 155 170 |
| MG Poster | 60 70 85 95 105 115 |

Some paper is called 'untrimmed' which means the dimensions of a sheet of paper before trimming and not specifically squared.

Trimmed paper means the final dimensions of a sheet of paper or board.

**Recommended untrimmed stock sizes for MG Poster Paper**

| mm | | mm | mm | | mm | mm | | mm |
|---|---|---|---|---|---|---|---|---|
| 510 | x | 760 | 760 | x | 1020 | 1015 | x | 1270 |
| 535 | x | 785 | 785 | x | 1040 | 1020 | x | 1520 |
| 570 | x | 890 | 585 | x | 1550 | 1040 | x | 1550 |
| 635 | x | 1020 | 890 | x | 1140 | | | |

## Quantities of paper

In Britain we have had our traditional ways of measuring and packing paper.

### Quire

A quire is twenty four sheets of paper. Originally it was named after a set of four sheets of paper or parchment folded into eight leaves as in Medieval manuscripts.

### Ream

This comprises 480 sheets of paper or twenty quires of paper. In practice often 500 or more sheets are sold as a ream to allow for any wastage that may occur.

### Printer's ream

This is 516 sheets of paper.

## Book sizes

Books vary in size as much as the sizes of paper, but can be divided into six main popular categories.

| Book Sizes | | | | | | |
|---|---|---|---|---|---|---|
| | mm | | | in | | |
| Royal | 234 | x | 156 | 9.1 | x | 6.1 |
| Demi | 216 | x | 138 | 8.4 | x | 5.4 |
| Large Crown | 198 | x | 129 | 7.7 | x | 5.0 | B Format |
| Crown | 186 | x | 123 | 7.3 | x | 4.8 |
| Crown Quarto | 246 | x | 189 | 9.6 | x | 7.4 |
| Large Crown Quarto | 258 | x | 201 | 10.1 | x | 7.8 |
| All conversions are approximate | | | | | | |

## Envelopes

Envelopes come in a huge range of shapes and sizes. There is no legislation at present regarding the size they must be, but there are certain sizes which are 'Post Office Preferred' (POP). When the sorting and franking of mail is done by machine, it is obviously easier if the envelopes fall into a limited number of sizes.

**'POP' envelopes are**
DL 110 x 220 mm
C6 114 x 162 mm

Greetings cards still vary a great deal in size, but there is increasing conformity between paper manufacturers to produce writing paper and envelopes which meet given recommended sizes for personal and business use.

## Business mail

A well presented private or business letter is not folded several times before being placed in an envelope. Choose the paper best suited to your needs and then buy envelopes which require that paper to be folded once or twice only.

Pages can be placed in large envelopes without folding if they would create too much bulk when folded or if the recipient is likely to prefer them flat for ease of filing and/or photocopying. However it can be expensive and a waste of paper to use an envelope far larger than is necessary.

## Quality of envelopes

Like paper, envelopes are available in various weights and quality.

Heaviest, strongest quality are 130 gm weight Manilla.

120 gm and 115 gm weight are still very strong for most normal purposes.

Highest quality are 100 gm heavy weight.

Good quality but lighter are 85 gm weight.

The lightest envelopes are very thin for airmail use to save costs.

The more expensive envelopes are lined or printed with a pattern to prevent the contents being revealed.

Self seal envelopes are also available.

| Sizes of Envelope | | | | | | | | | | | |
|---|---|---|---|---|---|---|---|---|---|---|---|
| **in** | | | **mm** | | | **in** | | | **mm** | | |
| 12¾ | x | 18 | 324 | x | 457 | 6 | x | 15 | 152 | x | 381 |
| 12 | x | 16 | 305 | x | 406 | 5 | x | 12 | 127 | x | 305 |
| 10 | x | 15 | 254 | x | 381 | 4¾ | x | 9¼ | 120 | x | 235 |
| 10 | x | 12 | 254 | x | 305 | 4½ | x | 6⅜ | 114 | x | 162 |
| 9 | x | 14 | 229 | x | 356 | 4¼ | x | 8⅝ | 110 | x | 220 |
| 9 | x | 12¾ | 229 | x | 324 | (standard size for use with A4 paper folded into three) | | | | | |
| 8½ | x | 10⅝ | 216 | x | 270 | | | | | | |
| 6⅞ | x | 9⅞ | 175 | x | 250 | 4 | x | 9 | 102 | x | 229 |
| 6⅜ | x | 9 | 162 | x | 229 | 3½ | x | 6 | 89 | x | 152 |
| (standard size for use with A4 paper folded in half) | | | | | | | | | | | |

### Manilla envelopes

These brown envelopes are popular for business use. Some open along the narrow end called pocket style and some along one long side called banker style. Some have a see-through pocket in the front for the address on the letter to show through.

Manilla envelopes are usually cheaper in price than white envelopes.

### Padded envelopes

The sizes of these envelopes or bags varies with each manufacturer and none of them are the same size as paper envelopes. It is the internal size which is important as the fibre or air bubble packing takes up space. When deciding what size to buy, remember that most objects sent in these envelopes such as videos, can be quite deep, so allow for this when measuring.

**MailLite Air Bubble envelopes** have guaranteed quality as they are manufactured to BS 5750 standards.

**They are available in the following sizes:**

| Sizes of Envelope | | | | | | | | | | | |
|---|---|---|---|---|---|---|---|---|---|---|---|
| in | | | mm | | | in | | | mm | | |
| 5¼ | x | 8 | 130 | x | 203 | 9 | x 12½ | | 229 | x | 318 |
| 6½ | x | 10 | 165 | x | 254 | 10¼ | x 14½ | | 260 | x | 369 |
| 8 | x | 10 | 203 | x | 254 | 12 | x | 17 | 305 | x | 432 |
| 8 | x | 12 | 203 | x | 305 | 13 | x | 17 | 330 | x | 432 |

## Labels

Labels are made in many sizes and their purchase depends upon the use to which they are to be put. General purpose labels are usually based on an A4 size sheet of paper. The largest label is A4 size, the next largest half A4 size and so on.

| Sizes of Labels | | |
|---|---|---|
| Imperial size | Metric size | Number of labels per sheet |
| 8¼ x 11¼ | 210 x 287 | A4 size 1 label per sheet |
| 8¼ x 5¾ | 210 x 148 | 2 labels per sheet |
| 5¾ x 4³/₁₆ | 148 x 105 | 4 labels per sheet |
| 2¹⁵/₁₆ x 4³/₁₆ | 74 x 105 | 8 labels per sheet |
| 1½ x 4³/₁₆ | 38 x 105 | 14 labels per sheet |
| 1⁷/₁₆ x 4³/₁₆ | 36 x 105 | 16 labels per sheet |
| 1⁵/₁₆ x 4³/₁₆ | 35 x 105 | 16 labels per sheet |
| 1½ x 2¾ | 38 x 70 | 21 labels per sheet |
| 1⁷/₁₆ x 2¾ | 36 x 70 | 24 labels per sheet |
| 1⁵/₁₆ x 2¾ | 35 x 70 | 24 labels per sheet |

## Large address labels

| Imperial Size | Metric Size |
|---|---|
| 3 x 1⁷/₁₆ | 76 x 36 |
| 3½ x 1⁷/₁₆ | 89 x 36 |
| 4 x 1¹⁵/₁₆ | 102 x 49 |

There are a huge variety of labels for specific purposes such as
• long narrow ones for labelling videos
• tiny labels with addresses on for placing on cards etc
• labels for labelling computer discs of varying sizes
• sticky coloured dots for colour coding.

## Postal tubes

Postal tubes are still sold in imperial measures to accommodate imperial sized paper and posters.

13½ inch tube to send or store A4 items

19½ inch tube to send or store A3 items

26½ inch tube to send or store A2 items

## Record cards

At present these are still made and sold in imperial sizes so they will fit into boxes with alphabet dividers.

Whether plain, ruled, white or coloured they are 5 x 3; 6 x 4; 8 x 5(inches)

# ROMAN NUMERALS

This numbering system is in use around the world yet is confusing for many. Can you sort out your 'D's, 'L's, 'M's and 'V's?

**Roman Numerals**

| | | | | |
|---|---|---|---|---|
| 1 is written as | I | | 11 | XI |
| 2 | II | | 12 | XII |
| 3 | III | | 13 | XIII |
| 4 | IV | | 14 | XIV |
| 5 | V | | 15 | XV |
| 6 | VI | | 16 | XVI |
| 7 | VII | | 17 | XVII |
| 8 | VIII | | 18 | XVIII |
| 9 | IX | | 19 | XIX |
| 10 | X | | 20 | XX |

From this list it can be seen that any number can be built up by writing the unit numbers, that is the Roman numeral I to IX (1 to 9) after the number of 'tens' required written as 'X'

**e.g. XI = 11   and   XVI means ten + five + one = 16.**

To prevent rows and rows of 'X's having to be written and counted up when writing a large number, groups of tens have been given other symbols.

Five tens (50) is written as L

Ten tens (100) is written as C

Five hundred (500) is written as D

One thousand is written as M

The numeral for the largest number is usually written first, so fifty one will be written as  LI (fifty + one)

sixty will be written LX  (fifty + ten)

six hundred and fifty will be DCL  (five hundred + one hundred + fifty).

To again shorten the number of symbols used the largest number is usually written first and the number built up as indicated. But if the large number is preceded by a smaller number then the value of the smaller number is subtracted from the large one to arrive at the number required. For instance:

LX is fifty + ten = 60          XL is fifty - ten = 40

## For quick reference

| | | | | | |
|---|---|---|---|---|---|
| 40 | XL | 400 | CD | 4,000 | $\overline{MV}$ |
| 50 | L | 500 | D | 5,000 | $\overline{V}$ |
| 60 | LX | 600 | DC | 10,000 | $\overline{X}$ |
| 70 | LXX | 700 | DCC | | |
| 80 | LXXX | 800 | DCCC | 50,000 | $\overline{L}$ |
| 90 | XC | 900 | CM | 100,000 | $\overline{C}$ |
| 100 | C | 1,000 | M | | |
| 200 | CC | 2,000 | MM | 500,000 | $\overline{D}$ |
| 300 | CCC | 3,000 | MMM | 1,000,000 | $\overline{M}$ |

## TIMES AROUND THE WORLD

Greenwich Mean Time is based on the meridian at Greenwich, London.

Greenwich Mean Time (GMT) was adopted all over the world in 1884 and became Universal Time. The Time in other countries is set by the number of hours they are ahead of, or behind GMT.

**+ indicates the number of hours the place is ahead of GMT**

**- indicates the number of hours the place is behind GMT**

| | | | | | |
|---|---|---|---|---|---|
| Abu Dhabi | + 4 | Beirut | + 2 | Cairo | + 2 |
| Accra | same | Belgrade | + 1 | Calcutta | + 5½ |
| Adelaide | + 9½ | Berlin | + 1 | Lisbon | same |
| Aden | + 3 | Berne | + 1 | Luxembourg | + 1 |
| Algiers | same | Bombay | + 5½ | Madras | + 5½ |
| Amsterdam | + 1 | Bonn | + 1 | Madrid | + 1 |
| Ankara | + 2 | Brisbane | + 10 | Manila | + 8 |
| Athens | + 2 | Brussels | + 1 | Melbourne | + 10 |
| Auckland | + 12 | Bucharest | + 2 | Mexico City | - 7 |
| Baghdad | + 3 | Budapest | + 1 | Montreal | - 5 |
| Bangkok | + 7 | Buenos Aires | - 4 | Moscow | + 3 |

| | | | | | |
|---|---|---|---|---|---|
| Nairobi | + 3 | Reykjavik | same | Tokyo | + 9 |
| New York | - 5 | Rio de Janeiro | - 3 | Toronto | - 5 |
| Oslo | + 1 | Riyadh | + 3 | Tripoli | + 1 |
| Ottawa | - 5 | Rome | + 1 | Tunis | + 1 |
| Panama | - 5 | San Francisco | - 8 | Vancouver | - 8 |
| Paris | + 1 | Shanghai | + 8 | Vienna | + 1 |
| Peking | + 8 | Singapore | + 7½ | Warsaw | + 1 |
| Perth | + 8 | Stockholm | + 1 | Washington | - 5 |
| Prague | + 1 | Sydney | + 10 | Wellington | + 12 |
| Quebec | - 5 | Tehran | + 3½ | Winnipeg | - 6 |

## Units of European Currency

| | | | | | |
|---|---|---|---|---|---|
| Belgian | franc | Irish | punt | Spanish | peseta |
| Danish | krone | Italian | lira | U. K. | pound sterling |
| French | franc | Luxembourg | franc | | |
| German | mark | Dutch | guilder | | |
| Greek | drachma | Portuguese | escudo | | |

# WEATHER FORECASTING

To understand a weather forecast it is necessary to understand what the signs and measurements mean on a weather map.

## Isobars, cyclones and anticyclones

When air is moving it is affected by the spinning of the earth and so moves in swirls rather than straight lines.

To get an accurate picture of the wind speed and direction, meteorologists measure the pressure exerted by the air. This is measured in millibars by a barometer. From this they can work out the speed and direction of the wind rather than by measuring the actual air speed and direction.

### Isobars

The curving lines with arrows on a weather map are called isobars. The lines join together places where the air pressure is the same.

An isobar measuring 760 mm of mercury on a barometer indicates an area of high pressure air. On a weather map the arrows on the line of the isobar will point in a clockwise direction. When a weather forecaster says there is a 'high' it means a high pressure area bringing good weather.

The closeness of the isobars on a weather map indicate the speed of the wind. The closer the isobars the stronger the wind force.

### Cyclone

An isobar measuring 735 mm of mercury indicates an area of low pressure air indicating a cyclone, often called a 'low' or 'depression' and meaning poor and usually rainy weather is expected. The arrows on the lines of the isobar will point in an anticlockwise direction.

### Anticyclone

When the air is spiraling clockwise it is called an anticyclone.

The movement of air in cyclones and anticyclones cover an area of 1,500 or more kilometres in diameter and move at between 2 and 18 metres per second.

## Fronts

When air masses move about, two different kinds may come together to form what is called a 'front'.

### Cold Front

In a cyclone the air swirls and rises before cooling and forming clouds and maybe rain.   As the air rises it can form a 'cold front' shown on a weather map as black triangles along a line.

### Warm Front

A 'warm front' will result from an anticyclone where the air moves slower causing less rain and cloud and more sun. This is shown on a weather map as black semicircles along a line.

## WIND FORCES

Winds from light breezes to hurricanes are measured using the Beaufort Scale.

| Force No | Description | Miles per hour | Kilometres per hour |
|---|---|---|---|
| 0 | Calm | 0 - 1 | below 1.5 |
| 1 | Light air | 1 - 3 | 1.5 - 5 |
| 2 | Light breeze | 4 - 7 | 6.5 - 11 |
| 3 | Gentle breeze | 8 - 12 | 13 - 18 |
| 4 | Moderate breeze | 13 - 18 | 21 - 29 |
| 5 | Fresh breeze | 19 - 24 | 30.5 - 38.5 |
| 6 | Strong breeze | 25 - 31 | 40 - 49.5 |
| 7 | Near gale | 32 - 38 | 51 - 61 |
| 8 | Gale | 39 - 46 | 62.5 - 73.5 |
| 9 | Strong gale | 47 - 54 | 75 - 86.5 |
| 10 | Storm | 55 - 63 | 88 -101 |
| 11 | Violent storm | 64 - 75 | 102.5 -120 |
| 12 | Hurricane | over 75 | over 120 |

## TYPES OF CLOUDS AND THEIR HEIGHTS

There are numerous types of clouds and the sky always looks different, but clouds have been divided into ten main types each with a special name of its own. Each type occurs within certain levels above the surface of the earth.

**Stratus** - layers of cloud resting on high ground, often as mist, appearing as streaks across the sky or as a hanging grey layer up to 2,000 feet (610 metres) in height.

**Nimbostratus** - dark grey layers of clouds which may be thousands of feet or metres thick. May be composed of ice crystals, snowflakes and raindrops. Occur below 6,500 feet (2,000 metres.)

**Cumulonimbus** - very large, round, black or dark grey clouds which are usually a sign of bad weather and thunderstorms to come. They are high, round masses at 2,500 - 3,000 feet (760 - 900 metres).

**Stratocumulus** - Thick, dark clouds at 3,000 - 6,000 feet (900 - 1,800 metres).

**Altostratus** - resemble a grey veil across the sky, thick enough to hide the sun or moon at a height of 6,000 - 12,000 feet (1,800 - 3,650 metres).

**Altocumulus** - greyish white speckly clouds in round formation at 6,000 - 15,000 feet (1,800 - 4,600 metres).

**Cirrostratus** - like a white veil around the sun or moon about 12,000 feet (3,650 metres) high.

**Cirrocumulus** - layers of small flaked or rounded clouds often called a 'mackerel' sky at 10,000 - 18,000 feet (3,050 - 5,500 metres) high.

**Cirrus** - white, feathery, delicate clouds made of ice crystals and formed at the highest level of clouds 20,000 - 25,000 feet (6,100 - 7,600 metres).

## OCEAN DEPTHS

Depths of oceans and seas are usually refered to in feet and fathoms even in countries where metric measures are in common use. This chart gives the depth of the largest oceans and seas in feet and metres.

| Ocean Depth | | |
|---|---|---|
| OCEAN OR SEA | AVERAGE DEPTH IN FEET | AVERAGE DEPTH IN METRES |
| Pacific Ocean | 14,040 | 4,282 |
| Atlantic Ocean | 12,880 | 3,928 |
| Indian Ocean | 13,000 | 3,965 |
| Arctic Ocean | 4,200 | 1,281 |
| Mediterranean Sea | 4,500 | 1,372 |
| South China Sea | 5,400 | 1,647 |
| Bering Sea | 1,665 | 508 |
| Caribbean Sea | 8,400 | 2,562 |
| Gulf of Mexico | 4,700 | 1,434 |
| Sea of Okhotsk | 3,000 | 915 |
| East China Sea | 610 | 186 |
| Yellow Sea | 160 | 49 |
| Hudson Bay | 440 | 134 |
| Sea of Japan | 4,835 | 1,475 |
| North Sea | 180 | 55 |
| Red Sea | 1,490 | 455 |
| Black Sea | 4,300 | 1,312 |
| Baltic Sea | 221 | 67 |

## RIVER LENGTHS

The lengths of rivers are usually given in miles but this chart gives the length in miles and kilometres.

## Longest Rivers in the World

| River | Country | Length in miles | Length in kilometres |
|---|---|---|---|
| Nile | Africa | 4,090 | 6,581 |
| Amazon | South America | 4,050 | 6,516 |
| Mississippi-Missouri | USA | 3,760 | 6,050 |
| Irtysh | USSR | 3,200 | 5,149 |
| Yangtze | China | 3,100 | 4,988 |
| Amur | Asia | 2,900 | 4,666 |
| Congo | Africa | 2,718 | 4,373 |
| Hwang Ho | China | 2,700 | 4,344 |
| Lena | USSR | 2,645 | 4,256 |
| Mackenzie | Canada | 2,635 | 4,240 |
| Mekong | Asia | 2,600 | 4,183 |
| Niger | Africa | 2,600 | 4,183 |
| Yenisey | USSR | 2,360 | 3,797 |
| Murray-Darling | Australia | 2,310 | 3,717 |
| Volga | USSR | 2,290 | 3,685 |
| Yukon | Alaska | 1,979 | 3,184 |
| St Lawence | Canada | 1,945 | 3,130 |
| Rio Grande | USA | 1,885 | 3,032 |

## NAUTICAL MEASURES

| | | |
|---|---|---|
| 6 feet | equal | 1 fathom |
| 100 fathoms | equal | 1 cable |
| 10 cables (6,080 feet) | equal | 1 nautical mile (1,852 metres) |
| 1 knot | equals | 1 nautical mile per hour |

The fathom - 6 feet or 1.8 metres - began as did many measurements by being compared to parts of the body. A fathom was the length of the outstretched arms between the finger tips. It is still used for measuring depths in the sea.

### Future legislation

After 31st December 1999 the fathom will cease to be a measure for marine navigation.

# GEOLOGICAL TIME SCALE

| Era | Period | Age in Millions of Years |
|-----|--------|--------------------------|
| Cenozoic | Quaternary | 1.6 |
| | Tertiary: Pliocene | 5.2 |
| | Tertiary: Miocene | 23 |
| | Tertiary: Oligocene | 35 |
| | Tertiary: Eocene | 65 |
| Mesozoic | Cretaceous | 146 |
| | Jurassic | 205 |
| | Triassic | 251 |
| Upper Palaeozoic | Permian | 290 |
| | Carboniferous | 353 |
| | Devonian | 390 |
| Lower Paleozoic | Silurian | 440 |
| | Ordovician | 510 |
| | Cambrian | 550 |
| Azoic | Pre-cambrian | |
| Origin of the Earth | | 4,500 |

# ASTROLOGY AND SIGNS OF THE ZODIAC

Astrology is the ancient art of foretelling the future of human beings from the positions of the stars and other heavenly bodies.

Astrologers divide the fixed stars into 12 different groups which are called the signs of the zodiac. To tell a person's fortune, an astrologer makes a map of the stars showing their position at the hour of the person's birth. The planet which is in the group at the time of the birth is supposed to have a strong influence over the person and planets which are far away at the time of birth have weak influences. Each planet has a special meaning. Some regard all this as superstition, but astrology has been an important influence throughout history.

## Signs of the zodiac

| | | | | | |
|---|---|---|---|---|---|
| Aries | March | 21 | to April | 20 |
| Taurus | April | 21 | May | 21 |
| Gemini | May | 22 | June | 21 |
| Cancer | June | 22 | July | 23 |
| Leo | July | 24 | August | 23 |
| Virgo | August | 24 | September | 23 |
| Libra | September | 24 | October | 23 |
| Scorpio | October | 24 | November | 22 |
| Sagittarius | November | 23 | December | 21 |
| Capricorn | December | 22 | January | 20 |
| Aquarius | January | 21 | February | 19 |
| Pisces | February | 20 | March | 20 |

## Wedding Anniversaries

| | | | |
|---|---|---|---|
| 1st | Paper | 14th | Ivory |
| 2nd | Cotton | 15th | Crystal |
| 3rd | Leather | 20th | China |
| 4th | Fruit/Flowers | 25th | Silver |
| 5th | Wooden | 30th | Pearl |
| 6th | Sugar/Iron | 35th | Coral |
| 7th | Wool/Copper | 40th | Ruby |
| 8th | Bronze/Pottery | 45th | Sapphire |
| 9th | Pottery/Willow | 50th | Golden |
| 10th | Tin | 55th | Emerald |
| 11th | Steel | 60th | Diamond |
| 12th | Silk/Linen | 70th | Platinum |
| 13th | Lace | | |

## Planets

### Order of the Planets and Distance from the Sun

| | kilometres | miles |
|---|---|---|
| Mercury | 58,000,000 | 36,000,000 |
| Venus | 108,000,000 | 67,000,000 |
| Earth | 150,000,000 | 93,000,000 |
| Mars | 227,000,000 | 141,000,000 |
| Jupiter | 778,000,000 | 484,000,000 |
| Saturn | 1,427,000,000 | 887,000,000 |
| Uranus | 2,869,000,000 | 1,784,000,000 |
| Neptune | 4,497,000,000 | 2,796,000,000 |
| Pluto | 5,888,000,000 | 3,661,000,000 |

# 12

# CAR AND GARAGE

## THE CAR

Cars built throughout Europe, including the United Kingdom, have been built to metric measures for many years. The import and export of models and parts have made this move essential. However in all other aspects of the car and garage the only switch has been at the petrol pumps where petrol is now sold in litres instead of gallons.

There are no plans by the Government to metricate further in this area. Documents state, 'There is authorisation for the continued use, without time limit, of the mile, yard, foot and inch for road traffic signs and related distance and speed measurement'.

Speed restrictions such as '30', '40' or '50' miles per hour seen on numerous signposts around the country will remain, as will the number of miles to the next town remain on signposts both on country lanes and motorways.

Maps will be printed in similar scales as at present, e.g. 1 inch to the mile. The use of the inch, foot, yard and mile will not be authorised units of measurement for any other general use.

Cars will continue to be fitted with dials indicating the number of kilometres per hour the car is travelling as well as miles per hour. This is essential, as British drivers take their cars to the Continent where kilometres per hour are used, and cars are built for the export market as well as home use.

## The efficiency of a car

One of the ways of estimating the efficiency of a car has traditionally been to find out how many miles it will travel on one gallon of petrol. This is more difficult to work out when the distance is in miles but we now put litres into the tank.

As it is a comparative test, one way to tell is simply to keep a note of how many litres of petrol you put in your car and the mileage reading on the milometre on each occasion you fill up. By deducting the first total from the second you find how many litres of petrol you have used to travel a certain number of miles. If you wish to still think in miles per gallon then turn the number of litres used into gallons using the table on page 189 and you will know how many gallons of petrol you have used to travel that number of miles.

## Calculating speed

With increasing numbers of people taking their cars to the Continent it is as well to become familiar with speed limits in European countries which measure their speeds in kilometres per hour. If a signpost states an 80 K limit do you realise what that is in mph?

| Miles per Hour Equal to Kilometres per Hour | | | | | |
|---|---|---|---|---|---|
| MPH | Exact equivalent | Nearest kilometre | MPH | Exact equivalent | Nearest kilometre |
| 1 | 1.609 | (2) | 20 | 32.187 | (32) |
| 2 | 3.219 | (3) | 30 | 48.28 | (48) |
| 3 | 4.828 | (5) | 40 | 64.374 | (64) |
| 4 | 6.437 | (6) | 50 | 80.467 | (80) |
| 5 | 8.047 | (8) | 60 | 96.561 | (96) |
| 6 | 9.656 | (10) | 70 | 112.654 | (113) |
| 7 | 11.265 | (11) | 80 | 128.748 | (129) |
| 8 | 12.875 | (13) | 90 | 144.841 | (145) |
| 9 | 14.484 | (14) | 100 | 160.934 | (161) |
| 10 | 16.093 | (16) | | | |

**For a rough estimate**

To convert miles per hour to kilometres per hour divide the miles by 6 and multiply that answer by 10.

**E.g. 18 miles ÷ 6 = 3 x 10 = 30 kilometres.**

You can do the same conversion for kilometres to miles.

| Kilometres per Hour Equal to Miles per Hour | | | | | |
|---|---|---|---|---|---|
| Km | Exact equivalent | Nearest mile | Km | Exact equivalent | Nearest mile |
| 1 | 0.621 | (½) | 20 | 12.427 | (12½) |
| 2 | 1.242 | (1) | 30 | 18.641 | (18½) |
| 3 | 1.864 | (2) | 40 | 24.854 | (25) |
| 4 | 2.485 | (2½) | 50 | 31.068 | (31) |
| 5 | 3.106 | (3) | 60 | 37.282 | (37) |
| 6 | 3.728 | (4) | 70 | 43.495 | (43½) |
| 7 | 4.349 | (4) | 80 | 49.709 | (50) |
| 8 | 4.970 | (5) | 90 | 55.923 | (56) |
| 9 | 5.592 | (5½) | 100 | 62.137 | (62) |
| 10 | 6.213 | (6) | | | |

**For a rough estimate**

To convert kilometres per hour to miles per hour divide the number of kilometres by 10 and multiply by 6.

E.g. 14 kilometres ÷ 10 = 1.4 x 6 = 8.4 or almost 8½ miles.

**Comparative Speeds**

| | | |
|---:|:---:|:---|
| 1 mph | = | 1.46667 feet per second |
| 1 mph | = | 0.447040 metres per second |
| 1 mph | = | 1.609344 kilometres per hour |
| 1 metre per second | = | 3.28084 feet per second |
| 1 km/h | = | 0.911346 feet per second |
| 1 km/h | = | 0.277778 metres per second |

## Conversion from miles to kilometres and kilometres to miles

| Miles | Kilometres | Kilometres | Miles |
|-------|------------|------------|-------|
| 1 | 1.609 | 1 | 0.609 |
| 2 | 3.219 | 2 | 1.243 |
| 3 | 4.828 | 3 | 1.864 |
| 4 | 6.437 | 4 | 2.485 |
| 5 | 8.047 | 5 | 3.107 |
| 6 | 9.656 | 6 | 3.728 |
| 7 | 11.265 | 7 | 4.350 |
| 8 | 12.875 | 8 | 4.971 |
| 9 | 14.484 | 9 | 5.592 |
| 10 | 16.093 | 10 | 6.214 |
| 20 | 32.187 | 20 | 12.427 |
| 30 | 48.280 | 30 | 18.641 |
| 40 | 64.374 | 40 | 24.855 |
| 50 | 80.467 | 50 | 31.069 |

## To convert litres to UK gallons

### ROUNDED TO NEAREST QUARTER GALLON

| Litre | Exact measure UK Gallon | Rounded measure UK Gallon | Litre | Exact measure UK Gallon | Rounded measure UK Gallon |
|-------|------------------------|--------------------------|-------|------------------------|--------------------------|
| 1 | 0.22 | ¼ | 20 | 4.39 | 4½ |
| 2 | 0.44 | ½ | 30 | 6.59 | 6½ |
| 3 | 0.66 | ¾ | 40 | 8.79 | 8¾ |
| 4 | 0.88 | 1 | 50 | 10.99 | 11 |
| 5 | 1.10 | 1 | 60 | 13.19 | 13¼ |
| 6 | 1.32 | 1¼ | 70 | 15.39 | 15½ |
| 7 | 1.54 | 1½ | 80 | 17.59 | 17½ |
| 8 | 1.76 | 1¾ | 90 | 19.79 | 19¾ |
| 9 | 1.98 | 2 | 100 | 21.99 | 22 |
| 10 | 2.20 | 2¼ | | | |

If the tank in your car holds 11 gallons of petrol how many litres of petrol will it hold?

This is worked out this way:

The chart shows that

10 gallons equals 45.460 litres

+1 gallon equals 4.546 litres

total 11 gallons equals 50.006 litres

## To convert UK gallons to litres

| UK Gallon | Exact Litres | Rounded to nearest Quarter Litre |
|---|---|---|
| 1 | 4.546 | 4½ |
| 2 | 9.092 | 9 |
| 3 | 13.638 | 13½ |
| 4 | 18.184 | 18 |
| 5 | 22.730 | 22¾ |
| 6 | 27.276 | 27¼ |
| 7 | 31.822 | 31¾ |
| 8 | 36.368 | 36¼ |
| 9 | 40.914 | 41 |
| 10 | 45.460 | 45½ |
| 20 | 90.922 | 91 |
| 30 | 136.383 | 136½ |
| 40 | 181.844 | 181¾ |
| 50 | 227.305 | 227¼ |
| 60 | 272.765 | 272¾ |
| 70 | 318.226 | 318¼ |
| 80 | 363.687 | 363¾ |
| 90 | 409.148 | 409 |
| 100 | 454.609 | 454½ |

## Tyre pressures

Correct tyre pressures are very important for safety. They are often now expressed in kilograms per square centimetre instead of pounds per square inch.

| Pounds per sq in | 20 | 22 | 24 | 26 | 28 | 30 | 32 | 34 |
|---|---|---|---|---|---|---|---|---|
| Kilograms per sq cm | 1.41 | 1.55 | 1.69 | 1.83 | 1.97 | 2.11 | 2.25 | 2.39 |

## Road signs and maps

No change will take place in the measurements used on roads or maps. The yard and mile will remain on all road traffic signs and signposts on country lanes and motorways. The use of the inch, foot, yard and mile will not however be authorised units of measurement for any other general use.

## Measures of gradients

When cycling, running or in a car it is often helpful to know how steep a hill or slope is. Lorries in particular need to know if a hill is steep so they can be sure to get up it with a heavy load. Contour lines give the height of a hill but it is the gradient that indicates its steepness.

### How the gradient is worked out

The gradient is calculated by taking two points, one at the top and one at the bottom of a slope, and then measuring the length of the slope between them. The horizontal distance between the same points is then measured.

The rise divided by the horizontal distance equals the gradient.

So if the rise is 70 metres and the horizontal distance 700 metres:

$$\frac{70}{700} \text{ metres} = \frac{1}{10}$$

This is expressed as a gradient of 1 in 10.

That means that for every ten metres you travel up the slope you will rise by one metre.

1 in 1 is virtually vertical and would only be experienced by a mountaineer or climber.

1 in 3 is a very steep climb for walkers and too steep for ordinary cars.

1 in 4 is very steep and cars usually have to change to low gear and drive with care.

1 in 7 is steep but is managed by walkers although cyclists would have to dismount.

1 in 15 is also steep for cyclists but easy for cars.

1 in 50 is easy for all motor transport although a special slow lane may be available for heavy lorries.

Although the gradient is worked out by measuring distances in metres or feet, the actual gradient is a ratio between two figures whatever the method of measure used.

## Lengths of cars

Motoring magazines list the dimensions of cars in feet and inches. These vary greatly between makes and between models within these makes. For exact dimensions of any car refer either to a car dealer or to the handbook.

When considering whether a certain car will fit into your garage remember to allow for the width of the doors, or at least the driver's door, when open to allow easy access. Allow at least two feet extra to the length of the car. To allow full access to the boot when the car is in the garage measure the height of the car with the boot door raised.

### Taking your car abroad

The average car is taken as being about 4.5 metres long although a few may measure nearer 5 metres long. The space usually allowed for each car is 6.5 metres in length. The details of the make of your car is written on the booking form but there is no difference in price for the length of space your car is taking up unless you have a vehicle which is something extraordinary.

## Trailers and vans

Most trailers and vans fall into the category of 3 metres for a short trailer or 6 metres for an average caravan. If you have a longer vehicle you pay the standard price plus an extra charge per metre over 6 metres.

There is a limit on the height allowed. The standard allowance is for a vehicle 2 metres high. Over that, if for instance you have a very high roof rack, you may have to pay a surcharge.

Various companies have slightly differing policies and of course costs change but basically everyone pays the same for the same space whether you have a small, medium or fairly large car.

## NAILS

Nails can be bought in small numbers in packets or in large numbers by weight which works out cheaper.

## Sizes and types of nails

**Round wire nail -** general purpose nail
sizes 20 - 150 mm (¾ - 6 in)

**Oval wire nail -** general purpose nail with a smaller head
sizes 25 - 150 mm (1 - 6 in)

**Lost head nail -** for finer carpentry and floors. The head can be banged below the surface and the hole filled in to give a good finish
sizes 25 - 150 mm (1 - 6 in)

**Cut clasp nail -** good for wood and masonry
sizes 25 - 200 mm (1 - 8 in)

**Clout nail -** used for roofing felt, window sash cords. May be bought in a galvanised form if to be used out doors
sizes 20 - 100 mm (¾ - 4 in)

**Panel pin -** used for cabinet, joinery and moulding work where the minimum size head pin is needed
sizes 15 - 50 mm (⅝ - 2 in)

**Tack -** to fix carpets and fabric to wood floors. May be bought as 'fine' or 'improved' which have larger heads
sizes (6 - 30 mm)(¼ - 1¼ in)

**Chair nail -** used in upholstery work and meant to be seen. So available in bronze, chrome, copper or antique finish
sizes of heads 3 - 13 mm (⅛-½ in)

**Masonry nail -** used in bricks, cement and breeze blocks to make a strong grip. May be in fine or heavy gauges
sizes 15 - 100 mm (⅝ - 4 in)

**Annular nails -** for fixing sheet materials like plywood. It has teeth which bite into wood to give a strong grip.
sizes 20 - 100 mm (¾ - 4 in)

**Hardboard pin -** used for fixing hardboard. Its head goes into the hardboard
sizes 15 - 50 mm (⅝ - 2 in)

**Galvanised nail -** used for corrugated iron on outside roofs
size - a large head size of 20mm (¾ in) and a length of 65 mm (2½ in)

**Plasterboard nail -** like an annular nail its ridged shank grips the nail in the plasterboard
size 30 mm (1¼ in) or 40mm (1½ in)

**Plastic headed nails -** can be bought for fixing plastic to wood. May be black, white or brown with flat or domed head
sizes 20 - 65 mm (¾ in -2½ in)

**Round wire nail**

**Oval wire nail**

**Lost head nail**

**Cut clasp nail**

**Clout nail**

**Panel pin**

**Tack**

**Chair nail**

**Masonry nail**

**Annular nails**

**Hardboard pin**

**Galvanised nail**

## SCREWS

Screws may be bought in small packets but are usually bought in boxes containing 100, 200 or 500.

Two measurements are necessary when determining which screw to use for a job. The length in mm (in) from the rim of the head to the tip and the diameter of its shank is called the gauge. The gauge is not an actual measurement but a figure. The smallest gauge is 0 and the largest 20. Different length screws are available within the same gauge. The most common gauge screws in use are gauge 4,6,8 and 10.

### Screw lengths

| | | |
|---|---|---|
| 6.5 mm (¼ in) | 32 mm (1¼ in) | 75 mm (3 in) |
| 10 mm (⅜ in) | 38 mm (1½ in) | 82 mm (3¼ in) |
| 13 mm (½ in) | 44 mm (1¾ in) | 90 mm (3½ in) |
| 16 mm (⅝ in) | 50 mm (2 in) | 100 mm (4 in) |
| 19 mm (¾ in ) | 57 mm (2¼ in) | 125 mm (5 in) |
| 22 mm (⅞ in) | 65 mm (2½ in) | 150 mm (6 in) |
| 25 mm (1 in ) | 70 mm (2¾ in) | |

Not all the screws illustrated are made in all these lengths but are made in the most suitable length and gauge combinations for the jobs for which they are likely to be needed.

**Countersunk screws** have a flat top which allows them to be screwed down until level with the surface. Countersunk with a single head have one slot across the top and are the most common type used for general woodwork and jobs such as fitting hinges. Countersunk screws with cross slot heads are the same as above but have two crossed slots across the top. A special screwdriver is needed for these.

**Round head screws** have one slot across the top and protrude above the surface as they are not countersunk.

**Raised head screws** have a single slot and need to be countersunk to the rim. They are often used as a feature as they can be seen.

**Dome head screws** have a round screw hole in the head into which is screwed a chromed cap to give an attractive appearance and hide the screw. They are mostly used when items such as bathroom mirrors are screwed to walls.

**Chipboard screws** have the thread going right up to the head in order to get a good grip.

**Dowel screws** can be used when an invisible join is required. One end is screwed into one piece of wood and the other piece of wood is wound onto the screw.

**Coach screws** are used in heavy construction work.

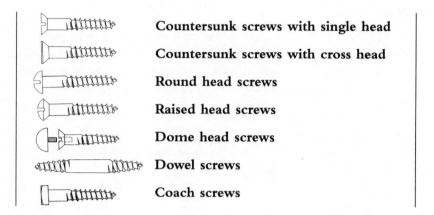

Countersunk screws with single head

Countersunk screws with cross head

Round head screws

Raised head screws

Dome head screws

Dowel screws

Coach screws

## BOLTS

Where two pieces of wood or metal may need to be separated at a later date they are best bolted together instead of screwed. As they are fixed by the tightening of a nut, it is essential that the threaded part of the bolt goes up into the hole a bit so that the nut can go right up to the surface of the wood. If the threaded part is too long it can be trimmed off with a hacksaw after the nut has been tightened.

## There are two main types of bolt

**Machine bolts** have flat heads and are suitable for use with wood or metal. Sizes are available up to lengths of 500 mm (20 in) and from 5 - 19 mm (³⁄₁₆ - ¾ in) diameter.

It is usual to add a washer at both ends of these bolts.

**Coach bolts** have domed heads but have a square collar underneath which locks into the wood when the nut is tightened. A washer is needed under the nut. Sizes are available up to lengths of 500 mm (20 in) and 5 - 19 mm (³⁄₁₆ - ¾ in ) diameter.

Rag bolts and masonry bolts are available for use in heavier masonry construction projects.

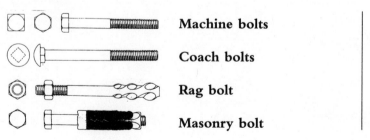

Machine bolts

Coach bolts

Rag bolt

Masonry bolt

# NUTS

Nuts are available in eight main shapes (see diagram). The tapped threads of the nut should match the die threads of the bolt on which it is going to be used. A suitable sized spanner or an adjustable spanner will be necessary to tighten the nuts while the wing nuts can be tightened by hand.

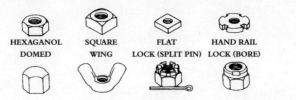

| HEXAGANOL | SQUARE | FLAT | HAND RAIL |
| DOMED | WING | LOCK (SPLIT PIN) | LOCK (BORE) |

# WASHERS

Washers are used beneath the heads of nuts and bolts to prevent them breaking the wood by tearing into it.

Use plain washers for woodwork and toothed washers for metal work.

**Plain washers** are flat smooth metal.

**Toothed washers** have a jagged edge all around which sink into the wood and give a better purchase.

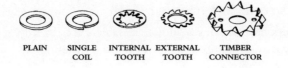

| PLAIN | SINGLE | INTERNAL | EXTERNAL | TIMBER |
| | COIL | TOOTH | TOOTH | CONNECTOR |

# 13

# THE BODY

• • • • • • • • • • • • • • • • • • • • • • • • • • • • • • • • • • • • • • • • • • •

## HEALTH

In the area of health and fitness there are numerous measurements which are crucial. Check your Body Mass Index to see if you are overweight; check how much energy you are using in various activities and how your pulse rate measures up under exercise; are you drinking too much; all vital information to achieve good health and fitness.

Where figures have been mentioned in this chapter it must be pointed out that these are average recommendations and are not intended to be exact targets that every individual must achieve. Always consult your doctor for advice on personal health and fitness, especially before commencing a new exercise regime or diet.

## BODY MASS INDEX

The Body Mass Index (BMI) is now the recommended method of assessing obesity. It is calculated by dividing the weight in kilogrammes by the square of the height in metres. Sometimes it is referred to as the Quartlet Index.

### To calculate your Body Mass Index

First weigh yourself carefully in kilograms and measure your height in metres. Then divide your weight in kg by your height squared in metres. So if you weigh 65 kg (10 stone 4 lb) and your height is 1.6 m (5 ft 4 in) $65 \div (1.6 \times 1.6) = 65 \div 2.56 = 25.4$. This means that you are a little bit overweight.

By using this system of measure it is easier to define the various grades of obesity. A BMI of between 20 and 24.9 is regarded as normal and indicates that no ill health will result from an excess of fat in or around the body.

| | |
|---|---|
| BMI 20 | underweight |
| BMI 20 - 24.9 | normal |
| BMI 25 - 29.9 | plump or Grade I obesity |
| BMI 30 - 39.9 | moderately overweight or Grade II obesity |
| BMI 40 | severe obesity or Grade III obesity |

# Are you the right weight for your height?

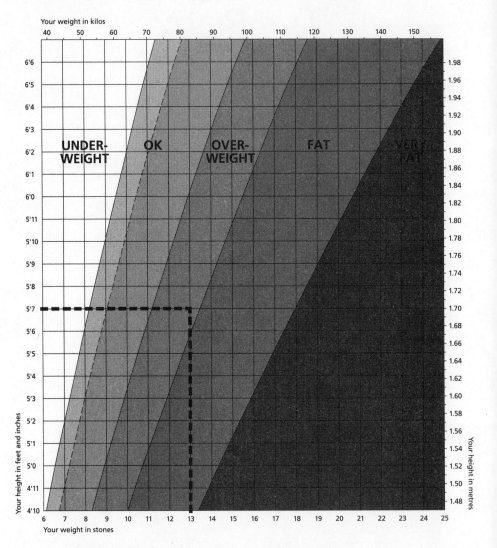

This chart gives a quick check on whether you are in the correct weight band for your height. It is designed for adult men and women, not children.

There are many reasons why one person weighs more than another and there is no single weight which is ideal for each person. Just because you weigh pounds or kilograms heavier than your friend of the same age does not mean you necessarily need worry. Just check your weight regularly to see that you are well within the correct weight band for your height.

### To use this weight chart

Weigh yourself without clothes, in stones and pounds or kilograms, whichever you prefer.

Draw a straight line from where your weight is marked on the edge of the grid until it crosses with another straight line drawn across from your height without shoes.

Where the two lines meet indicates the weight band into which you fall.

### Underweight

Maybe you need to eat a bit more. But go for well-balanced nutritious foods and don't just fill up on fatty and sugary foods. If you are very underweight see your doctor about it.

### OK

Your weight is in the desirable range for health. You are eating the right quantity of food but you need to be sure that you are getting a healthy balance in your diet.

### Overweight

Your health could suffer. You should try to lose weight.

### Fat

It is really important to lose weight.

### Very fat

Being this overweight is very serious. You urgently need to lose weight. Talk to your doctor or dietitian.

### Children's weights

Childrens' weights vary considerably as they are growing. Boys and girls develop and grow at different speeds. The weight will vary for differing reasons and there is no 'ideal' exact weight everyone should be. (Any sudden or excessive weight gain or loss noticed should be reported to your doctor who should take any action required.)

### Your weight

For those who like to put a figure on their weight, a guide is given in the charts on pages 200 and 201. However there is no need to try to be an exact weight; it is quite sufficient to check into which band you fall in the chart on 198.

| IDEAL WEIGHT TABLE MEN 25 - 59 YEARS | | | |
|---|---|---|---|
| **Weight in kg (in indoor clothing)★** | | | |
| HEIGHT (IN SHOES)♦ (cm) | SMALL FRAME | MEDIUM FRAME | MID POINT | LARGE FRAME |
| 158 | 58.3-61.0 | 59.6-64.2 | 61.9 | 62.8-68.3 |
| 159 | 58.6-61.3 | 79.9-64.5 | 62.2 | 63.1-68.8 |
| 160 | 59.0-61.1 | 60.3-64.9 | 62.6 | 63.5-69.4 |
| 161 | 59.3-62.0 | 60.6-65.2 | 62.9 | 63.8-69.4 |
| 162 | 59.7-62.4 | 61.0-65.6 | 63.3 | 64.2-70.5 |
| 163 | 60.0-62.7 | 61.3-66.0 | 63.7 | 64.5-71.1 |
| 164 | 60.4-63.1 | 61.7-66.5 | 64.1 | 64.9-71.3 |
| 165 | 60.8-63.5 | 62.1-67.0 | 64.6 | 65.3-72.5 |
| 166 | 61.1-63.8 | 62.4-67.6 | 65.0 | 65.6-73.2 |
| 167 | 61.5-64.2 | 62.8-68.2 | 65.5 | 66.0-74.0 |
| 168 | 61.8-64.6 | 63.2-68.7 | 66.0 | 66.4-74.7 |
| 169 | 62.2-65.2 | 63.8-69.3 | 66.6 | 67.0-75.4 |
| 170 | 62.5-65.7 | 64.3-69.8 | 67.1 | 67.5-76.1 |
| 171 | 62.9-66.2 | 64.8-70.3 | 67.6 | 68.0-76.8 |
| 172 | 63.2-66.7 | 65.4-70.8 | 68.1 | 68.5-77.5 |
| 173 | 63.6-67.3 | 65.9-71.4 | 68.7 | 69.1-78.2 |
| 174 | 63.9-67.8 | 66.4-71.9 | 69.2 | 69.6-78.9 |
| 175 | 64.3-68.3 | 66.9-72.4 | 69.7 | 70.1-79.6 |
| 176 | 64.7-68.9 | 67.5-73.0 | 70.3 | 70.7-80.3 |
| 177 | 65.0-69.5 | 68.1-73.5 | 70.8 | 71.3-81.0 |
| 178 | 65.4-70.0 | 68.6-74.0 | 71.3 | 71.8-81.8 |
| 179 | 65.7-70.5 | 69.2-74.6 | 71.9 | 72.3-82.5 |
| 180 | 66.1-71.0 | 69.7-75.1 | 72.4 | 72.8-83.3 |
| 181 | 66.6-71.6 | 70.2-75.8 | 73.0 | 73.4-84.0 |
| 182 | 67.1-72.1 | 70.7-76.5 | 73.6 | 73.9-84.7 |
| 183 | 67.7-72.7 | 71.3-77.2 | 74.3 | 74.5-8S.4 |
| 184 | 68.2-73.4 | 71.8-77.9 | 74.9 | 75.2-86.1 |
| 185 | 68.7-74.1 | 72.4-78.6 | 75.5 | 75.9-86.8 |
| 186 | 69.2-74.8 | 73.0-79.3 | 76.2 | 76.6-87.6 |
| 187 | 69.8-75.5 | 73.7-80.0 | 76.9 | 77.3-88.5 |
| 188 | 70.3-76.2 | 74.4-80.7 | 77.6 | 78.0-89.4 |
| 189 | 70.9-76.9 | 74.9-81.5 | 78.2 | 78.7-90.3 |
| 190 | 71.4-77.6 | 75.4-82.2 | 78.8 | 79.4-91.2 |
| 191 | 72.1-78.4 | 76.1-83.0 | 79.6 | 80.3-92.1 |
| 192 | 72.8-79.1 | 76.8-83.9 | 80.4 | 81.2-93.0 |
| 193 | 73.5-79.8 | 77.6-84.8 | 81.2 | 82.1-93.9 |

★ Indoor clothing weighing 2.3 kilograms for men
♦ Shoes with 2.5cm heels

## IDEAL WEIGHT TABLE WOMEN 25 - 59 YEARS

### Weight in kg (in indoor clothing)★

| HEIGHT (IN SHOES)◆ (cm) | SMALL FRAME | MEDIUM FRAME | MID POINT | LARGE FRAME |
|---|---|---|---|---|
| 148 | 46.4-50.6 | 49.6-S5.1 | 52.4 | 53.7-59.8 |
| 149 | 46.6-51.0 | 50.0-55.5 | 52.3 | 54.1-60.3 |
| 150 | 46.7-51.3 | 50.3-55.9 | 53.1 | 54.4-60.3 |
| 151 | 46.9-51.7 | 50.7-56.4 | 53.6 | 54.8-61.4 |
| 152 | 47.1-52.1 | 51.1-57.0 | 54.1 | 55.2-61.9 |
| 153 | 47.4-52.5 | 51.5-57.5 | 54.5 | 55.6-61.9 |
| 154 | 47.8-53.0 | 51.9-58.0 | 55.0 | 56.2-63.0 |
| 155 | 48.1-53.6 | 52.2-58.6 | 55.4 | 56.8-63.6 |
| 156 | 48.5-54.1 | 52.7-59.1 | 55.9 | 57.3-64.1 |
| 157 | 48.8-54.6 | 53.2-59.6 | 56.4 | 57.8-64.6 |
| 158 | 49.3-55.2 | 53.8-60.2 | 57.0 | 58.4-65.3 |
| 159 | 49.8-55.7 | 54.3-60.7 | 57.5 | 58.9-66.0 |
| 160 | 50.3-56.2 | 54.9-61.2 | 58.1 | 59.4-66.7 |
| 161 | 50.8-56.7 | 55.4-61.7 | 58.6 | 59.9-67.4 |
| 162 | 51.4-57.3 | 55.9-62.3 | 59.1 | 60.5-68.1 |
| 163 | 51.9-57.8 | 56.4-62.8 | 59.6 | 61.0-68.8 |
| 164 | 52.5-58.4 | 57.0-63.4 | 60.2 | 61.5-69.5 |
| 165 | 53.0-58.9 | 57.5-63.9 | 60.7 | 61.0-70.2 |
| 166 | 53.6-59.5 | 58.1-64.5 | 61.3 | 62.6-70.9 |
| 167 | 54.1-60.0 | 58.7-65.0 | 61.9 | 63.2-71.7 |
| 168 | 54.6-60.5 | 59.2-65.5 | 62.4 | 63.7-72.4 |
| 169 | 55.2-61.1 | 59.7-66.1 | 62.9 | 64.3-73.1 |
| 170 | 55.7-61.6 | 60.2-66.6 | 63.4 | 64.8-73.8 |
| 171 | 56.2-62.1 | 60.7-67.1 | 63.9 | 65.3-74.5 |
| 172 | 56.8-62.6 | 61.3-67.6 | 64.5 | 65.8-75.2 |
| 173 | 57.3-63.2 | 61.8-68.2 | 65.0 | 66.4-75.9 |
| 174 | 57.8-63.7 | 62.3-68.7 | 65.5 | 66.9-76.4 |
| 175 | 58.3-64.2 | 62.8-69.2 | 66.0 | 67.4-76.9 |
| 176 | 58.9-64.8 | 63.4-69.8 | 66.6 | 68.0-77.5 |
| 177 | 59.5-65.4 | 64.0-70.4 | 67.2 | 68.5-78.1 |
| 178 | 60.0-65.9 | 64.5-70.9 | 67.7 | 69.0-78.6 |
| 179 | 60.5-66.4 | 65.1-71.4 | 68.3 | 69.6-79.1 |
| 180 | 61.0-66.9 | 65.6-71.9 | 68.8 | 70.1-79.6 |
| 181 | 61.6-67.5 | 66.1-72.5 | 69.3 | 70.7-80.2 |
| 182 | 62.1-68.0 | 66.6-73.0 | 69.8 | 71.2-80.7 |
| 183 | 62.6-68.5 | 67.1-73.5 | 70.3 | 71.7-81.2 |

★ Indoor clothing weighing   1.4 kilograms for women
◆ Shoes with 2.5cm heels

## BASAL METABOLIC RATE (BMR)

The Basal Metabolic Rate is the number of kilocalories or kilojoules used by a body to stay alive, to breathe, to grow, to digest food and similar functions that the body does automatically without any conscious effort being necessary.

**To calculate your Basal Metabolic Rate**

Find your weight in kilograms. If you only know your weight in pounds divide the number of pounds by 2.2 to get the number of kilograms you weigh.

**For instance – if you weigh nine and a half stone (133 pounds) 133 ÷ 2.2 = 60½ kilograms.**

Each person requires for his/her Basal Metabolic Rate, 1 kilocalorie for every kilogram he/she weighs for every hour in the day. So 1 cal x 60½ kg x 24 hours = 1452 calories.

1452 kilocalories will need to be eaten to provide the requirements for your personal basal metabolic rate.

Kilocalorie requirements for activities carried out during the day have to be added to the BMR requirement to find the total that need to be eaten per day (see page 203).

## Measurement of energy used by the body

Every movement made by the body uses energy. (see above. See page 204 for energy used in various forms of exercise). Some gentle movements use very little energy whereas others such as running use a lot of energy. Energy used by the body can be measured in two ways, in kilocalories or kilojoules.

### Calories or joules

Several years ago it was decided in Britain that the Continental measure for dietary energy, the kilojoule, should be used in place of the kilocalorie as a unit of energy. However this change has not generally occurred and the British people continue to use kilocalories, commonly known as calories, to measure the energy they obtain from food and the energy their muscles use when performing various tasks.

Kilojoules are used on the Continent and often appear on food labels in Britain. Sometimes both calories and joules are to be seen on a label, but it is necessary to know how to convert from one to the other, especially if you are counting the calories/joules in order to lose or gain a little weight or wish to compare the value of one food with another.

### Conversion of kilocalories to kilojoules and megajoules

1 kilocalorie (kcal) equals 4.184 kilojoules (kJ).

For convenient quick reckoning this is usually rounded up to 4.2.

So 1,000 kilocalories (kcal) equals 4,184 kilojoules or rounded up, equals 4,200 kilojoules (kJ).

By multiplying calories by 4.2 the number of joules in the answer can be very large. To avoid working in such large numbers the megajoule can be used.

1 megajoule (MJ) equals 1,000 kilojoules (kJ) therefore 4,200 kilojoules could be written as 4.200 megajoules (MJ).

1 megajoule (MJ) also equals 239 kilocalories (kcal).

1 kilojoule (kJ) equals 0.239 kilocalories (kcal).

### Calculating how many calories/joules you can eat

If you wish to follow a diet providing 2,200 kilocalories, this is how to work out how many kilojoules you can eat:

2,200 kilocalories multiply by 4.2 equals 9,240 kilojoules or 9.240 megajoules.

Similarly on a slimming diet of 1,150 kilocalories you can eat:

1,150 kilocalories multiply by 4.2 equals a diet of 4,800 kilojoules or 4.800 megajoules.

## Calorie/joule content of Foods

If the daily amount of energy required is being calculated in joules then the joule content of all foods needs to be known.

### Energy obtained from food nutrients

Calories or joules are obtained from the fat, alcohol, carbohydrates and protein in food.

| | |
|---|---|
| 1 gram of fat | supplies 9 kilocalories or 37 kilojoules |
| 1 gram of alcohol | supplies 7 kilocalories or 29 kilojoules |
| 1 gram of carbohydrate | supplies 4 kilocalories or 17 kilojoules |
| 1 gram of protein | supplies 4 kilocalories or 17 kilojoules |

The official scientific reference book to look up the calorie *and* joule content of foods is called *The Composition of Foods* by Professor McCance and Dr Widdowson published by The Royal Society of Chemistry and the Ministry of Agriculture, Fisheries and Food.

Small booklets one can buy only give the calorie content of the most popular foods and do not usually give the joules content. To find the joules content simply multiply the calorie content by 4.2 as described earlier.

For instance, 100 g (about 4 oz) of cheddar cheese provides 412 kilocalories. Multiply this by 4.2 and you find that the same amount of cheese provides 1,730 kilojoules. As the figure 4.2 is rounded up from 4.184 it must be remembered that where large amounts of energy or food are involved the final figure will not be absolutely accurate. If an accurate figure is required the actual conversion figure of 4.184 should be used.

| Calories used up in 15 minutes by a 70 kg (11 stone) adult doing the following activities | | | |
|---|---|---|---|
| **ACTIVITY** | **CALORIES SPENT IN 15 MINUTES** | **ACTIVITY** | **CALORIES SPENT IN 15 MINUTES** |
| Sitting | 20 | Skating | 90 |
| Sweeping the floor | 30 | Gentle jogging | 90 |
| Sitting and writing | 35 | Basketball | 90 |
| Archery | 40 | Fencing | 95 |
| Croquet | 40 | Gymnastics | 100 |
| Driving a car | 48 | Hockey | 100 |
| Rifle shooting | 50 | Climbing | 110 |
| Playing table tennis | 50 | Competitive swimming | 110 |
| Sailing | 50 | Playing tennis | 120 |
| Walking slowly | 55 | Jogging | 120 |
| Ironing | 60 | Digging the garden | 130 |
| Cycling slowly | 65 | Playing football | 140 |
| Polishing the floor | 68 | Cycling fast | 168 |
| Playing badminton | 70 | Skiing downhill | 175 |
| Bowling (10 pin) | 70 | Hard running | 200 |
| Canoeing and rowing | 70 | Water polo | 210 |
| Playing golf | 75 | Wrestling | 210 |
| Walking fast | 80 | Playing squash | 230 |
| Doing ballet | 80 | Water polo | 235 |
| Surfing | 80 | Swimming fast | 255 |
| Dancing energetically | 85 | Climbing uphill when skiing | 280 |

N.B. The above figures are an average guide. It should be noted that someone proficient in something, especially a sport, will generally spend fewer calories doing it than an amateur. Do not suddenly take up strenuous exercise just to use up energy and loose weight without consulting your doctor.

# MEASURING BLOOD PRESSURE

Everyone has blood pressure. Every time the heart contracts it is pumping blood along the arteries to all parts of the body. Some pressure is essential to force the blood through the circulatory system to all the tissues. A heart problem occurs when the pressure is higher than it should be due to the blood vessels being partially blocked. Then the heart has to work harder to push the blood through. This can happen with increasing age and in some diseases.

**Systolic pressure**
At each contraction of the heart the pressure rises rapidly and reaches a maximum pressure called the systolic pressure.

**Diastolic pressure**
The minimum pressure is when the heart is resting before beating again. This is called the diastolic pressure.

The pressure is measured in terms of the height of mercury in millimetres which the pressure can maintain.

## Normal ranges of blood pressure

A typical blood pressure for a young healthy person is 110/80.

(Systolic pressure of 110 mm mercury and a diastolic pressure of 80 mm mercury).

**Low blood pressure**
is under 110/60 mm

**High blood pressure**
As some of the elasticity of the blood vessels decreases, so the resistance increases, along with the blood pressure which might rise to something like 140/90, or even higher to 160/110 and above which can be serious. Someone with blood pressure consistently rising above 160/110 is often said to suffer from hypertension. A high diastolic pressure is more serious than a high systolic pressure.

# PULSE RATES

The pulse rate is the number of times the heart beats in one minute and is one of the main indicators of fitness.

## Normal pulse rate

A normal resting pulse rate for someone who is not doing anything is between 70 and 80 times a minute. The pulse is lowest when you are lying in bed.

## Raised pulse rates

As soon as any movement starts, the pulse rate rises and in strenuous exercise it can rise to be very high. The move from a low pulse rate to a high pulse rate should be a gradual process. No harm should occur if care is taken to gradually work up to a high level. However, harm can be done if the heart is placed under too much stress too quickly upon exertion.

## Safe pulse rates

The safe maximum pulse rate for a young fit man in good physical condition is around 200 a minute.

For most people the pulse rate should fall within the limits shown in Table below.

### Pulse Rate Chart

| AGE | 50% Easy Effort | 65% Steady Effort | 75% Hard Effort | 85% Athletic Effort | AGE | 50% Easy Effort | 65% Steady Effort | 75% Hard Effort | 85% Athletic Effort |
|-----|-----|-----|-----|-----|-----|-----|-----|-----|-----|
| 16 | 102 | 133 | 153 | 173 | 47 | 86 | 112 | 130 | 147 |
| 17 | 101 | 132 | 152 | 173 | 48 | 86 | 112 | 129 | 146 |
| 18 | 101 | 131 | 151 | 171 | 49 | 85 | 111 | 128 | 145 |
| 19 | 100 | 130 | 150 | 170 | 50 | 85 | 110 | 127 | 144 |
| 20 | 100 | 130 | 150 | 170 | 51 | 84 | 110 | 127 | 144 |
| 21 | 99 | 129 | 149 | 169 | 52 | 84 | 109 | 126 | 143 |
| 22 | 99 | 129 | 148 | 168 | 53 | 83 | 109 | 125 | 142 |
| 23 | 98 | 128 | 148 | 167 | 54 | 83 | 108 | 125 | 141 |
| 24 | 98 | 127 | 147 | 167 | 55 | 82 | 107 | 124 | 140 |
| 25 | 97 | 127 | 146 | 166 | 56 | 82 | 107 | 123 | 139 |
| 26 | 97 | 126 | 146 | 165 | 57 | 81 | 106 | 122 | 138 |
| 27 | 96 | 125 | 145 | 164 | 58 | 81 | 105 | 122 | 138 |
| 28 | 96 | 125 | 144 | 163 | 59 | 80 | 105 | 121 | 137 |
| 29 | 95 | 124 | 143 | 162 | 60 | 80 | 104 | 120 | 136 |
| 30 | 95 | 124 | 142 | 162 | 61 | 79 | 103 | 119 | 135 |
| 31 | 94 | 123 | 142 | 161 | 62 | 79 | 103 | 118 | 134 |
| 32 | 94 | 122 | 141 | 160 | 63 | 78 | 102 | 117 | 133 |
| 33 | 93 | 122 | 140 | 154 | 64 | 78 | 101 | 117 | 132 |
| 34 | 93 | 121 | 140 | 158 | 65 | 77 | 100 | 116 | 131 |
| 35 | 92 | 121 | 139 | 157 | 66 | 77 | 100 | 115 | 130 |
| 36 | 92 | 120 | 138 | 156 | 67 | 76 | 99 | 114 | 130 |
| 37 | 91 | 119 | 137 | 155 | 68 | 76 | 98 | 114 | 129 |
| 38 | 91 | 118 | 136 | 155 | 69 | 75 | 98 | 113 | 128 |
| 39 | 90 | 118 | 136 | 154 | 70 | 75 | 97 | 112 | 127 |
| 40 | 90 | 117 | 135 | 153 | 71 | 74 | 96 | 111 | 126 |
| 41 | 89 | 116 | 134 | 152 | 72 | 74 | 96 | 111 | 125 |
| 42 | 89 | 116 | 133 | 157 | 73 | 73 | 95 | 110 | 124 |
| 43 | 88 | 115 | 133 | 150 | 74 | 73 | 94 | 109 | 124 |
| 44 | 88 | 114 | 132 | 150 | 75 | 72 | 94 | 108 | 125 |
| 45 | 87 | 114 | 131 | 149 | 76 | 72 | 93 | 108 | 122 |
| 46 | 87 | 113 | 130 | 148 | | | | | |

Checking regularly on these rates will mean that you should not be harming yourself when you are exercising. If you are overweight, unfit, pregnant or just had a baby, or have any history of heart trouble or other medical problem, you should consult your doctor before starting on any new exercise programme or sport which may cause your pulse rate to rise far higher than through previous activity.

| Average Safe Pulse Rate for Healthy People in Different Age Groups | |
|---|---|
| **AGE IN YEARS** | **BEATS PER MINUTE** |
| 20 - 25 | 140 - 180 |
| 25 - 30 | 130 - 170 |
| 30 - 35 | 125 - 165 |
| 35 - 40 | 110 - 150 |
| 50 - 55 | 110 - 145 |
| 55+ | 110 - 140 |

### How to take your pulse

The pulse can be felt where a large artery passes just under the skin and the most usual place to take a count is on the wrist at the base of the thumb. Use the fingers, not the thumb, of the other hand as shown in the diagram. Count the beats for 15 seconds and multiply by four to get the pulse rate in one minute.

### Pulse rates during exercise

During exercise the pulse rate rises depending on the effort used.

See page 206 for the pulse rates for each age compared to effort.

## Body temperature

Normal body temperature is now more usually referred to as 37°C (actual figure 36.9°C) in place of the more familiar figure of 98.4°F.

There is no need to buy a different thermometer if you have a perfectly good one which measures in degrees Fahrenheit. Just read from whichever scale you wish.

| °Fahrenheit | °Celsius | °Fahrenheit | °Celsius |
|---|---|---|---|
| 95.0 | 35 | 102.2 | 39 |
| 96.8 | 36 | 104.0 | 40 |
| 98.6 | 37 | 105.8 | 41 |
| 100.4 | 38 | | |

## Healthy cholesterol levels

The average body contains about 140 g (5 oz) of cholesterol in the blood and body cells. It is a vital substance, much of it made in the body but some obtained from foods eaten in the diet.

Experts agree that for good health we should aim to have a blood cholesterol level of below 5.2 mmol per litre.

Kits can be bought to enable cholesterol levels to be checked at home but if you think you have a problem it is wise to see your doctor and have your level of cholesterol checked professionally. Advice on any desirable change in diet can then be given by a dietitian.

## FITNESS

How fit you are depends on your stamina, strength and suppleness.

Each kind of activity gives different benefits and will also vary according to the amount of effort you put into the activity.

For best overall fitness choose activities with the most stars.

| Fitness | | | |
|---|---|---|---|
| ACTIVITY | STAMINA | STRENGTH | SUPPLENESS |
| Aerobics | ★★★ | ★★ | ★★★ |
| Badminton | ★★ | ★★ | ★★★ |
| Climbing stairs | ★★★ | ★★ | ★ |
| Cycling | ★★★★ | ★★★ | ★★ |
| Dancing | ★ | ★ | ★★★ |
| Disco dancing | ★★★ | ★ | ★★★★ |
| Digging the garden | ★★★ | ★★★★ | ★★ |
| Football | ★★★ | ★★★ | ★★★ |
| Golf | ★ | ★ | ★★ |
| Housework | ★ | ★ | ★★ |
| Jogging | ★★★★ | ★★ | ★★ |
| Squash | ★★★ | ★★ | ★★★ |
| Swimming | ★★★★ | ★★★★ | ★★★★ |
| Tennis | ★★ | ★★ | ★★★ |
| Walking | ★★★ | ★★ | ★ |
| Weightlifting | ★ | ★★★★ | ★ |
| Yoga | ★ | ★ | ★★★★ |

**Stamina** is necessary to keep going at the activity without gasping for breath.

**Strength** is necessary to move through the activity whichever part of the body is involved.

**Suppleness** allows the joints of the body to be able to bend, stretch, twist and turn whatever the activity.

## Stress Factors

The higher the number in the chart below the higher the stress. It should be remembered that usually more than one stress factor is present at any one time

| | |
|---|---|
| Death of a spouse | 100 |
| Divorce | 73 |
| Marital separation | 65 |
| Jail sentence | 63 |
| Death of a close family member | 63 |
| Personal injury or illness | 53 |
| Marriage, engagement or living together | 50 |
| Loss of job | 47 |
| Marital reconciliation | 45 |
| Retirement | 45 |
| Change in health of family member | 44 |
| Pregnancy | 44 |
| Sex difficulties | 39 |
| Birth of a baby | 39 |
| Business changes | 39 |
| Changes in financial position | 38 |
| Death of a close friend | 37 |
| Change to a different job | 36 |
| More rows with spouse | 35 |
| Taking out a large mortgage or loan | 31 |
| Promotion or demotion at work | 29 |
| Son or daughter leaving home | 29 |
| Trouble with in-laws | 29 |
| Outstanding personal achievement | 28 |
| Spouse begins or stops work | 26 |
| Beginning or end of school or college | 26 |
| Change in living conditions | 25 |
| Change in routine | 24 |
| Trouble with the boss | 23 |
| Change in work hours or conditions | 20 |
| Moving house | 20 |

| | |
|---|---|
| Change in school or college | 20 |
| Change in recreation | 19 |
| Change in Church activities | 19 |
| Change in social activities | 18 |
| Change in sleeping habits | 16 |
| Change in eating habits e.g. dieting | 15 |
| Holiday | 13 |
| Christmas | 12 |
| Minor violations of the law | 11 |

## ALCOHOL AND HEALTH

### 'Healthy' measures of alcohol

There have been several studies carried out in recent years to discover the maximum amount of alcohol it is safe to drink. Some have resulted in suggestions that the levels listed below are too low and that people could safely drink a little more than this.

Of course there are some medical conditions such as pregnancy which make it advisable not to drink at all. Until there is firm evidence to the contrary, the following advice from the Health Education Authority should be followed.

#### Units of alcohol

It is advisable to consume not more than a certain number of units of alcohol a week. Men should have no more than *28 units* a week. These should be spread throughout the week with one or two drink free days. Women should have no more than *21 units* a week spread throughout the week with one or two drink free days.

### What is a unit?

One unit of alcohol is - 1 single measure of spirits

*or* 1 small glass of sherry

*or* one glass of wine

*or* ⅓ pint strong beer,

lager or cider

*or* ½ pint ordinary beer,

lager or cider

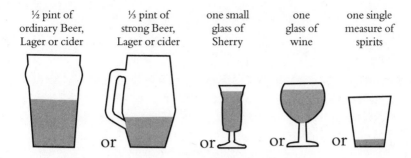

½ pint of ordinary Beer, Lager or cider    ⅓ pint of strong Beer, Lager or cider    one small glass of Sherry    one glass of wine    one single measure of spirits

Check this list to see just how many units you are drinking when you enjoy your favourite drink. Remember that when drinks are poured at home they are invariably larger than those served at a bar! It is worth noting that the same amount of alcohol is consumed from a glass of sherry, a glass of wine, a standard measure of gin or half a pint of beer so there is little advantage in changing the type of drink you choose in order to reduce the alcohol consumed.

| Beers and Lagers | Units |
|---|---|
| 1 pint of Export beer | 2½ |
| 1 can Export beer | 2 |
| 1 pint ordinary beer or lager | 2 |
| 1 can ordinary beer or lager | 1½ |
| 1 pint of strong ale or lager | 4 |
| 1 can of strong ale or lager | 3 |
| 1 pint of extra strong beer or lager | 5 |
| 1 can of extra strong beer or lager | 4 |
| | |
| **Ciders** | |
| 1 pint of cider | 3 |
| 1 pint of strong cider | 4 |
| **Spirits** | |
| 1 standard single measure | 1 |
| **Table Wine** | |
| 1 standard glass | 1 |
| **Sherry** | |
| 1 standard small measure | 1 |

| Low alcohol Lagers and Beers | Units |
|---|---|
| Half pint | ⅓ |
| 1 pint | ⅔ |
| 1 can = 16 fl oz = 440 ml = ¾ pint | ½ |
| **Low alcohol Cider** | |
| Half a pint | ⅓ |
| 1 pint | ½ |

## Metrication legislation regarding drinks

Certain legislation on units of measurement will result in the following changes. After 31st December 1999 the fluid ounce and pint will cease to be authorised for beer, cider, mineral waters, lemonades and fruit juices in returnable containers. They will be sold in litres or other metric measures. However the pint will still be authorised for continued use, without time limit, for dispensing draught beer and cider and for milk in returnable containers.

## Buying drinks

When drinks are bought outside the home strict weights and measures are enforced. Capacity serving measures for use by the trade for measuring and serving liquor for consumption on or off the premises at which it is sold have been changed.

35 ml 'thimbles' of intoxicating liquor, gin, rum, vodka and whisky, are permitted since 1st January 1995.

Fluid ounces (fl oz) will no longer be used in this context.

Measures will be      ⅓ pt = 175 ml

½ pt = 250 ml

1 pt = 500 ml

1 quart (2 pints) and ½ gallon (4 pints) will no longer be used.

When buying drink it is wise to check that you have a measure which takes the drink to the brim of the glass or that it measures exactly along the horizontal line marked on the glass. Measures should be clearly marked with the capacity they are measuring.

As metric measures become fully implemented it is feared by many that some traditional measures will be abandoned. This has led to various groups lobbying to keep the measures they have used for centuries. One of these groups is the whisky lovers in Scotland. The Government has decided to allow them to retain their traditional dram which is larger than the usual public house tot of whisky.

# 14

# SPORTING MEASURES

As sport is such an international pastime it is important that all countries and players understand the size of all pitches and equipment whether in imperial or metric measures. Many measures were put into place many years ago and use measuring terms that have long since disappeared from public usage. For instance the length of a cricket pitch was originally one chain. They have been officially adapted in various ways and it should be noted that while the figures given here are accurate they cannot be fully comprehensive. On occasions when serious competition is involved it would be wise to check both measurements and rules with the headquarters or association of the sport concerned.

In some events strict rules are in place regarding the thickness of wood to be used for various pieces of equipment, thickness of the lines painted on boundaries, minimum distances to be allowed for run-up to jumps etc.

There are competitive occasions when the relationship between miles and kilometres has to be known. For some time now athletic events have been referred to as the 100 metre hurdles, the 5,000 metres race and so on, so most people are becoming more aware of the approximate distances involved when metric terms are used in these situations.

Whether lengths of cricket pitches and football pitches will be measured in metres in the future remains to be seen.

To find out the equivalent distance in metric measures, measure the distance in miles, yards or feet, whichever is most appropriate, and refer to the conversion charts in chapter one.

For instance, to calculate how far you have swum in metres - multiply the number of lengths swum by the number of yards in each length and refer to the conversion chart on page 24.

Or, instead of telling friends you went for a five mile walk at the weekend you will now have to say you went for a 8.047 kilometre walk!

## American Football

The field is 360 ft long and 160 ft wide.

The ball should be inflated to a pressure of between 12.5 and 13.5 pounds per square inch. The weight should be 14-15 ounces. The length must be between 10 and 11 inches. The larger circumference should be not less than 27¾ inches and not more than 28½ inches.

The smaller circumference should be not less than 20¾ inches and not more than 21¼ inches.

# Archery

Laws regarding the sport are the responsibility of the Grand National Archery Society.

The diameter of outdoor targets may be 122 cm or 80 cm.

The centre circle on a 122 cm face should be 24.4 cm surrounded by four concentric bands, the breadth of each being 12.2 cm.

The centre circle of an 80 cm face should be 16 cm ringed by four concentric bands each measuring 8 cm.

The bands of all targets are coloured, being from the centre outwards gold, red, blue, black and white. Each colour zone is divided into two zones of equal width by a line not exceeding 2 mm in width.

The centre of the gold area is termed the pinhole and is marked with a small cross, the lines of which should not exceed 2 mm in width. When the targets are set up the pinhole should be 130 cm (4 ft 3 in) above the ground.

The safe minimum spacing between each target centre should be 2.5 m (8 ft 2 in) if one or two archers are shooting or 3.66 m (12 ft) if three archers are shooting.

**The distance of the shooting line from the targets should be within:**

**Metric**      up to and including 50 m distance ± 15 cm

distances above 50 m ± 30 cm

**Imperial**      up to and including 50 yd distance ± 6 in

distances above 50 yd ± 12 in

Scoring for GNAS rounds is as follows - an arrow in the gold target scores 9, red 7, blue 5, black 3 and white 1.

Scoring points for metric rounds are inner gold 10, outer gold 9, inner red 8, outer red 7, inner blue 6, outer blue 5, inner black 4, outer black 3, inner white 2 and outer white 1.

# Indoor Archery

The same GNAS rules apply as for outdoor archery but the diameter of the standard target faces may be 40 cm, 60 cm, and 80 cm. The 40 cm face has a circle of 8 cm in the centre ringed by four concentric bands each 4 cm wide. The 60 cm face has a circle in the centre of 12 cm diameter ringed by four concentric bands each being 6 cm wide. The 80 cm face is as for outdoor archery.

Scoring is determined by the distance and accuracy of the shot.

# Association Football

A football field should be a minimum of 100 yards(90 metres) and a maximum of 130 yards(120 metres)long. It should be a minimum of 50 yards(45 metres) and a maximum of 100 yards(90 metres)wide. The penalty area is 18 yards(16.5 metres) out from the goal line and the same amount on either side of the goal posts. The goal posts are 8 yards(7.3 metres) apart joined by a horizontal crossbar 8 feet(2.4 metres) from the ground. The game is started from a point in the centre of a circle in the centre of the pitch and this circle is 10 yards (9 metres) diameter.

International matches call for more specific dimensions and the field of play is then measured in metric measures and is a maximum 110 metres x 75 metres  and a minimum 100 metres  x 64 metres.

The weight of the ball must be between 14 and 16 ounces (396-453 grams). The circumference of the ball should be between 27 and 28 inches (0.68 and 0.71 metres).

# Athletics

This term covers a wide range of activities each requiring different facilities.  Metric measures are used in all major international meetings but some meetings in the USA are still measured in imperial measures.

### Track events
Sprinting events are usually over 100 and 200 metres.

Middle distance running falls between 400 and 1,500 metres, 400 metres being a long sprint and the 800 and 1,500 metres middle distance races.

Long distance races are 5,000 and 10,000 metres.

The marathon is 26 miles 385 yards long.

### Hurdles
The main hurdle events are the 110 metres hurdles when the top bar is 106 centimetres high and the 400 metres intermediate hurdle with the top bar at 91 centimetres high.
Women run 100 metres with the hurdle 84 centimetres high or 200 metres with the hurdle 76 metres high.
In international competitions strict rules are laid down regarding the weight of the hurdles and the resisting force.  Each hurdle must not weigh less than 10 kg and the width should be 1.2 metres.
Adults jump over 10 hurdles while young people jump over 8 hurdles during the course of one race. The distance between the flights over the hurdles varies according to the length of the course and the number of hurdles being jumped.

### Relay races

Relay races may be four people each running 100 metres, 4 people each running 400 metres or the medley relay in which the first runner runs 800 metres, the second and third 200 metres each and the fourth 400 metres.

### Pole vaulting

The metal, bamboo or fibre glass poles are usually about 4.5 metres long. The distance between the uprights holding the bar should be between 4.30 metres and 4.37 metres.

### Discus

The person throwing a discus throws it from a circle 2.5 metres diameter.

### Javelin

A javelin may be made of any material, the most favoured being light metal alloy or Finnish birch wood. It must not weigh less than 750 grams and it must be not less than 2.5 metres long with a sharp metal point at one end.

## Badminton

A badminton court is 13.4 metres long and 6.1 metres wide. The top of the net from the surface of the court should be 1.524 metres at the centre of the court and the depth of the net should be 760 mm.

The shuttle should weigh between 4.74 and 5.50 grams and should have 16 feathers fixed in the base so forming a circle with a diameter between 58 mm to 68 mm.

## Bowls

A bowling green should be a square of not less than 120 ft (36.58 m) and not more than 132 ft (40.23 m) a side.

Wooden bowls should have a maximum diameter of 5¼ in (133.35 mm) and a minimum diameter of 4⅝ in (117 mm).

The weight must not exceed 3 lb 8 oz (1.59 kg).

## Boxing

A boxing ring must be a minimum of 12 ft (3.6 m) square and a maximum size of 20 ft (6.10 m square) measured inside the line of ropes.

Boxers weighing below 67 kg wear gloves weighing 8 oz and boxers weighing over 67 kg should wear 10 oz gloves. In boxing championships these weights may be changed.

The categories below refer to boxers over 17 years.

| Boxing | | |
|---|---|---|
| **Boxing class** | **Metric weight** | **Imperial weight** |
| Light-flyweight | 48 kg | 7 stone 7 lb |
| Flyweight | 51 kg | 8 stone |
| Bantamweight | 54 kg | 8 stone 7 lb |
| Featherweight | 57 kg | 9 stone |
| Lightweight | 60 kg | 9 stone 7 lb |
| Light-welterweight | 63.5 kg | 10 stone |
| Welterweight | 67 kg | 10 stone 8 lb |
| Light-middleweight | 71 kg | 11 stone 2 lb |
| Middleweight | 75 kg | 11 stone 11 lb |
| Light-heavyweight | 81kg | 12 stone 10 lb |
| Heavyweight | No limit | |

## Cricket

The distance between two wickets on a cricket pitch is one chain or 22 yards (20.12 metres).

Each wicket is made of three stumps of wood, each 28 in (71.1 cm) high and 1¼ in (4 cm) in diameter. These are placed 9 in (22.86 cm) apart. The bails should be 4⅜ in (11.1 cm) long. The position of the batsman at the popping crease is 4 ft (1.22 m) in front of the wicket.

A cricket ball weighs not less than 5½ oz (155.9 g) and not more than 5¾ oz (163g) and should not be more than 9 in (22.9 cm) in circumference.

The bat should be not more than 38 in (96.5 cm) in length and not longer than 4½ in (10.8 cm) in width.

## Golf

Golf courses, distance between holes, and hazards on a course vary from course to course. Golf clubs also vary.

A golf course usually consists of 9 holes or 18 holes which may vary in length between 100 and 600 yards. An 18 hole course measures between about 5,000 and 7,000 yards. Golf clubs vary; 4 or 5 clubs are often adequate for a beginner while the maximum allowed is 14 clubs. The irons are numbered 1 to 9 according to the slope of the blade. A club called a putter is used on the green.

The hole for the ball to drop into must be 4¼ in (108 mm) in diameter and at least 4 in (100 mm) deep.

## Gymnastics

The beam is 4 ft (1.2 m) from the ground.

It is 16 ft (4.9 m) long and 4 in (10 cm) wide

The mat for floor exercises is 39 ft (12 m) square.

## Hockey

A hockey pitch is 100 yards (91.4 metres) long and 60 yards (55 metres) wide. The goal posts are 4 yards (3.66 metres) apart and the cross bar 7 ft (2.14 m) from the ground. The shooting circles are taken 16 yards (14.63 metres) from the goal line.

A woman's hockey stick should weigh a maximum of 23 oz (652 g) and minimum of 12 oz (340 g). A man's stick should weigh a maximum of 28 oz (794 g) and a minimum of 12 oz (340 g).

The ball is the same size and weight as a cricket ball but is white instead of red. The weight of the stick should not exceed 28 oz (794 g) nor be less than 12 oz (340 g) and should not be bigger in diameter anywhere along its length than 2 in (5.1 cm).

## Horse racing

Horse racing may be flat racing or jumping. Jumping may be hurdling or steeplechasing, the steeplechasing being done by older horses over higher and stouter fences than hurdles. Jumping is mainly a winter sport and flat racing a summer one, but the two seasons are long and overlap a lot. Despite the change to metric measures in many areas the distances over which the horses race remain in miles and furlongs.

Flat races vary in length from five furlongs to two and three quarter miles.

### Lengths of the best known races

The races known as the 'classics' which are the 2,000 guineas and the 1,000 guineas run at Newmarket are run over one mile.

The Derby and the Oaks are run at Epsom over one and a half miles.

The St Ledger is run at Doncaster and is run over one and three quarter miles.

All the above races are for three-year-old horses.

The 1,000 guinea and the Oaks races are for fillies, young female horses, only.

The King George VI and Queen Elizabeth Stakes is run at Ascot over a mile and a half and is for three-year-old horses upwards.

In England a horse's age is always counted from the 1st January of the year in which he or she is foaled. The earliest age at which horses run on the flat is two years. They may start hurdling at three years and racing over fences at four years old. By seven years a horse is a bit old for flat racing and a bit young for steeplechasing.

## Dressage

The size of an arena for dressage is 198 ft (60 m) by 66 ft (20 m).

## Ice Hockey

An ice rink on which ice hockey is to be played should be a maximum size of 61 metres long and 30 metres wide with a minimum size of 56 metres long and 26 metres wide. The corners are rounded in the arc of a circle with a radius of 7 - 8.5 metres. The safety boards around the rink should be at least 1.2 metres high and not more than 1.22 metres above the ice surface. The game is played with a flat disc called a puck which is 2.5 cm thick and 7.5 cm wide. It should weigh not less than 156 g and not more than 170 g.

## Lacrosse

A lacrose playing field should be 110 yards (100.58 metres) long and 60 yards (54.86 metres) wide. The goals which should be 100 yards (92 m) apart consist of two vertical posts 6 ft (1.83 m) apart with a top cross bar 6 ft (1.83 m) from the ground. The goal circle should have a radius of 2.6 m (8.5 ft) measured from the centre of the goal line to the outer edge of the goal line.

The ball is of white, yellow or orange rubber and must be between 7.75 in (19.69 cm) and 8 in (20.32 cm) in circumference. It should weigh between 5 and 5.25 ounces and when dropped from a height of 72 in (1.83 m) it should bounce to a height of between 45 in (114.3 cm) and 49 in (124.46 cm).

## Netball

A netball court is 100 ft (30.5 m) long and 50 ft (15.25 m) wide. A circle 3 ft (0.9 m) in diameter marks the centre of the court. The goal circle is in fact a semi-circle with a radius of 16 ft (4.9 m) with its centre at the midpoint of the goal line. Each goal post is 10 ft (3.05 m) high with the metal ring through which the ball passes for a goal 15 in (3.8 cm) in diameter attached horizontally 6 in (1.5 cm) out from the upright. The netball is the same as an association football size 5, measuring between 27 in (6.9 cm) and 28 in (7.1 cm) in circumference. It weighs between 14 oz (400 g) and 16 oz (450 g).

## Rugby League Football and Rugby Union Football

Although there are differences between the two games the pitch is of similar size. The playing field should be no larger than 100 metres long and no more than 68 metres wide. The goal shaped like an H has its cross bar 3 metres above the ground. The ball is similar for both games, the desired dimensions being length 28 cm, longest circumference 74 cm, widest circumference 59 cm and dry, clean weight 410 g.

## Squash Rackets

The court is a room with four walls 32 feet long and 21 feet wide. All along one of the shorter end walls of the court is a board whose upper edge needs to be 19 inches from the ground. The ball used is a hollow rubber squash ball.

## Table Tennis

The playing surface area of the table is 2.74 metres long and 1.525 metres wide. It should be perfectly level and 76 cm above the floor. The playing surface is important to allow the standard ball to bounce correctly at 23 cm when it is dropped onto it at a height of 30 cm.

The table is dark but a white line 2 cm wide should be painted along each edge. The top of the net stretched across the centre of the table should be 15.25 cm above the table surface. The white or yellow celluloid ball has a diameter of 38 mm and should weigh 2.5 g.

## Tennis

The size of a tennis court for singles games is 78 ft (23.77 m) long and 27ft (8.23 m) wide. The court for a doubles game should be 36 ft (10.97 m) in width and the same length as the singles court. The height of the net at the centre of the court is 3 ft (0.91 m) held down taut at the centre by a strap. The service lines are placed 21ft (6.4 m) back from and parallel to the net. Tennis balls should be more than 2½ in (6.35 cm) and less than 2⅝ in (6.67cm) in diameter and weigh more than 2 oz (56.7 g) and less than 2¹/₁₆ oz (58.5 g). The ball should have a bounce of more than 53 in (135 cm) and less than 58 in (147 cm) when dropped 100 in (254 cm) onto concrete.

# INDEX